LONG JOURNEY HOME

A Prague Love Story

HELEN NOTZL

 FriesenPress

Suite 300 - 990 Fort St
Victoria, BC, V8V 3K2
Canada

www.friesenpress.com

ISBN
978-1-5255-0818-9 (Hardcover)
978-1-5255-0819-6 (Paperback)
978-1-5255-0820-2 (eBook)

1. BIOGRAPHY & AUTOBIOGRAPHY, PERSONAL MEMOIRS

Distributed to the trade by The Ingram Book Company

*To Walter, with the deepest love and gratitude,
and to Adam, life's gift to us both*

Table of Contents

⨎⨎⨎ Acknowledgements

WORK ON THIS BOOK BEGAN MANY YEARS AGO, WHEN I'D SIT with my sister Irene in various restaurants and cafés, pumping her for details about the shadowy, mysterious people and places that haunted my imagination. Being thirteen years older, she had vivid memories of everything we had left behind. I am most grateful for her sharing, painful though many of those memories were for her.

Years later, on the other side of the ocean, I did the same, asking endless questions of my beloved niece, Helena Nekulová. Míša Zavadilová generously filled in many blanks over coffee at the Slavia Café.

I am deeply grateful to Beth Kaplan, writer, teacher, editor, mentor and dear friend, whose support and belief in me and my writing gave me the courage and persistence to keep going. Without her this book would never have been written.

I am most indebted to Christopher Cameron for his brilliant editing, several times over, and for his incisive and generous on-going comments and suggestions.

I wish to thank my dear friend Veronika Ambros, professor in the Department of Slavic Languages and Literatures, University of Toronto, for her expert correcting and editing of my Czech grammar.

I am very grateful to Gordon Harris for his brilliance at image processing and photo enhancement and for his unending patience - "I want your photos to be *great*," he'd insist when I thought they were good enough.

Most of all, I am grateful to my family, in Canada and in Prague, and for the rest of the characters that people this book, who made my life so rich and dramatic that the story had to be told.

〰〰〰 Introduction

ONE EVENING SOME YEARS AGO, I'D BOOKED A BOX AT THE magnificent Prague State Opera. *Rusalka* was being performed, the Czech composer Antonin Dvořák's most celebrated opera. I was familiar with his most famous aria, the "Song to the Moon," but had never seen the entire work. My father had loved opera, and when I was a child I'd heard its haunting music emanating from behind the closed door of his den at our home in Toronto.

I was born in Prague, but at the age of four was torn away when the Communist party took over Czechoslovakia and my family fled to Canada, leaving everything and everyone behind. As a child listening to my mother's stories, I fell in love with that mythical place and the mysterious characters – my extended family – that she described. Her grief and longing for that lost paradise set me on a quest that was to run like an underground river through my life.

Over the years, I'd been drawn to Prague again and again, living in Canada but driven by an urgent longing that would not let me go. Coming to see *Rusalka* was part of my search.

I sat listening, entranced by the soaring, lyrical music. Suddenly I caught my breath and had to stop myself from crying out. This was my story! Rusalka, a water nymph, has fallen in love with a human prince and longs to be with him. Dissatisfied with her lot, she dreams of being human. Her wish is granted. The libretto tells the story of their two incompatible worlds colliding and in their case, since it is an opera, their inevitable tragic end.

Walking home a daze, I realized I needed to write down the story of my own two worlds colliding and the fallout from that collision. A story of exile and the search for my own resolution.

And, perhaps, redemption.

⅄⅄⅄ Prologue

I WAS BORN IN THE CITY OF PRAGUE IN 1944, DURING THE final year of the Second World War and of the Nazi occupation of Czechoslovakia.

The war ended the following year. Czechoslovakia erupted in frenzied jubilation at its liberation from the Nazi horrors, only to endure the pillaging and brutality of its Soviet "liberators." For the next three years, the country's fate hung in the balance. Would the enlightened and cultured democracy that had flourished before the war, the most free and prosperous nation in all of Europe at that time, be restored, or would this small country in the heart of Europe fall to the Soviets? The communist coup of 1948, and the probable murder of the Minister of Foreign Affairs, plunged the country into a darkness from which it wouldn't emerge for forty years. In 1948 the persecution – firing, imprisonment, disappearance, torture and execution – of the middle and upper classes, of professionals, executives and intellectuals, had begun.

I was four years old in 1948 when the event occurred that was to set the course for the rest of my life.

We lived in Prague, in a penthouse apartment in the residential district of Královské Vinohrady, the Royal Vineyards, and also had a villa in Černošice, a wealthy neigbourhood on the outskirts of the city. My father, Pavel Albert Karel Notzl, was the director of Česká Eskomptní Banka, one of the largest banks in Prague. A tall, handsome man of fifty with dark brown eyes and greying black hair, he exuded confidence and sophistication. My mother, Martha (neé Kratochvílová), was his third wife, a blonde, blue-eyed beauty eight years younger, the daughter of a judge. They had two children together, my brother Peter, a year older, and me.

As a bank director, my father was in danger, sure to be persecuted and possibly killed. It was imperative that we flee the country. The borders were sealed; barbed-wire fences had been erected, patrolled by police armed with machine guns. To be caught meant certain imprisonment and possible death.

This is how my mother told me the story over the years, burning it into my imagination until it was as potent and vivid as a memory of my own. An official-looking envelope arrived one day – a document my father had applied for and was anxiously awaiting. It was a summons to Nuremburg, requiring him to testify at the International War Crimes Tribunal in June of 1948, and informing him that the exit visa requested by the Tribunal had been granted – a precious document that would allow him to leave the country legally.

My mother always cried telling the next part of the story – my father convincing her they had to go, and soon. No goodbyes, despite knowing they might never return, leaving everyone and everything behind. "It's over," my father said. "Life will never be like this again."

"How can you ask this of me?" she cried. "Crossing the border by myself with two small children! We could be shot!"

"We have to risk it," he said, promising to make all the arrangements before he went. A guide, a car and driver waiting on the other side.

He left for Nuremburg.

One morning soon after, my grandparents hurried through the door of our apartment. Our nanny Giselle brought Peter and me into the living room. We were excited, having been told we were going on a train trip with our beloved *Babi* and *Děda*. My mother took Giselle's hands in her own, prayed nothing would happen to her, and made her promise not to say a word, no matter what happened. Giselle swore on her life, she'd known nothing – an outing.

We found a compartment to ourselves. Peter and I watched the countryside race by and begged for treats at village stations. Finally the train stopped; the end of the line. We climbed down and stood on the platform amidst the belching steam, the soot, the smell of coal.

We were in a town several kilometres from the German border. The same train would make its way back to Prague momentarily; our goodbyes had to be quick. Our grandparents held us tight and kissed us again and again. My mother clung to them, unwilling to let them go. A whistle blew. With many a backward glance, Babi and Děda climbed up the steps and into the train. Another whistle and the train began to move. We stood waving until it disappeared into the tunnel.

A man sidled past and signalled my mother to follow. Keeping a careful distance, she took our hands and led us out to the street. After several blocks the man stopped. He looked around, opened the rear door of a car parked by the curb and nodded. We ran and tumbled in. One last quick look and he jumped into the driver's seat. We drove through the town and into the countryside.

Much later the car slowed and swerved onto a track that led through deep woods. It ended abruptly and we stopped. We got out and followed the driver into the forest, the pine needles spongy and fragrant under our feet. Except for the chirping of birds, all was silent.

My mother told how I suddenly pulled my hand free and ran forward, crying out, "*Maminko, podívej se – houby!*" Mommy, look, mushrooms! She caught me, clapping a hand over my mouth.

At last the man stopped. "This is as far as I go." Horrified, my mother begged, "Please, no, you can't leave us here!" He was adamant. He gave her instructions, wished us luck and disappeared back into the woods. She fell to her knees and buried her face in her hands. Whimpering, Peter and I patted her hair, her shoulders. Finally she took a deep breath and knelt in front of us. We had to be very brave, she told us. She would take care of us. But we mustn't talk and we mustn't cry, we had to be as quiet as little mice. She got up and took our hands.

On and on we walked, stopping to rest every now and then. Suddenly ahead of us, between the trees, a high chain-link fence appeared, its top strung with coils of razor wire. We kept it to our right, as the guide had instructed, and crept forward until we spied a low hut and a wooden watchtower, and between them a laneway blocked by a double set of barriers.

We crouched, hidden by the thick trees. "Come," my mother whispered, and taking a firm hold of our hands, she pulled us closer and closer, darting from tree to tree. There were no windows on our side of the hut and no one was in sight.

Suddenly a voice broke the silence, a door slammed and boot heels crunched on the gravel. A man in a green uniform with a gun slung over his shoulder crossed the laneway and climbed the ladder up the watchtower. We waited, hardly breathing. My mother closed her eyes, took a deep breath and prayed. Several minutes later the man came down and went back into the hut. We heard laughter.

"Now!" my mother said.

There was a narrow opening between dense bushes and the barriers. We ran towards it, pausing for a split second to listen. Voices, another burst of laughter as we dashed into the open. We flew towards that narrow space, ducked as the leaves and branches slapped our faces, past the first barrier, past the second, past the wire fence with the deadly razor wire. We ran and ran until the hut and the fence were behind us, through the underbrush and into the woods, the German woods, where we collapsed on the ground, my mother sobbing as she held us tight and stroked our cheeks, our hair.

Eventually we got up and emerged onto the road. Not far ahead, a black car was parked. A man jumped out, calling my mother's name – the car and driver my father had arranged, the car that would take us to him.

In a nearby town we stopped in front of a hotel and ran inside. The driver spoke to the man at the reception desk, and there was my father running down the hotel stairs and sweeping my mother into his arms.

"And my two darlings!" he cried, lifting Peter and me and twirling us until we were dizzy with joy. "Safe and sound, thank God."

We all spoke at once. "Let's get you something to eat," my father said and led us into the dining room.

"They were very brave," my mother said, and we went on to tell him everything that had happened.

Our ordeal wasn't over yet, my father warned. We still had to get through Germany to Zell am See in Austria; he'd booked us into a pension there where we were to stay until we knew where we'd eventually settle. The roads were full of checkpoints, too many people moving around, and everyone was suspect. Don't say a word, he said to us; he'd do all the talking. He spoke fluent German. We made it through all the checkpoints and arrived safely at the *Pension Olga*, where we were to stay for the next year.

————

We were in Austria, so close, not much more than a hundred kilometres from the border, yet our country was sealed off from the rest of Europe as tightly as if behind high prison walls. The gates had clanged shut, imprisoning everyone inside and forbidding any access. My father raged at the bastards, the criminals who had stolen our country, vowing to never set foot in it again. He couldn't in any case, having been labelled an enemy of the regime for being a banker, a capitalist.

————

In Czechoslovakia we'd been part of a large and complex family. What can a child of four know about the dynamics of family relationships? What I knew was that I'd been embedded in a large, loving clan who cared for me – and suddenly they were gone and my world shrank to a paltry few. We'd left so many people behind. My father had been married twice before and had two sons from his first marriage and a daughter from the second. We'd left my parents' siblings, beloved aunts and uncles to Peter and me, my father's mother, and my mother's parents, Babi and Děda. The extended family we left behind was to become a cast of mysterious characters shrouded by distance and secrecy, mysteries that years later I became determined to solve.

———

My mother had a daughter, Irene, from her previous marriage, who was seventeen and had lived with us in Prague. A few days before my father left, Irene disappeared. During one of my parents' late-night conversations planning their escape, my father had declared emphatically that Irene was not to come with us. My mother was afraid Irene had overheard him and had run away to escape on her own. She was distraught, having no idea if Irene had made it or where she might be.

One day at the Hotel Olga we heard though the refugee grapevine, secret yet everywhere, that Irene had succeeded in escaping, guided by a friend, and was in a refugee camp in Germany. My mother pleaded with my father to try to find her. He set out, visiting camp after camp, each teeming with refugees. He finally found her, filthy and dressed in rags. He insisted she hide in the trunk of his car. He was stopped several times and waved on. But at the Austrian border, the car was searched and he had to open the trunk. He explained over and over that Irene was his step-daughter whom he was reuniting with her mother, rather than a case of abduction or white slavery. His visa and documents from the Nuremburg trials helped to establish his credibility and they were released.

Word came that Rudy, my father's twenty-four-year-old son from his first marriage, also wanted to escape and join us. Irene, through that same grapevine, contacted her friend and begged him to lead Rudy out. He simply arrived at the pension one day. We learned later that Irene's friend was caught going back and imprisoned.

The six of us lived at the Pension Olga for a year. Being a banker, my father had known what to do before leaving for Nuremburg to transfer money out of the country.

———

One day years later and far away, I watched a little boy and girl who looked to be about the same age Peter and I had been at the time of our escape. They were walking hand in hand with their mother, talking happily together and smiling up at her. The scene of our escape came back and a chill ran through me. I saw just how small that girl was, how vulnerable, and I was overwhelmed with terror to the point of nausea on their imagined behalf, and finally, my own.

———

My parents had impassioned discussions about where we should go. It came down to Canada or South America. My mother pleaded to stay in Austria – or anywhere in Europe – but my father insisted it was imperative that they leave. "We have to get as far away as possible," he said. "This communist blight could take over the entire continent." He prevailed. They applied for visas to Canada and were accepted. My father signed an agreement that he would farm, which was at the top of Canada's wish list. Of course he had no intention of becoming a farmer. He figured he'd finesse that when we got there.

One year after we'd arrived in Zell am See, the required documents came through. The six of us made our way to Liverpool and sailed to Montreal in 1949 on the Empress of Canada. I have several small black and white photographs of us on the ship, sitting on a staircase on the upper deck. We don't look like refugees, we look like adventurers. My mother, a hand raised to shield her eyes from the sun, is wearing a silk scarf to protect her hair from the breeze blowing across the bow of the ship.

PART ONE

Chapter I

THE EMPRESS OF CANADA STEAMED UP THE ST. LAWRENCE River and its massive bulk drew alongside the wharf in Montreal. Lines were thrown and secured, the gangplank was lowered and passengers began to stream off. We looked out at the country that was to become our home. Montreal looked raw. Low warehouses and storage buildings sprawled across the harbour.

We found a rooming house where we stayed for several weeks, then boarded a train to Toronto. My parents had Czech friends who had come to Toronto, some of whom my father considered potential business partners. In Toronto, we rented a modest house on Douglas Drive in Rosedale, across from Chorley Park.

Since my father was the only one who'd left with a legitimate visa, only he had brought luggage with things from home. One was a leather suitcase full of family photos, coffee table books of photographs of Prague and the Czech countryside, and several albums of 78 rpm records of Czech folk songs. A lifeline to everything we had left behind.

It was 1950. Peter and I were enrolled in kindergarten at Whitney Public School in north Rosedale. That first terrifying day, my mother walked us hand in hand along Summerhill Avenue, past Marshall's Drugstore, past the grocery store and the hairdressing salon, across the bridge over the train tracks and up the hill to the school. She had dressed us in our best clothes, as she would have in Europe, clothes bought in shops in Zell am See and Vienna. I wore a white blouse, a short grey knit wool skirt with straps, woolen knee socks and sturdy leather ankle boots. There was a large white taffeta bow in my hair, which was drawn back into two braids down my back. Peter wore a white shirt, *lederhosen* – leather shorts with suspenders – and ankle boots.

My mother kissed us goodbye, turned and left us standing in the cinder-covered yard amidst the shrieks and laughter of children running and playing, who, when they saw us, stopped in their tracks and stared. I stared back. Some stuck their tongues out. A boy came over and said something, laughing. I turned my back to him. His friends surrounded us, pointing, jeering. I clutched Peter's hand and we ran away, up a grassy hillside, where older children sat together under clumps of pine trees. A few smiled at us. We waited there until the bell rang, then followed as children streamed towards the school. A teacher separated me from Peter, as boys and girls had to line up at different doors, but once inside, an adult led me to the kindergarten classroom. Peter was there and I ran to him.

I was lucky to have a teacher who was kind to me. Miss Anglin introduced us to the class and must have said something that made the other children behave better – at least within earshot of a teacher. Those first years I endured ongoing

taunting from schoolmates and children in our neighbourhood. Toronto was not used to immigrants, especially not in
WASP Rosedale.

"What does DP mean?" I asked my father at dinner
one evening.

My parents were to speak to us in Czech for years, though
my father's English improved quickly and he understood it
well. My mother spoke to us only in Czech, wanting us to not
lose our language. Inevitably, Peter and I shifted from speaking
Czech the more we learned English, and it was from us that my
mother picked it up.

"Where did you hear that?" my father asked, frowning.

"Everywhere. Bill Bustard up the street. Kids at school."

"It stands for Displaced Person," he told me. "A person who
had to leave his own country and has no home. Refugees. But
we're not displaced," he went on. "We're here as immigrants,
not refugees." It didn't make much difference in the Toronto of
the 1950s.

Our next door neighbours seemed nice and had a girl my
age; they invited Peter and me to visit a relative's farm, and I
was thrilled to discover they had goats, the first time I'd been
close to such animals and I spent the afternoon playing with
them. A few weeks later that same neighbour knocked on our
front door. My mother opened the door.

"In Canada we do not let children play outside with no
clothes on," she said to my mother, slowly and loudly, as though
that would help her understand English. "I have seen your
children in your back yard without any clothes on. We don't
do that here."

My mother slammed the door, and that was the end of any
potential friendship.

My mother hated Toronto, hated Canada.

One day when I came home from school, my mother, in the kitchen preparing dinner, was in a rage. "That stupid cow of a neighbour!" she cried. Potato peelings flew from her hands. "I was sweeping the front steps. She was in her garden and came over, holding up a tulip. She said, *'Do you know what this is?'*" The knife slashed through the white flesh of the potatoes. "I just stared at her. She said, *'This is a tulip. Do you have tulips where you come from?'* I wanted to slap her face, to scream at her, 'What do you know of flowers and beauty in this hideous place? You have nothing like Wenceslas Square, its masses of tulips and roses, or our villa in Černošice. Our own gardener, our orchards of fruit trees, deer wandering through our woods.' But I couldn't say a word of it ..." She was crying now. "So I turned my back on her, to show her what a stupid woman she is."

Sometime later, we bought and moved to 300 Glen Road, two blocks away, with Chorley Park, which I had come to love, just down the street. Chorley Park, where the residence of Ontario's Lieutenant Governor had once stood, was an expanse of grass, flowering shrubs and pine trees perched on the edge of a deep ravine. A wide, open hillside was crisscrossed by paved paths curving their way down. Flagstones led under a small stone bridge and a steep trail wound down through the woods to the very bottom of the ravine. I thought there must have been a quarry down there once, as a section that dropped precipitously had been fenced off and posted with No Trespassing signs.

———

Having convinced the Canadian authorities that as a former bank director, he was not suited to farming, my father explored various business ventures. He tried importing knitting machines, but finding there was no market for them, he brought in European jewelry, rhinestone and filigree necklaces. No luck there either.

A community of Czechs who had also fled developed around Masaryk Hall at Queen Street West and Cowan, named after Tomáš Garrigue Masaryk, the founder and president of the previous democratic Czechoslovak republic. Many were friends whom my parents had known in Prague, like the Jelineks who lived in Oakville. My father had been associated with Mr. Jelinek's cork business in Prague, and they explored forming a partnership together. Though it didn't work out, our families visited one another often and Peter and I would play with Otto and Maria, who were the same ages as we were. I spent happy hours playing at paper dolls with Maria, chattering in Czech. One day the two of them would become Canada's Olympic skating champions and Otto a minister in the federal government.

My father had another Czech friend, Mr. Gora, whose family had settled in Guelph. Mr. Gora and my father created a successful business called Top Paper Products, headquartered at 77 York Street in downtown Toronto, supplying laundries with gummed tape for sealing packages of folded shirts and gummed tape handles for carrying the packages home. As president of Top Paper Products, my father would drive off to his office every morning in his two-tone green Studebaker and appear again at dinnertime. He was a patrician figure, tall and broad-shouldered, with very dark brown eyes. He'd stand smoking, one hand in his pocket, his teeth clamped down on a black cigarette holder with a gold band.

My mother pined for her parents and the life she had known. She learned English slowly and rarely ventured from the house. She was ashamed of not speaking English, yet she didn't seek out English classes or study on her own. We became members of Rosedale United Church. When she went shopping up Summerhill Avenue, she'd keep an eye out for someone from the church who might recognize her and would scurry to the other side of the street to avoid having to speak to them.

She was contemptuous of Canadians' stupidity about Europe, about arts and culture. "They look down their noses at me, those Rosedale ladies," she'd say. "But what have they got to be smug about? There's no culture here. Where are the cafés, the theatres and concert halls? Where are their opera houses? I detest this backward place!"

She told me once, "I didn't want to leave Prague. I begged my mother not to expect me to go. But she said, 'Your place is with your husband now, and your children.'"

When I came home from school, she'd be sitting at the dining table where she'd set up her sewing machine, and launch into a litany of complaints.

"At home," she'd say – Prague was and would forever be home – "your father would return from business trips in Vienna or Paris and bring me silks and fine lace, which I'd take to my dressmaker. Now look at me, having to sew my own clothes, and yours!"

But when she spoke of Prague, her voice was soft and full of yearning. "Do you remember," she'd ask, "the Vltava River, that wide, slow-moving river that runs through the very heart of Prague?" I'd sit down at the table, watching her, mesmerized, hanging on every word. "When I was little," she'd continue, "my parents would take me to the *kavárna* – the café – on Kampa Island and we'd sit and have ice cream and then go to the edge of the river and feed the swans. The linden trees were in full bloom. Oh, the sweet scent of linden blossoms! Will I ever smell that again?" She'd sigh. "Do you remember the castle? We took you there often with Babi and Děda, and strolled through the castle gardens. Everywhere you looked, such beauty, such magnificence! The National Theatre, the opera, the museum at the top of Wenceslas Square, all the parks, the church spires." She was close to tears.

Suddenly she'd wake from her reverie. "But that's all gone now," she said, the light fading from her eyes. "The days when we were surrounded by family, by music and laughter, and life was happy." She rose heavily from her chair. "Gone are the days when Cook would come in and say, 'Dinner is ready, madam.' I'm no longer madam. I'm the maid now, having to do everything." She put her sewing machine away and went into the kitchen.

***

My father's business was growing, and he was travelling often to the States. My mother envied his life outside the home. He controlled the money and gave her an allowance of $100 a week for groceries and other necessities. Thursday evenings they shopped together at the Loblaws supermarket in Leaside, my father feeling entitled to approve every purchase. This became another of her complaints.

One day I came running home, clutching blossoms I'd picked off a neighbour's hyacinth plants, hoping they might make her happy. As usual, she was at her sewing machine. Before I could say a word, she started on one of her tirades. "I am trapped in the house all day while the rest of you are out there busy doing things. At home I had friends and places to go, lovely places. Here I have nobody and nowhere to go but shopping. I told your father I wanted a job. Do you know what he said? 'No wife of mine is going to work!' And then added, 'Besides, what could *you* do?'

"Just like my parents!" she went on. "I told them I wanted to be an actress. They were horrified. 'That's no better than a prostitute!' they said. I gave up that dream."

I fidgeted. "So now your father flies off to Fort Wayne in his tailored suit," she continued, "his nails manicured by some charming manicurist at the King Edward hotel, while I'm having to make ends meet on a hundred dollars a week. I don't allow myself a cup of coffee when I go shopping, telling myself I'll save the ten cents and have my coffee at home." She started up the sewing machine. I dropped the squashed pink flowers on the dining table and went into the kitchen.

"Have you been picking neighbours' flowers again?" she shouted. "You mustn't steal from other people's gardens!" I stood in the kitchen, looking out at the cherry trees and strawberry beds my father had planted that spring. My mother's unhappiness washed over me like poison.

There were good times too. So we didn't lose our Czech heritage, Peter and I were sent to Masaryk Hall every Saturday morning. There were classes with Mr. Honza, who taught us Czech grammar, basic literature and history. After the lessons, there was Sokol, Czech gymnastics. This was my favourite part. I discovered I was good at somersaults and headstands, at leaping over the leather horse and hanging from my knees and swinging high and fast on rings suspended from the ceiling. At Masaryk Hall I didn't feel like an alien; with Sokol I felt I could fly.

Every third Saturday was bridge night at 300 Glen Road. I loved watching my mother sitting at her dressing table, putting on her makeup, dabbing perfume behind her ears, closing the clasp of her gold bracelet, heavy with charms. Her hair was soft and brown, her cheeks red and her blue eyes shining. She'd dress in one of the fine dresses she'd sewn. "Back home I used to win beauty contests," she'd tell me. "They'd drape lovely red sashes over me and present me with armfuls of roses."

Their friends the Masaryks and the Bermans would arrive. The Masaryks – no relation to the former president – were loud and funny, and at Christmas they gave Peter and me lavish gifts: a record player or a pair of budgie birds, my first pets. Mr. Masaryk used to take my father up to northern Ontario to fish. Old Mr. Berman had thick glasses and hunched shoulders. Mrs. Berman wore extravagant dresses and big gold rings on her gnarled hands.

I loved the father I saw at these bridge games. He laughed aloud, told stories and jokes and when they took a break from cards and listened to our Czech 78 rpm records, he'd burst into song and bang the table in time with the music. He could also erupt in anger, swearing at his partner when he made a mistake. The others would laugh and tell him to calm down. He'd laugh it off. My mother didn't play bridge. She kibitzed, brought the players drinks and served the midnight supper when the games were over. It amazed me that she wasn't keen to learn to play.

My father loved classical music, especially the Czech composers Dvořák and Smetana, and Czech folk songs. The house would reverberate to the sounds of Dvořák's Cello Concerto, his Humoresques, Smetana's *Má Vlast*. I loved singing along with him, and sometimes my mother joined in when they played the old recordings of *Ta Naše Písnička Česká*, "That Czech Song of Ours," or *Ty Staré Zámecký Schody*, "Those Old Castle Stairs," and the Czech-Canadian bass Jan Rubeš' deep, booming voice singing *Teče Voda, Teče*, "The Water Flows and Flows."

My mother read Peter and me Czech bedtime stories. My favourite was *Broučci*, an illustrated children's book they'd brought with them, its edges in tatters from a bomb that had destroyed a building across the street towards the end of the war, shattering every window in our apartment, I an infant and a near casualty. *Broučci* was a beautiful tale about the adventures of a family of fireflies. I would prop myself up in bed, crying, "Mommy, show me the pictures!" I loved that firefly family – gentle, loving and brave, even in the face of danger.

But most of the time my mother was lost in grieving for home and my father was preoccupied with starting all over again. I was left to cope by myself with school bullies and the enormous loss of having been uprooted. My parents didn't seem to realize how desperately lonely I was. At four, I had lost everything – my large and close extended family, my beloved nanny, my home, my language, and most of all, the loving, caring parents I had known for the first four years of my life. A teacher's report from the end of my kindergarten year reads, "Helen is finally becoming a little less dependent on Peter and has started to speak a few words."

————

Irene, my half-sister and Rudy, my half-brother, lived with us briefly at 300 Glen Road. Rudy wanted to go to college, and my father paid his way, but he skipped classes and failed. My father hired him to work in his company, starting at the bottom, but that didn't last long and my father fired him. He moved out and lived with a friend. Irene stayed with us longer and found a job as a salesgirl at a downtown department store. My father insisted that she give a portion of her wages to my mother to help with household expenses. At twenty-one, at Rosedale United Church, she married Jim Vogan, a Canadian accountant who worked for Revenue Canada. I served as her flower girl. She moved out of our house and in quick succession they had a girl, Debbie, and two boys, Dennis and Jeff.

When I was seven, two years after our arrival in Canada, my mother disappeared and it was my father making our dinner. I was frightened, despite my father's reassurances. "When she comes back, she'll bring you a present," he told me.

"A skipping rope!" I cried. "Daddy, please, tell her to bring me a skipping rope!"

A few days later, my father's green Studebaker pulled into the driveway and my mother got out. I threw the front door open, almost swooning with relief to see her. But something was wrong. She was carrying an armload of something and sat on the sofa, the bundle still in her arms. "Come here, Helen," she said. "See what I have brought you."

I stood where I was.

"Remember I told you Mommy would bring you a present?" my father said. I dragged my heels over to where she sat.

"This is your new baby brother," she said, pulling aside the corner of a blanket. There was a tiny face. "His name is Tommy."

I stared in horror and pulled away.

"Did you bring me my skipping rope?"

"Who cares about a silly skipping rope? You have a new baby brother!" my mother said.

I ran to my room.

I hated Tommy with all the hate a lonely child can muster. I'd stand in the corner and watch her changing his diaper as he lay on the bassinet, his fat legs waving. They set up his crib in their bedroom. My mother was endlessly feeding him, walking around with him in her arms, taking him out in his carriage.

There was a flat roof covered with tar and small round pebbles above the garage of our house. I discovered I could shinny up there, braced against the neighbour's house. I hid there often. No one knew where I was.

One summer's day, I climbed up there on a mission – to stay on the roof until they noticed I was missing. I sat breathing in the hot tar smell, watching through the leaves of our silver maple tree as a group of boys, including Peter, played road hockey.

Soon my mother would realize how long it had been since she'd seen me. She'd call out, and when there was no answer, she'd start searching. She'd summon my father, who'd come running. The two of them would look everywhere, and stricken, they would realize how dreadfully neglectful they'd been, and how much they loved me. I imagined the joy, the immense relief when I finally returned.

After what seemed like a very long time, I began to feel sorry for making them suffer, so I shinnied back down. My heart pounded as I stepped into the kitchen. My mother was at the sink, scrubbing carrots. "Hi," I said in a small voice.

"Set the table," she said, scarcely turning.

————

Shortly after Tommy was born, a black cloud descended on our house, and nothing was ever the same again. My mother had been desperately unhappy before, but this was different. When I came home from school, I could tell she had been crying. She looked broken. I would burst into the house, full of some new triumph – "I won a spelling bee today and Mr. Allen gave me a pear as a prize!" – or some new grief – "Bill Bustard called me a DP again!" – and she would look up blankly from her sewing machine, silent, the lines along the sides of her mouth etched deep.

She flew into sudden rages, once smashing a pot full of Lipton's chicken noodle soup against the kitchen counter, noodles and hot broth flying everywhere.

I was active and full of energy, a tomboy, and did handstands all over the house. One day I did a somersault over the back of the living room sofa and my shoe caught the corner of the coffee table, breaking the glass. My mother flew in from the kitchen, her blows raining on my head as she screamed, "Neřáde! Hajzlíku! Prevíte!" The shock of hearing those swear words from my mother's lips would linger forever. The shock of discovering she hated me.

One terrible day I came home from school and found her sitting at her dresser, her eyes blank. Suddenly she was struggling for breath, the veins on her neck standing out like ropes. She turned white and fell back on the bed, her eyes closed.

"*Maminko!*" I cried again and again, patting her cheek, shaking her shoulder.

Her eyes fluttered open briefly. "It will soon be over," she whispered.

I threw myself across her body, screaming, "No! Mommy, no, please don't leave me!" I lay on her, sobbing, certain she was dying. Eventually, she opened her eyes, pushed me off and slowly sat up. Holding on to the edge of the dresser, she darted a shamefaced look in my direction, pulled herself to her feet and walked slowly out of the room. She never spoke of it, never explained what had happened.

My father became a shadow. He'd come home from work, walk slowly up the stairs to change, then disappear until dinner to the backyard where he knelt tending to his horseradish patch and strawberries. He sat at the dinner table, his shoulders slumped. My mother's eyes narrowed when she looked at him and if he caught her glance, he'd look down, shamefaced. Tommy's arrival in our family must have caused this terrible change, I concluded, and I hated my brother all the more.

My mother gathered her children in to herself, away from my father. We looked out at him from under her angry, possessive embrace. Her voice was sharp and bitter when she spoke to him. I didn't know what he'd done, I only knew he was bad and it would be a betrayal of my mother to love him. With her attitude towards him and her behaviour, I knew I must not love him, not openly. I could only love him secretly and from a distance. He was lost to me.

One day, when I was nine, my father was listening to music in his den in the lower level of our house, where he'd set up a hi-fi sound system and an entire wall of records which he'd painstakingly indexed. I could hear beautiful music drifting up into the house. My mother was in the kitchen. I tiptoed downstairs and gathering my courage, I knocked on the door. No answer. I started to turn away, then turned back and knocked again, louder. I heard his chair creak, footsteps. The door opened and my father stood there.

"Could I come in and listen?" I asked tentatively.

His expression moved from surprise to a smile of welcome. "Come," he said, stepping aside. I took a seat on the sofa. He sat down at his green felt-covered table and continued to play solitaire. The music swelled. I knew it was an opera, though I didn't know the name, and the exquisite music filled my ears. Everything in me expanded and I felt blissful, the luckiest child in the world, sitting there with my father.

Suddenly the door opened, and my mother's head poked into the room. There was silence as she took in the scene. "What are you doing here, Helen?" she said.

"Listening to music," I said.

"Have you done your homework?"

"Most of it."

"Well, go finish it."

My father was silent. I rose, head down, and left the room. My mother closed the door and followed me up the stairs.

———

It was many years before I learned what had happened. My father had had an affair with a married woman in his office. She'd become pregnant and had given birth to their child close to the time when Tommy was born. My mother found out shortly after she came home from the hospital. Rudy, my father's son, was the one who told her, his revenge for my father having fired him. Rudy was ousted from the family; we had nothing to do with him for many years. My father ended the affair and my parents stayed together, but my mother never forgave him. Never again did I see her make a warm or loving gesture towards him.

She was trapped. She had loved my father and was utterly dependent on him. She couldn't work, didn't speak English yet and had few friends of her own. She couldn't return home; she'd be arrested. And how could she leave her children? Later I understood her helpless rage and profound depression, yet I hated to see my father, whom I adored, so diminished. As a teenager, I wished they would separate, so each could find happiness. I came to the conclusion, observing them, that I wanted a life like his, a life nothing like hers. Never, I vowed, would I be helpless and dependent as she was. Never.

———

How unfortunate that children only know their parents as parents: older, and then old. My father was already forty-six when I was born, still a handsome man. In one photograph I found years later, a photograph from before we left Prague, he is strolling down a street just outside the bank where he was president. He's wearing a bowler hat, a jacket, tie and dapper brown and white shoes, and in one hand he holds a pair of soft leather gloves. It's his elegant stance that is eye-catching. No wonder women fell for him. It was too bad my mother wasn't able to be his match, though she might have been had they stayed in Prague. Her inability to cope with living in exile, with life in Canada, her depression and complaints, must have made her unattractive to him. She had been beautiful and brave once.

⁂ Chapter 2

AS A YOUNG GIRL, I STRUGGLED WITH TWO CONFLICTING
messages from my mother about my future. The first was
hopeless: since I was a girl, I was doomed to a constricted life
as a wife and a mother, dependent on my husband, fortunate if
he was kind to me. I developed a hatred for anything domestic,
resentful when I had to wash dishes while my brothers played
outdoors. I refused to learn to cook and avoided housework.

The second message was her fervent wish for me. "Don't be
like me," she'd say. "Aim higher, have a life different than mine."
But if the first was inevitable, I wondered, how could she
exhort me to the second?

I became a loner and a rebel, both arrogant and vulnerable.
I told myself I was better than these stupid Canadian girls. Yet
I was lonely and anguished, afraid there was something wrong
with me that made them not like me.

I spent many hours alone in Chorley Park. I'd scramble
over the fence with the No Trespassing sign and climb trees,
explore, lose myself in a book. Or at the top of our street, I'd
climb the wire mesh fence and walk along the railway tracks to
school, instead of taking the long way up Summerhill and over
the bridge. The No Trespassing signs were for others.

When I was ten, my parents did something that made all the difference; they sent me to Camp Shawanaga in Georgian Bay for an entire month. They deposited me and my big steamer trunk on a train that travelled north through exotic-sounding places like Port Severn, Victoria Harbour, Waubashene. We flew across the water and landed on a wild and rocky island covered with leaning pine trees. At camp I discovered I was fast, courageous and athletic. I learned to swim, to dive from high towers, to sail, to solo canoe. I played the Tin Man in a production of *The Wizard of Oz*. Going off by myself to read, I'd pick blueberries and lie on the moss and watch the clouds sail by. I was reprimanded again and again for going barefoot. But for me, camp was about freedom, and to me that included running barefoot.

I adored Camp Shawanaga, but after I'd been there for two summers, my mother received a letter from the camp director, advising that if my defiant behaviour didn't improve, I wouldn't be welcome back. Sure enough, the letter arrived the next autumn, confirming I was not to come back. My mother found other camps for me – Wahcahmie, Tapawingo – but I never loved them as much as Shawanaga. I grieved and didn't know what I had done wrong. I wanted to be accepted and to belong, but on my own terms.

I was becoming strong and self-sufficient, yet underneath was a core of grief and profound loneliness. No one held me close. Casting around for solace, I took my mother's stories of Prague and created a vision of paradise lost – the place where I'd been loved, where we'd been happy. If only I could be there, everything would be good again.

My mother enrolled me in Brownies, but my new friend Linda and I got thrown out for being disruptive, and then when we were caught smoking behind Rosedale United Church, we were thrown out of Girl Guides as well.

I wanted to be popular, yet I despised most girls as silly or stupid. But by Grade Five, to my surprise, I'd earned a place in the main clique of girls: Sharon MacIntosh, Irene Dennie, the kind of girls I'd seen on my first day of kindergarten, sitting together under the pines. I was invited to their parties, which included boys, and we played spin the bottle.

I had an entrepreneur's mind. When my father brought home large rolls of gummed tape, I rewound them into small rolls of one or two yards each. Out of a cardboard box I fashioned a tray, attached a ribbon to either side and filled the tray with the small gummed tape rolls. Then I went door to door in my neighbourhood, selling the rolls for five cents "or whatever you'd like to donate," explaining the proceeds were for the Red Cross. If challenged, I'd say, "We have a Red Cross donation box in my classroom and I put all the money in that box." But that Red Cross box never saw a penny.

In Grade Six, at the yearly visit to the school nurse to read the eye chart, all I could see was the top E. I'd had trouble reading it the year before and had talked the girl next to me into whispering the letters to me. This time I didn't get away with it. My mother took me to an optometrist and to my horror, chose glasses with hideous pale brown frames. I looked ugly, with glasses and pigtails down to my waist, as no amount of begging convinced my parents to let me get my hair cut or to wear it free. A cute, athletic boy named John Thomas that I had a secret crush on sat in front of me. John Thomas wore glasses, but on him they looked good. Now and then he'd take them off and place them on his desk. I took mine off whenever he did and casually placed them on my desk too.

I also liked John Sakaris, who lived nearby, and I'd pick him up on the way to school. We and a few others would go over to Colin Crowe's after school to practise kissing in the room above his garage.

At field days I'd enter everything and come home with ribbons. My report cards were good, but my teachers' comments said, "Could do much better if she applied herself." There were too many other things on my mind.

I graduated from Whitney School and my parents sent me to St. Clement's, an academically demanding private school for girls, to which I was awarded a scholarship. I accused my mother of sending me there to get me away from boys. All the other girls seemed content, whereas I felt like an alien, waiting to be unmasked. I wore a white blouse, a red blazer and a navy tunic whose crest bore the school motto: *Vincit Omnia Veritas.* Truth conquers all. But I was an imposter, a wild child tamed by a scarlet and navy uniform. A Bohemian in Canadian disguise.

And yet I flourished and came to love that school. The requirement for teachers at St. Clement's seemed that they all be old, unmarried women. I learned to open the door with a little bow and say, "Good Morning, Miss Waugh. Good morning, Miss Conway." I loved Miss Henry, the math teacher, the ugliest woman I'd ever seen, with sallow skin, wire-rimmed glasses and a mouthful of crooked teeth. I was thrilled when I could shoot up my hand to answer a question and be rewarded by a brief nod and the ghost of a smile. Classes were small, the girls were smart and I made friends. I played on the ice hockey and basketball teams against other private girls' schools, and in Grade Thirteen played Puck in *A Midsummer Night's Dream.*

My first serious boyfriend, whom I met at a party when I was eighteen, was Bob Bradley. Bob was strikingly good looking with short red hair and jet black eyebrows. Bob went to Jarvis Collegiate and drove a motorcycle. He'd pick me up after school every day, revving his motorcycle out front. I'd run out in my tunic and oxfords and leap on the back, feeling the glares from the prefects and teachers standing on the school steps burning into my back. No wonder I wasn't a prefect despite my marks being among the top in my class.

One evening after Bob and I had been to the movies and he'd driven me home, I decided to invite him in for a coffee. My parents hadn't met him, had no intention of meeting him and were opposed to the idea of my having a boyfriend at all – or in fact having friends at all. My mother in particular was critical of every friend I had.

"Are you sure it's all right?" Bob said.

"We'll have to be quiet," I said.

My parents always left the door unlocked until my curfew, and it was my job to lock it when I came home. I opened the door and listened. Yes, they were in bed. I signalled him in and we crept across the hall into the kitchen. I made coffee and we sat at the kitchen table, whispering. We always had a million things to say to one another.

Suddenly a floorboard creaked upstairs and my father's voice boomed from the top of the stairs, "Who's there?" We both froze. "What's going on down there?"

"It's just me," I said. "I've invited Bob in for a coffee. We're just talking."

My father was marching down the stairs – in his pyjamas. I ran to stop him. Bob stood up. My father charged into the kitchen and grabbed the back of Bob's jacket.

"Stop that!" I yelled. "We weren't doing anything!"

My father marched Bob to the front door, opened it and threw him down the porch steps. He slammed the door shut, locked it, turned on me. "Don't ever invite anyone here again without my permission!" he said and climbed back up the stairs. I hated him at that moment, him and his accent and his suspicious European ways. I had become pretty. It made him want to control me, and it agonized my mother.

I ran to my room and slammed the door, convinced I'd never see Bob again. But he came after school the next day, and over a milkshake at Paul's Ranch House on Bloor Street, he consoled me for my bad luck in the parent department.

Several weeks later I found a solution. Bob brought me home on time. My parents were in bed but wouldn't fall asleep until they'd heard the lock click. I locked the door and deliberately made noise as I climbed the stairs and closed my bedroom door firmly. After waiting a few minutes, I took the sheets off my bed, knotted them together and tied the end to one foot of the radiator beside my window. My bedroom was on the second floor at the back, overlooking the garden. I opened the window wide, let myself down the rope, and ran to Chorley Park where Bob was waiting for me. We lay together among the bluebells under the bridge.

Hours later, I crept to the side of the house, stuck my arm through the milk box, and turning the Yale lock, pulled the door open. I tiptoed up the stairs, avoiding the ones that creaked, and in my room I'd remake my bed and go to sleep. My parents never found out.

I stole. On the way home from school, a group of us would cluster around the Garfield News stand in the subway station. When the harried clerk turned her back, I and a few like-minded classmates shoved chocolate bars and gum into the pockets of our red blazers. At Simpson's, on my own, I'd take an armload of clothes into a fitting room and slip my favourite things into a bag containing one item I had paid for, returning the rest to the salesclerk with a shrug of disappointment.

But one day, I had just left the store when a heavy hand landed on my shoulder, and a voice said, "Excuse me, Miss, I believe you have something that doesn't belong to you. Come with me."

In the office upstairs, frightened out of my wits, I apologized and swore I'd never do it again. The man regarded me silently. Finally he spoke. "I'm going to let you off this time," he said, "but if we ever catch you stealing again, I won't hesitate to call the police." He picked up the phone. "I am, however, going to call your parents."

His assistant drove me home, a silent car ride. I was in a panic at what my parents would do. They fought. My father blamed my mother for spoiling us, my mother blamed him for being so miserly that I had to steal to have nice things. I watched them, relieved and sad. But I never stole again.

I graduated with good marks and went off to Queen's University. Bob gave way to football heroes and hockey players, during four giddy years of independence, parties, football games, drinking, wild nights, hard work, boyfriends, a few girlfriends and sports. I played left winger on the Queen's girls' A hockey team and forward on the girls' basketball team. I loved the intellectual challenge of my classes and worked as hard as I had to, eventually earning a degree in English and philosophy.

During my childhood, my father had taken us up to Chinook Lodge in Haliburton for the month of August. It had a main lodge with a huge fireplace, a ping-pong table, and shelves full of books and games; a dozen cabins, a wonderful beach, swings and shuffleboard courts. We went swimming every day, walked along the road picking raspberries, and sat around the bonfire, roasting marshmallows and singing campfire songs with the other guests. My summers were glorious, July at camp, August at Chinook. My father was doing well; another company he'd founded, Pines Plastics, had taken off. When I was fourteen, the owner of Chinook Lodge put it up for sale, and my father bought it, not to operate commercially, just for our family. My parents had the larger cottage, and each of us had our own cabin – Peter, my younger brother Tom (with whom I'd become not only reconciled but close friends), me, Irene and her husband Jim, and their three children.

One summer, when I was in my early twenties, a young foreign girl, whose name was also Helen, suddenly appeared at Chinook. My parents spoke with her in Czech. My father was friendly with her, while my mother tolerated her. I followed my mother's example. Though busy with my boyfriend, I was upset by this interloper and was puzzled by the secrecy surrounding her. Nobody explained to me who she was. Years later, I was to discover the existence of my father's eldest son, Malý Pavel, or Little Paul, the son who'd joined the Communist party, had been left behind and whom my father had disowned. This young girl, with the same name as mine, it turned out, was his daughter. My niece.

In 1964 we were living on Banbury Drive in Don Mills, in a larger house with a swimming pool. I was home from university for the summer and had a job as a waitress in a café in Yorkville. When I came home from work one day, my mother met me at the door, waving an airmail letter. "They're coming! They've finally been given visas and they're coming!"

My mother had tried to invite my grandparents and Uncle Paul many times, but their applications for a visa were denied every time. The only way citizens were allowed out of Czechoslovakia was if they were invited by an immediate family member who guaranteed to pay all their expenses. Czech citizens were not allowed to take crowns out of the country; the currency was worthless internationally in any case. Most had no access to hard currency, so they were trapped in the country monetarily as well as physically. My grandmother had died in 1962, two years earlier. My mother, unable to attend her funeral, grieved terribly. It was my grandfather and my Uncle Paul who were coming. My mother raced around the house, preparing the guest bedroom, making the house shine. We talked about nothing but the upcoming visit.

"How come they're letting them out?" I asked.

"Uncle Paul's finally married now, at sixty-two." my mother said. "He married a widow named Růža – Rose – who has written to me and seems very nice."

"She's being left behind as a hostage," my father said, "to make sure they come back. As if at 86 and 62 they're going to make a break for it!"

The day came and my parents left for the airport. Irene came over, and she, my brothers and I watched out the living room window until our car pulled into the driveway. We raced to the door. My father and Uncle Paul carried their suitcases, while my mother held her father's arm, her face radiant. They were ushered into the hall, and choked with emotion, my mother introduced us all.

My grandfather had white hair in a brush cut, his pink scalp shining through. He carried a silver-handled cane and wore a suit and vest that must have been elegant once. He had the kindliest eyes I'd ever seen. My uncle was tall, gaunt and severe. His eyes shocked and frightened me. They were pale blue, sunk deep into their sockets, yet protruding and wide.

One after the other, they took us in their arms and spoke to us in Czech. "*Helenko, dítě drahá, konečné Tě zas vidím!*" my grandfather whispered. Helen, dear child, at last I see you again. I felt his love envelop me. My uncle held my arms and stared at me, wordless, then clasped me to him, repeating, "*Helenko, Helenko!*"

Over the two weeks of their stay, I remained shy with them. I understood what they said but, not having spoken Czech for many years, could barely speak to them. They were foreign, yet dear. They smelled of mothballs and sweat, yet I wanted to be with them. I watched and listened to them hungrily, taking in every word.

When my mother took them to the supermarket, they were astonished by the abundance, the fruits and vegetables beautifully displayed, the variety of meats and cheeses. We went to dinner at the Victoria Room of the King Edward Hotel, where my father would take us to celebrate birthdays and other special occasions. My grandfather and uncle stared in awe at the beauty and elegance of the room and at the profusion of food available, amazed by the graciousness of the servers.

When we sat in our living room, the drapes wide open behind us, they kept glancing over their shoulders. "Shouldn't we close the curtains?" they said.

"No, it's fine," my parents assured them. "No one's watching us here."

One day we were sitting all together. My grandfather was speaking; his smile lit up his face, my uncle was nodding, my mother happy, animated. I thought, "I am sitting in the presence of God and his angel." I felt a profound attachment I had never felt before. I loved them deeply – and I felt loved.

When we took them to the airport, I cried, and when they were gone, I was bereft. I vowed to see them again one day.

———

Two years later, in the spring of 1966, I graduated from Queen's. I was twenty-two. My boyfriend, Larry Jones, tall, dark-haired with black-rimmed glasses, was a star Queen's hockey player and graduated in law the same year.

The graduation ceremonies over, my proud parents stood on the lawn outside Grant Hall, waiting to drive me home. Larry and I sat on a picnic table, talking about what the summer would bring. Separation. Looking for jobs, I in Toronto, he in Guelph. It was hard saying goodbye to our university days but not, we hoped, to one another.

"Why don't we forget about looking for jobs until the fall?" I said, suddenly excited. "Let's go to Europe!"

A grin spread across Larry's face.

"I've wanted to go for so long," I said. "Now's the perfect time. What do you think?"

"I think ... that would be grand," he said.

Through sheer determination, I convinced my parents to let me go. I'd saved money from my summer jobs and my father gave me the rest. My parents saw us off at the airport.

Chapter 3

WE LANDED AT THE LONDON AIRPORT, AND THUMBING through our copy of *Europe on Five Dollars a Day*, found an inexpensive B&B in Knightsbridge. We agreed we'd stay three weeks before heading to the continent.

"I don't want to be just a tourist," I said to him as we strolled hand in hand around London one day. "I want to live like a Londoner. I'm going to find a job."

I landed a part-time job as a waitress in a posh hair salon. Five days a week I left the B&B and rode the crowded Tube to work, where I put on my black uniform and white apron and cap, and served tea and scones to ladies under their hair dryers. When my hours were up, Larry and I met and we explored London together.

"I can't wait to get to the continent – the real Europe," I said as the three weeks were drawing to a close. "Let's head for Paris next."

"I'm not that keen on Paris," Larry said.

"What? In Europe and you don't want to go to Paris!"

He shrugged. "France isn't that high on my list."

"I definitely want to go to Paris, and to France generally," I said. "Here's an idea. Why don't we each go where we want to and meet regularly in between? We can stay in touch through American Express offices." Larry agreed.

Several days later I left my job and, having done a little research in the local papers, I drove back to the B&B on a used blue Lambretta scooter I'd just bought. "Here's how I'm going to travel," I called as he came out. "What do you think?" He laughed and shook his head.

It was hard parting with Larry, but bursting with excitement, I took off for Dover on a warm, sunny July day. I flew along, the wind in my hair, my one small suitcase strapped to the luggage rack behind me. I was free, and I was heading to the continent. Every adventure was waiting for me.

At Dover I met three young American guys on motorcycles and we exchanged travel plans as we crossed the Channel. We waved farewell in the sombre port of Calais, where I had the sense that the war still loomed large, and I set off into the French countryside.

In Paris I stood in the Louvre with tears in my eyes staring at Picasso's *Guernica*, a print of which I'd hung in my apartment at university. I sat in outdoor cafés smoking Gitanes, drinking in the bustle and elegance of Parisian street life along with my espresso. Then down the A1 to Lyon, through Provence, all melons and lavender, flying down the highway in my shorts and t-shirt – no helmet required back then – stopping for meals of French baguettes and brie, a glass of burgundy or chablis, and overnighting in inexpensive village *gites*.

Larry and I were reunited in Rome. He hopped on the back of my scooter and we drove across to the Adriatic, swam in that brilliant green sea, and up to Venice, where we stayed for a few wonderful days. No matter how much I loved every place we went, I was being drawn by a powerful magnet pulling me to Central Europe, into the heart of the continent where I was convinced my own heart lay.

We went to the opera in Vienna, sat in cafés enjoying the sound of zither music – I was so close I could hardly bear it. I found the Czech consulate and succeeded in getting a tourist visa. Larry and I parted, agreeing to meet in Munich in ten days. Finally, finally I set off for Czechoslovakia, and Prague.

———

As I drove through the Austrian countryside, farmers raked rows of sweet-smelling hay to dry in the sun, while herds of cows grazed high on hillsides. In villages, houses looked freshly painted, immaculate, flowers spilling from every window.

The stark contrast when I reached the border was shocking.

A chain-link fence stretching into the distance on either side of the road separated the two countries. The road ahead was blocked by two striped barriers and between them, a sunken bit of pavement. A low cement-block building with a corrugated metal roof guarded the road. Beyond, drab buildings, grey with dirt.

I pulled up to the first barrier, and turned off the ignition. I waited. Some minutes later, two guards in green uniforms sauntered out of the guardhouse, one hand on the rifles slung over their shoulders. They looked me over. My tentative smile was not returned.

"*Dokumenty*," one of them barked. He was older, short and swarthy, his shirt sweat-stained. The other one, thin, blond, walked around my scooter, examining it and me. I fumbled in my backpack and produced my Canadian passport with my tourist visa.

"What's the purpose of your visit?" demanded the older man, flipping through my passport.

"Do you speak English?" I tried. Annoyed, he shook his head. I hadn't spoken Czech for years.

"*Turist*," I said tentatively. "*Jedu do Prahy.*"

"Who are you visiting? Where are you staying?" he asked, his eyes narrowing.

"No one. Hostel."

"You were born here. Don't you have relatives?"

I shook my head, gestured like it was nothing to me.

"Why did you leave?" he continued.

How torn I was! They were speaking Czech, the language I loved, a language like music to me. Yet frightening now.

"I was small," I managed.

"And now?" he asked.

I struggled to answer. Finally, "I just want to visit."

The two guards looked at one another.

"Wait," ordered the one holding my passport, and they turned and went into the guardhouse. Could they still turn me away? Where is the place my mother spoke of so longingly, the place it broke her heart to leave? Anger welled up. What have they done to my country?

Eventually the older guard came out and with a curt nod, handed back my documents. I started the engine. The first barrier went up. I drove carefully down the steep incline and the barrier descended behind me. I waited. The second barrier rose. I eased my scooter up the other side and drove forward, the barrier crashing down behind.

I was reliving the reverse of that day eighteen years before, when my mother had hauled Peter and me across the border.

I headed for a drab stucco-covered building with a plain sign above the door. *Hospoda.* Pub. Potholes in the road. A strange, oppressive silence. As I drove, the few people out on the street turned to stare at me. Taking my suitcase with me, I pulled open the grimy door and stepped inside. Every head turned as I made my way to a table and sat down. The room was thick with smoke, a dingy room with rough wooden tables. The other patrons were mostly men, talking loudly, gesturing. Work-worn faces, sunken cheeks, bad teeth, unkempt hair. An odd heaviness to them. They looked at me with suspicion.

A waiter in a soiled apron and shiny black pants came over, carrying a tray of beer. I nodded. He set a stein down, drew a stroke on a slip of paper in front of me and moved on. I settled into my chair, drank my beer, listening to the sound of home, to that magic, musical language. This is a provincial town, I told myself. Wait and see. For despite the squalor around me, I felt joyful. Home at last.

A youngish man, a few years older than I, was standing at the tap. He wore dirty blue coveralls, like most of the men in the room. His hands were rough and his hair greasy. But when he turned in my direction to pick up a fresh beer, I caught my breath. He looked like me! I recognized myself in his face. He had high cheekbones and his nose was just like mine, a little up-tilted at the tip, with a small bump at the bridge. So this was a Czech nose I'd been sporting all these years.

What might he have been like if he'd grown up with the opportunities I'd been given? And who might I have become had I been raised here?

———

Back on the road, I encountered very little traffic. Every now and then a large black Tatra with darkened windows slid past me, or a rusty truck rattled by, its canvas cover flapping. When I drove through villages, every head turned to stare. My smiles weren't returned. It didn't matter. I was back and I was heading for home.

The contrast with the rest of Europe was devastating. How could a country be so ruined? Who benefitted from the destruction? Rusty ancient tractors stood in neglected fields. Garbage littered the sides of the road. In villages the houses were dilapidated, paint peeling off window frames. Clay tile roofs had holes in them like missing teeth.

As I drove north through the countryside of southern Bohemia, the rolling hills were beautiful, as were the deep pine forests. My mother's eyes would shine as she described them to me, forests that were tended and cared for, unlike what she saw as the crude forests of Canada. Each was managed by a forester; no undergrowth allowed to sprout, so that a person could stroll on the carpet of pine needles, searching for mushrooms – *bolety, václavky, lišky* – to their heart's content.

Here and there were fields that had been planted, patchwork squares of green grass or waving grain sloping across the hillsides, and dark jade ponds nestled in valleys. There were towns I drove through whose former glory was still recognizable. Magnificent churches with thin spires, pale green copper domes, bell towers sounding the hours. I avidly read the signs above shop windows, the signposts along the road, the names of towns and villages, saying them aloud, tasting the language in my mouth.

Suddenly, at the top of a hill, I rounded a curve and slammed on my brakes, skidding to the shoulder on the loose gravel.

Prague lay below me, shimmering in the sunlight. I burst into tears, taking in the breathtaking panorama below. It was as if my entire life had been leading up to this moment. Now that I was home, the years of loneliness and longing, the sense of profound loss that had dogged me, all that would be washed away. I cried with joy.

The city below was familiar from the books I'd pored over so often: the wide meandering river, spanned by many bridges; thousands of church spires; undulating waves of red clay tiles that graced every roof. Prague Castle spread majestically across the hillside overlooking the river. And the parks! Oases of lush green everywhere. Here was my city.

Suddenly in a hurry, I swept into town, following the signs to *Centrum*, bumping along cobblestones and avoiding tram tracks. And then there I was, in the heart of the heart of Europe. I drove wide-eyed, slowly, gazing with wonder at the sights. Here was the wide kilometre-long boulevard of Wenceslas Square with its huge statue of the Czech patron saint on his horse at the top of the square. Behind it, as backdrop, the magnificent museum.

I navigated the cobblestones to Old Town Square, overwhelmed by the beauty of the architecture, one building more awe-inspiring than the next. In all my travels throughout Europe, I hadn't seen such magnificence. There were Gothic, Baroque, Rococo and Art Nouveau buildings, gloriously decorative. Most of the apartment buildings that lined the streets were of the Renaissance style, adorned with balconies, statues and frescoes. Ancient stone churches abounded, with gargoyles leering from up high. I found the river and, parking my scooter, I stood on Charles Bridge and gazed up at the castle, the seat of the ancient kings of Bohemia who had once ruled most of Europe.

I crossed the bridge into Malá Strana, the Little Quarter, and explored its winding gas lit lanes and houses nestled against one another. Ancient Prague, mysterious, seductive. Its power claimed me.

Everywhere I saw ancient beauty, legacies of the past, hidden under decades of dirt and neglect. The sidewalks, constructed years ago with intricate patterns of grey, pink and white square stones, were in disrepair. Missing stones had been patched with rough gobs of asphalt. But here were the old castle steps that I knew from the song.

Nothing prepared me for the magnificence of Prague Castle. I stared in awe at the soaring gothic St. Vitus Cathedral within the castle walls. I walked from courtyard to courtyard and discovered the Golden Lane, its impossibly tiny houses that I had to bend over to enter; houses, I read, that in the sixteenth century were homes to castle craftsmen.

I walked down Nerudova Street, retrieved my scooter, and inquiring at one of the larger hotels in Wenceslas Square, was directed to a hostel on a side street nearby, a university residence during the school year, a hostel in the summer. Once settled in, I was back on the street, love battling rage and grief. Shops were utilitarian, ugly, with meagre goods on display. A fruit and vegetable shop had nothing but potatoes, onions and a few wilted carrots in cardboard boxes in the window. Inside, the shelves were empty. Many buildings were hidden behind scaffolding covered with torn rags of netting flapping in the breeze, but no work was being done.

What broke my heart were the people. There was no laughter. Grim, careworn and closed, faces sallow and doughy, bodies heavy. Everyone looked exhausted and old. Passersby scurried about their business, eyes downcast, backs bent, their clothes shapeless and drab. How could an entire people be so ruined? I wandered the streets, drinking in the sound of Czech all around me, staring into the faces I passed. I wanted them to recognize me, to acknowledge me as one of them. I was searching for welcome in the eyes of these strangers. I didn't find it.

The next day, I set out to find where Grandfather, Uncle Paul and Růža lived, the apartment where my mother had grown up. Jugoslávská 11. Number eleven Yugoslavia Street. Consulting my map, I realized I could walk there. Up the broad sweep of Wenceslas Square, around the museum, and up Bělehradská. I was in the neighbourhood called Královské Vinohrady – the Royal Vineyards, the neighbourhood, I recalled my mother telling me, where I'd been born. Several blocks further, I found Jugoslávská, and there, on the corner, was the building.

This was the apartment my grandparents had come back to after that final train journey accompanying my mother, Peter and me to the border town eighteen years before. A five-storey building, it was shabby now, its stucco dark with soot, the marble facing on the street level cracked, the concrete balusters on the balconies crumbling. I stood across the street looking up at the windows, wondering which one might be theirs. What if they were at their window just then, looking out over the square, seeing a young woman standing here but not knowing it was me? I'd asked my mother not to write them that I was coming, in case I didn't get a visa. What if they were away? And if I did knock on their door, how could my limited Czech do justice to the enormous significance of my reunion with my grandfather and Uncle Paul?

I crossed the street. There on the two rows of buttons was the name Kratochvíl, my mother's maiden name. I hesitated, fearful again of no answer, of having to explain myself into a metal grid. I nudged the street door and found it wasn't locked. Pushing it open, I was assaulted by the smell of cooking in the musty hallway. To my right, circular cement steps wound around a wrought iron elevator shaft that rose up the centre of the building. I climbed the stairs, my heart pounding.

There were only two apartments per floor, and on the second floor, I found my grandfather's name on a brass plate. František Kratochvíl, Advokát. I stood there for a few moments, and then, my hand shaking, I pressed the doorbell.

Silence. I waited. And then I heard footsteps, the sound of slippers on an uncarpeted floor, a chain being removed. Another one. Yet another. The rattle of a set of keys, and fumbling hands pushed a key into a lock. Through the door I could hear the sound of breathing, a bolt sliding, then a doorknob turning. My Uncle Paul stood there, with his shock of white hair, his pale blue protruding eyes. His face was greyer now, his body a bit stooped. It took him a moment, then his eyes opened wide and tears sprang into them. "*To je Helenka!*" he whispered hoarsely, opening his arms and enfolding me. "*Vítám Tě, dítě,*" he said. Welcome, child. He pulled me inside and closed the door behind us.

"Růža, come here!" he called over his shoulder. "It's Helen, from Canada!" A tiny, round, grey-haired woman emerged and came running down the dark hallway. She grasped both my hands and, pulling me down, wrapped her arms around me and kissed me on both cheeks.

Uncle Paul secured the many locks and hurried me through the narrow hallway. He gestured toward a closed door on our right, one finger to his lips. "Strangers," he whispered. We entered a small anteroom. There sat my grandfather, snoozing in an armchair beside the coal stove, looking just as I remembered him, though thinner. He still had that snow white brush cut. Uncle Paul gently touched his arm and he awoke with a start.

"We have a visitor," my uncle said. "Look who is here!"

My grandfather and I looked at one another. Recognition shone in his eyes, and he struggled to get up. Instead I knelt by his chair and we embraced and wept.

My uncle ushered me to a lace-covered table and the four of us sat gazing at one another, taking each other in. Růža disappeared and soon reappeared with coffee and pastries. Uncle Paul produced four small glasses and a bottle of Becherovka, Becker Bitters, a sweet and tangy liquor, and we toasted. They wanted to know everything about their Canadian family. I cursed my rusty Czech.

Uncle Paul pointed at the wall and whispered, "The Communists allocated so many metres per person, and with just Grandfather and me, before Růža, they decided we had too much space and gave half our flat to strangers. We have to share the bathroom with them." He shuddered with distaste.

"Much as we grieved your family's departure, you were right to leave," he continued. "It's been a nightmare here. Purges, people hauled in by the police and never seen again. We live in a prison. We never know when a knock on the door will come and one of us will get dragged away. False charges, often no charges. No better than under the Nazis. Worse, because these are Czechs, our own people! We live in constant fear. Anyone could be an informer. So could they, for all we know," he said, pointing to the wall. "You can't trust anyone.

"They say it's going to get better now. This fellow Dubček whose star is rising, he's a communist, but he talks about 'socialism with a human face.' A contradiction in terms, in my opinion. But he's challenging the harshness of the regime and advocating a lowering of restrictions and prohibitions. Some people are hopeful; I'm not so sure. But for now, a few things are loosening up. Perhaps we can breathe a little easier."

How extraordinary that I understood everything he said, yet could barely formulate an adequate response. It didn't matter. We toasted again.

"Did your mother ever tell you I knew the exact moment of your birth, even though I was away?" he asked, fixing me with his unnerving eyes. I shook my head. That was one story she hadn't told me. "I knew exactly, not only the date but the hour. She confirmed it when I came home."

I had difficulty looking at him. He had the eyes of someone who has seen things that couldn't be spoken aloud. What had happened to my Uncle Paul was a mystery that no one talked about when I was young. It was my sister Irene who told me years later, since she had been there. After divorcing her first husband, Irene's father, my mother had returned with Irene, then ten, to live with her parents and brother, Uncle Paul.

It was 1941, during the Nazi occupation. One night there was a loud banging on the apartment door. Two Nazis burst in, shouting in German. Shoving Uncle Paul and Grandfather aside, they tore through the apartment, ransacking every room. Not a word about what they were looking for. Irene knew they had a radio tube for receiving Radio Free Europe, and while the Nazis were in the next room, she found it and hid it in her pocket, knowing they'd all be arrested if it were found. She wasn't searched. My grandmother watched as the apartment was torn apart.

What they pounced on were two antique muskets, unusable collectors' items, mounted on the wall among other curios. My grandfather and uncle were arrested and led away. My grandfather was released the next day, but my uncle was sent to a concentration camp, charged with unlawfully owning firearms. It was suspected a spiteful neighbour had informed on him.

He endured four years of the most horrific forced labour, loading the bodies of people – men, women, children who had been gassed – into wheelbarrows and dumping them into pits dug by other prisoners.

When the Allies drew near, the Nazis abandoned the camps and any survivors who could walk straggled out. The long march homeward began. They were emaciated and many fell by the wayside. Learning of these death marches, the allies sent trucks to pick up the survivors and take them home. Irene remembered vividly the day she, my mother and my grandparents stood on the sidewalk outside, having received news that the transports were coming. Uncle Paul was deposited on the sidewalk, a skeleton, his hair white and that ghastly expression in his eyes. Slowly they nursed him back to health, feeding him spoonsful of soup and thin porridge until he regained his strength.

But back then, as we sat around the table, I didn't know the details of the story, I only experienced the chilling expression in my uncle's eyes.

"I see you still have that scar on your forehead," Uncle Paul said to me. I reached up and felt the small bump above my left eye. "Do you know how that happened?" he asked.

I nodded.

Uncle Paul turned to Růža. "It was 1945, before I came home. Helen, less than a year old, was lying in her basket out on their balcony on Blanická, covered by a fur rug. It was getting cool, so her nanny brought her inside. Perhaps something boiled over in the kitchen – nanny put the basket down in the hall and ran. Peter and Irene were in the living room with their mother. Just then a bomb fell on the building across the street. Every window in their flat was shattered. The balcony was destroyed. The nursery was destroyed. There was glass everywhere. Even Helen's basket in the hall was covered with shards of glass. Thank God for that fur rug. One large piece jutted from her forehead. Her father pulled it out, and they all dashed out to the bomb shelter up the street. The dead and wounded lay everywhere. No more bombs fell. Some said it was the Germans in retreat. Others said it was the Americans, mistaking Prague for Dresden."

My aunt spoke. "How lucky you were! This poor country has lived through terrible times. Such cruelty. Such evil. One thing after another. We pray things will get better now, with Dubček in charge."

"I hardly dare hope," my grandfather said from his chair. "Will it come in my lifetime?"

My uncle shrugged. "What's been done to this country will take a long time to undo – if it's possible at all. Imagine ...." he turned to me, his voice dripping with contempt. "You should see these workers, as they call them – as though the rest of us didn't work. They go to the opera in their sweat pants and sit there slicing their salamis and cracking hard-boiled eggs on their armrests!"

They insisted I stay for dinner. "And you must come often," Uncle Paul said. "You're here for such a short time. But tomorrow, we'll take you to Zlatá Studna, our favourite restaurant once – to celebrate our reunion!" he beamed.

The next evening I arrived in time to have a drink with my grandfather, who wasn't up to joining us. "Don't worry, I've given him his favourite meal," Růža assured me, and after waving to him at the window, we climbed aboard the number 22 tram in the square outside their building. My uncle wore an old-fashioned, three-piece brown pin-striped suit, shiny now, and a striped beige tie. The collar of his white shirt made his neck look thin. Růža was also dressed up in a dark flowered dress, a cameo brooch and small gold earrings. I sat between them. My uncle leaned towards me, put his hand on my arm, and whispered, "I'm wishing you were our daughter, the daughter we never had." Růža nodded, took my hand and held it. Oblivious to the stares of fellow passengers, we rode alone, entwined. My heart was singing.

Chapter 4

ONE EVENING A FEW DAYS LATER, AFTER DINNER AT UNCLE Paul's, I was reading in the hostel bar, sipping a glass of white Moravian wine. The tables were full of students and travellers. I happened to look up as a man came in the door. I caught my breath. He was gorgeous – tall, slim, broad-shouldered and blond. He wore jeans, a denim shirt and boots, all rare commodities in Prague. Our eyes met and he raised his eyebrows and smiled. A group sitting at a table near me called out to him and waved. He waved back, strode across the room and joined them at their table. I sighed, took a sip of wine and went back to my book.

"Are you American?" asked a voice beside me a while later, in Czech. It was him.

"No, Canadian. And Czech, way back. You?"

He pulled out a chair and sat down. "Greek. And Czech. Here on holidays?"

"Yes – and finding relatives."

"I'm Vasilis Sidovsky." He held out his hand.

"Helen."

"Like to join us?"

I moved to his table, where he introduced me to his friends. Despite the language barrier, we talked. He told me he was born in Greece of Czech parents and was studying Czech, living in this hostel. We shared our love of Prague, our disgust at its squalor.

"You're lucky your parents chose Greece," I said. "Like Bohemia, it too has ancient roots, and is passionate about music, and life. Canada is raw and very proper."

As the evening grew late, the others drifted away. The bar closed.

"Let's go out," he said.

The night was warm and still as we walked through the mysterious streets of Prague. He put his arm around my shoulders. I moved closer, my heart hammering. I was walking with a Czech Adonis.

At three in the morning we walked back to our hostel. Outside in the dark street, he kissed me.

"Come to my room with me," he said. I could only nod.

There were posters of Greece and posters of Prague – shining whitewashed houses against brilliant blue skies, the wide majestic river and the castle under a full moon; a Greek flag draped over the window, a Czech flag on the wall.

We made love that night and the next. In between, when we weren't together, I wrote in my journal. I'd been keeping a journal of all my travels, and now my happiness overflowed onto the page. Discovering Prague, being enfolded by my family, and now finding a Czech lover, one who understood the irresistible draw towards roots and home. Prague held me in its embrace and gave me everything. I'd experienced the ugliness and the rudeness – and now I'd found the magic. My heart was open, enthralled. This was a world out of time. Or perhaps this was my real life from which I'd been exiled since childhood.

On my last night I waited for him in the bar but he didn't come. His friends arrived and were surprised to see me. "He thought you were leaving today!" they told me. "He's gone."

We must have misunderstood one another, speaking our patched-together combination of Czech, English and Greek. I got over it. My other life was waiting. It never occurred to me that he and I might stay in touch. Our brief affair was like an event out of time and space, as though Prague was on a different plane entirely. But my lifelong love of this city had been affirmed. I knew I had to come back.

I spent my last evening wandering those beloved streets and in the morning set off to bid farewell to my family.

After lunch together in their apartment, Uncle Paul and Růža came out to the square where I'd parked my scooter, and my grandfather blew kisses from the window. "I'll be back," I promised, "as soon as I can." We held one another. I started my scooter and with many a backward glance, I drove off. They stood waving until I was out of sight.

———

A letter from Larry was waiting for me at the American Express office in Munich. I called his B&B from the office.

"I'm here!" I cried, happy to hear his voice.

"Come get me and we'll hit the road," he said and gave me directions. "Munich has been wonderful, but I'm lonely for you."

"Be there as soon as I can." And I raced out to my scooter.

There he was. I threw myself into his arms. We strapped his duffel bag on top of my suitcase.

"How about Spain?" I said.

"Sure," he said. "I'll get to see France after all."

We drove through the breathtaking Swiss and French Alps, the blazing sun and sophistication of the Riviera, the fish markets of Marseille, and the vineyards and lavender fields of Provence, crossing into Spain at Perpignan, and found a charming seaside village called Sitges. We took a room in a small hotel near the ocean and settled down to spend four quiet days before having to head back to London and home. We lay on the beach, ate tapas and drank wine in the afternoon, strolled hand in hand through the village, and made love at night.

I went out alone one afternoon – to shop, to sit in a café by myself – and when I came back, Larry was sitting on the bed in our room, his face ashen.

I stopped in the doorway. "What's the matter?" I asked.

He didn't answer. He wouldn't look at me.

"Larry! What is it?" I cried.

He said nothing. I looked around. There on the night table lay my journal, which I had kept in my drawer, under my clothes.

"I read it," he muttered. "I'm sorry I did."

———

He wouldn't speak to me for the rest of our trip. I tried to explain. "Larry, it was Prague! What happened has nothing to do with you and me. Being there was so intense. I can't explain it – I got caught up. It's a different world, like a dream. A different universe!"

Nothing could change his heart. He left the next day, flying back to London alone. I drove to Marseille and sold my scooter – for more than the 25 pounds I had paid for it – and took the train to London. I didn't see Larry until we were at the airport. We had to sit in our pre-assigned seats, side by side. I tried abject apologies, entreaties, further attempts to explain. He wouldn't speak to me.

At home, I continued to try to win Larry back, but he didn't return my phone calls or answer my letters. Once I'd started working for the National Film Board, I actually set up film courses and lectures at the Guelph library to give me an excuse to be in his hometown and track him down. It was useless. I didn't regret my magical affair with Vasilis. But I ached for Larry, sorry to have hurt him, sorry he had taken it so hard, sorry to have lost him.

⟆⟆⟆ Chapter 5

MY PARENTS WERE IMMENSELY RELIEVED TO HAVE ME BACK. Over dinner at home, I regaled them with stories of my visit, of finding my grandfather, Uncle Paul and Aunt Růža, and with what love and joy they had welcomed me.

"I'm going back the first chance I get," I said.

"You were lucky this time," my father said. "You frightened me, going to Prague. I'm telling you, it's dangerous."

I told him of the hope that was dawning with Dubček in power.

"'Socialism with a human face,'" my father scoffed, as Uncle Paul had. "What a joke. We've been reading about it. First of all, it isn't socialism, it's not even communism. It's state totalitarianism, orchestrated by the Soviets. Believe me, it won't be tolerated."

"I want to go too," my mother said. She turned to my father. "Nothing happened to Helen – there's no reason not to go."

"I wouldn't set foot in that godforsaken country for anything in the world," my father snorted.

"The country is run down, terribly neglected," I said. "It's depressing. But it's also very beautiful."

"What's beautiful is the country they stole. What's hideous is what they've done to it." My father sat back, folding his arms across his chest.

"I'd still like to go," my mother said. "I'd stay with Grandpa and Uncle Paul."

"I don't want you to risk it," he said.

"It's changing, like Helen said. And they don't have anything against me, it's you they'd have their eye on."

"I'll believe those changes when I see them."

———

She did go the very next year, 1967. She applied for a visa, got it, and returned home after nineteen long years. She came back shocked by the state of the country but thrilled at her reunion with her father and brother, and happy to meet Růža for the first time. They became very close over the years.

———

I began looking for work. I fought hard for a job at the National Film Board, in the distribution branch of their Hamilton office, for which there were many applicants. I succeeded at my first interview but had a sense I'd not done well at the second. I wrote a letter to the interviewers asking for another chance, and was invited to a third meeting and got the job.

It was a marvellous first job for someone twenty-four years old and just out of university. For the first few months, my main responsibility was sitting in the small theatre in our offices day after day watching movies, to familiarize myself with NFB films. Wonderful films – documentaries, shorts and features about Canadian artists and Canadian life, and brilliant animated films, especially the work of Norman McLaren; his *Neighbours* and the sensuously beautiful *Pas de Deux*, delayed images of two ballet dancers, a man and a woman, dancing to the haunting flute of a Romanian orchestra.

My portfolio was working with arts groups, teachers and university professors, instructing them on the power of film – this was the era of Marshall McLuhan and I had a lot to say about the power of media to shape our world and our perception – and encouraging teachers to use NFB films in their programs. I could carry out my portfolio in any way I might invent; a wonderful opportunity. I created and taught courses at local community colleges, ran weekly film series such as Canadian Artists and Canadian Experimental Filmmakers in the NFB's theatre and started a newsletter called *Pot Pourri*, describing films on offer and new releases. I had to buy a car to take the job. The perks were a secretary, an expense account and a salary of a whopping $13,000 a year. I couldn't believe my good fortune. In the late sixties in Canada, opportunities and jobs abounded.

My first apartment was a one-bedroom walk-up in an older three-storey building in a residential section of Hamilton. Hamilton was Steeltown – an industrial town with one smelter after another lining the shore of Lake Ontario, their smokestacks belching out yellow smog. Dismayed that this would be my home for the next few years, I drove around searching for places of beauty, oases where I might spend my free time. There were few cafés or restaurants to lure me. But I discovered the Royal Hamilton Yacht Club. It looked inviting. "Members Only," the sign at the entrance read.

I phoned the next day. "I'd be interested in a social member-ship," I said to the woman who answered the phone.

"For whom?" she asked.

"Why ... for me," I said.

She announced frostily, "Membership is open to men only."

"What!"

I hung up, furious. That she, a woman, could have said that to me so smugly. A red flag waved in front of me.

It took me a couple of days to craft the letter. I sent it to the president, requesting a meeting, voicing my arguments and my reasoning. The meeting took place in the bar at the yacht club. A handsome man in his fifties, he listened to me respect-fully, agreed to take my request to the board, and we parted. Several weeks later, he called to congratulate me on being the first woman member of the Royal Hamilton Yacht Club. For weeks afterwards, whenever I hosted a male friend or client in the dining room or bar, the cheque was invariably delivered to the man. When I said to the waitress, "No, I'm the member," she'd look at me dubiously.

———

Then came 1968. Though my life was full and demanding, I'd been following the events in Czechoslovakia. Exciting things were happening there, a relaxing of some restrictions, a freer press, just as Uncle Paul had described.

One evening, I was in my kitchen, preparing dinner. The television was on in the living room and the evening news came on.

The word *Prague* – and I was on the floor, up close, staring at the grainy black and white images on my small screen.

Crowds of people filled Wenceslas Square. The commentator was speaking words I could barely take in. Down the wide boulevard, between the throngs of people, rolled tank after tank. The faces in the crowd were masks of disbelief, rage, defiance, defeat. Another camera: a street lined with people, young, old, women, men. A close-up of a young woman, tears streaming down her face, both hands over her mouth. An old man shaking his cane in helpless rage, as the tanks trundled over the cobblestones. People stood bewildered. Others ran alongside, screaming. And then I saw a young couple. They stepped forward as a tank came to a stop in front of them. The young woman was carrying a bouquet of flowers. She took one and placed it into the barrel of a rifle a soldier held across his lap. The soldier looked confused. The tank rolled on.

The Soviets and their allies had responded to Prague Spring by invading the country. Tears of grief and rage ran down my face, as Prague was stolen from me again.

———

Two years later I'd been promoted and transferred to Toronto and was living in a house on Maitland Street, which I shared with two women friends. I had a small black part lab, my first dog ever, named Lawrence, after Margaret, D.H. and Durrell. I had begged for a dog as a child, but my mother refused. Too much heartache, she said, and told me the story of Prince, a beloved Irish setter we'd had back home. She'd promised him all the meat he could dream of once the war ended. "Instead we abandoned him," she said, "and he died without my keeping my promise."

Every day I'd race home from work to take Lawrence for long walks in the park, and had the chef and waiters at the expensive steak house on the corner trained to save me pieces of steak patrons left on their plates. Having that dog was a revelation to me. I had never loved anything or anyone the way I loved him. My mother was jealous. "You love that dog more than you love me," she said. "You'd grieve for him more than for me."

"How can you say such a thing?" I shot back. But I knew what she meant. I was reserved and wary, especially with her. People, I feared, would hurt me, or ask too much of me, or not be interesting. I loved my family, had friends and colleagues and was lucky to have had lots of boyfriends, but I'd never loved anyone so freely and joyfully as I loved that dog. Having Lawrence showed me I was capable of a love that intense.

Despite my charmed life, below the fun and hard work, there was a profound yearning, a grief than ran like a silent river under everything. It grabbed me most deeply when I listened to music. I'd put on a record of Dvořák's Cello Concerto and cry out with an old, old pain.

My housemate introduced me to a friend named John Zichmanis, a writer and photographer with Maclean's magazine and the Star Weekly. He was strikingly good looking in a rugged way – tall, with prominent cheekbones, a wide forehead and brown hair down to his shoulders. By his appearance he could have been an aboriginal Canadian. It turned out he was Latvian, and like me, had been born in Europe and came to Canada with his family as a child. He had a way of sitting back, a hint of a smile on his lips, his head tilted to one side, looking at things from under that strong brow, as though weighing everything. We soon became lovers.

One night when we were in the park walking Lawrence, John stopped in his tracks.

"What do you say we quit our jobs and move to Europe?"

I caught my breath.

"Why not?" he smiled in that lazy way of his.

Prague! I thought. But no. He wouldn't be able to stand it. He'd never had any interest in going back to Latvia, also now a Soviet satellite.

"Where would we go?" I asked.

"How about Spain?" he said. "Ibiza. I spent a week there a couple of years ago. An amazing quality of light there, a photographer's dream."

"I don't speak Spanish," I said.

"We'd learn. There's a terrific expat community, mostly English-speaking. Great beaches, outdoor cafés, Sandy's Bar."

"What would we do? How would we live?"

"We'd live!" he laughed aloud. "We'd live off our savings as long as we could. And then we'd decide what to do next."

In my letter of resignation to the National Film Board, I wrote, "There are times when we have to choose between work and life. And right now, I'm choosing life."

My father was furious with me for throwing away a job most young people would have given anything to land. He had no sympathy for the powerful draw of Europe. But I was determined and overrode his objections.

John went on ahead while I served out my month's notice at the Film Board. I bought a large steamer trunk and booked passage on a freighter, Young America, heading from Newark, New Jersey to Lisbon, Portugal, a crossing that took seven days. I thought nothing of leaving my family behind or of the pain it caused my parents. My mother was frightened on my behalf and grief-stricken at my leaving. My father maintained his stance of anger and disapproval. But Europe! Europe was a powerful draw, as were John and my lust for adventure.

"Don't worry, I'll be fine! I promise I'll write often," I assured them as we stood on the platform at Union Station. My trunk was loaded on board. My mother clung to me, crying, my father gave me an awkward hug, and with Lawrence in my arms, I climbed aboard the overnight train bound for Newark. I'd booked a couchette that accommodated us both.

Once in Newark, a taxi delivered us to the docks and came to a stop directly beside a freighter whose grey hull towered beside us. Tax incentives made it advantageous for freighters to carry a few passengers. This one had six double staterooms.

The taxi driver unloaded my trunk and I stood, Lawrence on his leash beside me, breathing in the thrilling smell of seawater, tar and oil. I had chosen to ignore the Dogs Are Not Allowed on Board in the material I'd received. I couldn't leave Lawrence behind. I figured I'd bring him and they'd have no choice but to let him board.

A man was coming down the gangplank, and I gave him my name.

"Welcome. I'm the first mate." He looked down at Lawrence. "Who's taking your dog?"

"Nobody," I said, as if shocked. "I'm bringing him with me."

"I'm afraid dogs aren't allowed on board."

"What? I didn't know. I'm moving to Spain – I have to bring him!"

"It said very clearly in the instructions you received: no pets."

"But what can I do? I'm here now."

"You'll have to find someone to put him on a plane in time to meet you in Lisbon," he said. "That's what the other family on board is doing."

"But I'm from Canada. I don't know anyone here."

He shrugged.

"Please," I said. "Look at him. He doesn't bark, he's friendly, clean, intelligent. He won't be a problem, I promise." I turned to Lawrence. "Sit!" He sat down. "Shake a paw!" Lawrence raised his right paw.

The man looked at Lawrence. "Wait here. It's up to the captain to decide." He climbed back up the gangplank.

I tried everything – praying, crossing my fingers, chanting. The first mate reappeared a short time later. "The captain says if it's okay with your cabin mate, it's all right with him. She hasn't arrived yet, so you'll have to wait. Everyone else is on board." It was 7:00 p.m. The instructions had requested we be there by 7:00. We were due to set sail early the next morning.

Lawrence and I walked along the wharf, breathing in the pungent, salty sea air. From a distance I saw the first mate descending that gangplank.

"I can't believe your luck," he said. "One passenger has cancelled. Your cabin mate."

Two men carried my trunk and I followed them up the gangplank, Lawrence trotting behind me.

The man led me through a maze of corridors, then stopped and opened a door. I stood staring. Mahogany walls, rich upholstery on the wing chairs, a desk, a bookcase, two beds, a luxurious bathroom. "It's beautiful," I told the first mate, and thanked him profusely. He left and Lawrence and I made ourselves at home.

Soon there was a knock on the door. A tall man in a uniform introduced himself. "I've come to welcome you to my ship," he said, "and to meet your dog."

Lawrence was sitting by my side. The captain reached down and stroked Lawrence on the head, which Lawrence accepted graciously. "He'll be fine, I'm sure. Dinner is at eight. I'll see you in the dining room," and he withdrew. I blessed my good fortune.

Dinner was a lavish affair. The dining room was beautifully appointed, the tables set with linen tablecloths and gleaming silverware. Early the next morning I heard the ship's horn blow and ran up on deck to watch us pulling away from the dock and making our way out to sea. North America receded behind us and ahead lay the wide and empty ocean.

———

The crossing was smooth and the weather fine as we cut through the water. Day after day, Lawrence and I walked the deck, the wind in my hair as I leaned on the railing and stared across the sea. Here I was, travelling halfway around the world to meet a man I'd been dating for a few months, to start a life I couldn't imagine. But I was heading for Europe.

Seven days later, I was overjoyed when my feet stepped onto European soil in the port of Lisbon. I rented a car, heaved my trunk into the back seat, and with Lawrence beside me, his ears flapping as he leaned out the window, we set off for Spain. I took the coastal road down to Gibraltar and up the Mediterranean, stopping now and then for a rest, a swim, a meal. I found a small seaside hotel for one night, and the next day, pulled into Barcelona. That evening once again, Lawrence and I shared a cabin in the overnight ferry to Ibiza, the end of our journey, where John waited.

I stood on deck early the next morning, watching what I knew from my map was the island of Majorca, the largest of the three islands of the Baleares, slide by on our starboard side, lush, green, rising high out of the sea, its rocky coast dotted with sandy beaches. Then another island came into view, small, high, round. Slowly we turned into the narrow mouth of a harbour and there in front of our bow a sparkling white city shone in the early morning sun, a tumble of whitewashed houses rising up the steep banks above the port. As the ferry navigated its way to the wharf, its bow thrusters churning, I searched the crush of people shouting and waving below. Passengers started streaming off the ship. I took Lawrence in my arms and walked carefully down the steep gangplank. And then I saw John, leaning on a motorcycle. His face was tanned, his hair long. Relief. Joy.

I set Lawrence down and stood my ground, looking at him. We threw our arms around each other.

"What now?" I asked, looking at his bike, Lawrence and the trunk, which porters had brought down to the wharf.

"I've rented a farmhouse for us in the country near Santa Eulalia, about ten kilometres from here. We'll get a taxi for your trunk."

"And Lawrence?"

"You hold him."

I pictured myself tumbling off backwards, unable to hang on, my arms full of dog.

"It'll be fine," John assured me.

He straddled his motorcycle and it roared into life. I took Lawrence in my arms and hopped on. We meandered slowly through the narrow streets, past squares where people sat at café tables under waving palms, and into the countryside, flying past whitewashed stone farmhouses and fields. I held Lawrence between us with one arm and grabbed a fistful of John's leather jacket with the other. I loved his strong and capable back, so solid there in front of me, his hair blowing back.

We turned onto a dirt road that wound up a hillside shaped into grassy terraces, walls of stone holding the earth in place, making every bit of land arable. We laboured up a steep incline, turned a sharp corner, and there stood a large whitewashed stone farmhouse surrounded by terraces of fig and olive trees. John braked to a stop and shut off the engine. I jumped off. Lawrence ran around like a wild thing, free at last.

"How do you like it?" John asked.

"Incredible," I said.

———

We lived in Ibiza for two years. We kept chickens. We sat in outdoor cafés in Santa Eulalia and made friends with other expats. John played chess with a local named Juan. He'd bought me a Mobylette – a small motorbike – to get around on. We went shopping by motorcycle, our straw Ibiza bags slung over our shoulders. We took picnics to the beach, where we swam and read our books.

We were living on our savings, but John started to worry about money.

"What's the point of worrying?" I said and went out and got a wonderful job as a tourist guide with Centrair, a Belgian tourist agency. That was me at the front of those large tourist buses, picking up clients at the airport, escorting them to their hotels, visiting them to make sure everything was satisfactory, selling them tickets to various excursions, and then accompanying them on those excursions – island tours, barbeque nights, flamenco bars – all in French, sometimes staying up the night before with a French-English dictionary, looking up the words I'd need.

At the end of our first year – it was 1971 – we went home to visit our families and on the spur of the moment, we got married. The wedding took place in my parents' backyard in Don Mills. I wore an ankle-length white cotton dress decorated with burgundy stitching and silver sequins. A friend of mine, a hippie-type minister, officiated. My parents liked John and were happy for me, but wished we were more serious about our futures.

When we returned to Ibiza, we moved to San Vicente in the north of the island, wilder and more remote than Santa Eulalia, to a large farmhouse that spanned a ridge, on one side a balcony overlooking a deep valley, and on the other side, the sea shimmering in the distance.

But our marriage was to last just one more year.

I went back to my tourist guide job. John continued to worry about money but took no action. I began to feel sidelined. Life was elsewhere, going on without me. My job was fun, but it wasn't enough; it wasn't a career.

"It's time we moved on," I said to John one day. "You can only lie on a beach for so long." Neither of us wanted to go back to Canada but we couldn't agree on where to go.

"France!" I suggested.

"You speak French. I don't," he said. "You'd have the advantage." We were unable to make a decision.

"Ibiza can do that to you, leave you like a squashed lemon, the will drained out of you," a friend of mine said.

Then came the most bitter loss. One day I called and called for Lawrence, who'd found paradise, wandering, exploring, free – but that day he didn't come. I thought I'd heard a sound from up the hill, a sound that frightened me. John went up behind our house while I waited. After a long time, I saw him walking down the rocky hillside, Lawrence in his arms.

"He's not okay, Helen," he said.

He'd been shot by hunters and was riddled with buckshot. There was nowhere I could take him. The nearest vet was in Ibiza Town, more than an hour's drive by motorcycle. I couldn't imagine hauling a wounded dog all that way, and we'd probably find it closed. All night I sat beside him where we'd laid him on thick towels. I talked softly to him, stroking his body, my hand coming away red with blood. There were moments when I thought he might recover, when his panting eased and his glazed eyes seemed to soften. Never had I experienced such pain. I cried over him all night, quietly, wanting only to soothe him. But when he finally lost the fight and died, I screamed with rage and grief. For days, after we'd buried him in the woods, I would burst into cries of pain. Riding on the back of John's motorcycle, I held onto him and howled into the wind.

I needed to move on. We argued, we fought. John started spending most of his days with an American friend, riding their Bultaco motorcycles through the countryside. He found another friend, a German named Gerhardt, who made leather goods, and became his apprentice.

I was home alone late one night when I heard John's motorcycle churning up the steep lane to our house. He staggered in, bleeding from wounds on his face and arms. He'd been drinking and his bike had skidded and fallen on the gravel road. That was the last time we made love. Soon after, he moved in with Gerhardt. I found a tiny house back near Santa Eulalia, two small rooms, perhaps once a grain storage shed, where I served out my notice with Centrair.

One day I was amazed to get a telegram from my mother informing me she was in Europe with my brother Peter and his wife Jane and that she was coming to visit me. I wondered how she would find me. A few days later, a friend pulled up at my front door on his motorcycle.

"Hey, Helen, your mother's in town looking for you," he called.

I jumped on my motorbike, rode into town and found her sitting at the café in the main square of Santa Eulalia. I was thrilled to see her. On her own she had taken the overnight ferry, arrived at the port of Ibiza, taken a taxi to Santa Eulalia, which she knew as my post office address, and then what?

"Well," she said, "I just asked after you in a couple of cafés, and your friend said he'd go tell you I was here!" She was beaming. "I left Peter and Jane in Marseille. I wanted to see how you live." She took a sip of her coffee. "Your last letter worried me. How is John?"

"We've separated. I'm living by myself now."

She looked stricken.

"I'll be all right. It's for the best."

"Was he angry that you kept your own name?" she asked.

"If he was, that's his problem," I said. "No, I think we just want different things. I actually don't know what he wants. But I need to move on." I stood up. "I'll show you around."

Valiantly she straddled the passenger seat on my bike. I strapped her small overnight bag to the back and we zipped around town, Sandy's Bar, the little *tiendas* where I shopped, a swing past the nicest beach, and then down the long lane toward my house – or shed.

She walked into the kitchen, ducking her head under the doorframe. An earthen floor, a low table, two small chairs, a plank of a counter, a rough wooden shelf for dishes, a hotplate fed by a canister of propane. She looked at me, unable to speak. We stepped back out into the sunshine.

"And here's my bedroom," I said. She ducked through the second wooden door into another small, dark room with a bed and two rough shelves. "Oh Helen," was all she could manage, close to tears. I laughed at the expression on her face.

"It's all right," I said. "I live mostly outside. Here's my desk" – a wooden table and chair under a fig tree – "and here's my shower," and I showed her a small tank suspended from an olive tree. "That's all I need."

I insisted she sleep in my bed at night, while I camped out in the kitchen. We explored the island together the next day. I took her with me on the island tour to Formentera and to a barbeque night, delighted to have her there, a mother I'd never known. An adventurer.

John joined us one evening when we went out to dinner. The evening was excruciating. I had such intense stomach cramps – something that used to happen to me as a teenager at home, and hadn't happened since – that I went outside and curled up in a grassy ditch outside the restaurant.

On the fourth day, I waved and waved as my mother's ferry pulled out of the harbour, and returned to my empty house, alone.

Of the horrible things I experienced in Ibiza, the worst all had to do with dogs.

While John and I were still together and after Lawrence's death, I went to Barcelona for a few days, and on that wild and festive square called Ramblas, I bought a small pretty dog I named Little Dog, and brought him home. He got sick a few weeks later. John was away. I took him by bus to a vet in Ibiza. Distemper, the vet said. Nothing can be done. Put him to sleep. The injection shouldn't hurt, the vet assured me, but Little Dog howled and howled before he died. There, the vet said. I paid him. "It's up to you to dispose of him," he informed me.

I had to put my dead dog in my straw Ibiza bag, sling the handles over my shoulder and walk to the bus stop. Boarding the bus, I imagined my dog, heavy now, breaking through the bottom of the straw bag and landing with a thud among the passengers. I trudged up the hill to our house, found a shovel and buried him next to Lawrence.

One day, alone now, sitting at my table under the fig tree by that small house, I heard a dog howling, on and on. Unable to bear it, I set off to see what was happening. My neighbour had just beaten his dog to death for killing a chicken. He was a little brown dog that used to come and visit me, I'd give him scraps and he'd lie beside me as I worked at my table.

I knew I had to leave.

I had a short affair with a German tourist named Heinz, a marketing executive. We'd spent one night in a tent on the beach and run naked into the sea. From Berlin, he wrote poems to me and asked me to come to Berlin to be with him.

One day, John found me in town. "Gerhardt is moving to England," he told me. "He's opening up a leather studio in Oxford." I waited. "I've decided to go with him." I nodded numbly.

I heard through the grapevine what day he was leaving on the overnight ferry. It left at eight in the evening. I went about my day, the hours ticking by. At six o'clock I was home, sitting at my table under the trees, thinking about that first arrival when I stood at the rail of the ferry, searching for John, Lawrence by my side. He was leaving me to figure out my future alone.

I jumped on my motorbike, sped to Ibiza and found him sitting alone at a low table at the back of a café, head down, shoulders hunched, a glass of *hierbas* in front of him. I sat down, my heart aching. "I had to come."

He ordered me a drink. We sat looking at each other. He was beautiful.

"Are we doing the right thing?" I asked.

He shrugged. "I don't know. All I know is, I'm going. I guess we'll see."

"Write to me," I said.

"What are you going to do?"

"I don't know."

Walking beside him to the wharf, I took his arm and waited in line with him; there was nothing more to say. When it was time to board, we held one another briefly, then he turned and climbed up the ramp. A horn sounded and the ferry pulled away.

I sat on a bench and stared out to where the ship had vanished. I was twenty-eight years old, my one-year marriage had just ended, and my life in Ibiza was also about to end. I had no idea what to do. Ibiza had been John's place, so that dream was over. Yet I wasn't ready to go back to Canada.

Letters came from Heinz inviting me to Berlin. I finished my contract with Centrair, sold my motorbike, packed the few things I wanted to keep and once again was on that ferry.

In Berlin I saw Heinz a few times, took myself to concerts and to the opera, but there was nothing there for me. I was alone.

One rainy day, walking along a downtown street surrounded by hurrying Berliners, I stopped in my tracks. An electric wave of joy and wild longing came over me. Yes, the route had been winding and painful, but suddenly I knew what I was doing there.

Not more than a few hours' train ride away was ... Prague.

Our villa in Černošice, 1942. From left: my grandfather, Irene, age 11,
Uncle Paul, my grandmother and my mother

My mother. Prague, 1943

My father's photo ID during the Nazi occupation

My sister Irene, 15, my brother Peter, 3, and me, 2. Prague, 1946

The Communist coup, Old Town Square, Prague, February 21, 1948.
Photo reproduced from the Czech textbook History for Grade 8 Elementary School / SPN

Sailing from Liverpool to Montreal on the Empress of Canada, 1949.
Clockwise from left: My father, me, Irene, Peter, and my mother

Father with cigarette holder

Mother with Tommy

Me at age 8, 1952

Grandfather and Uncle Paul during their visit to us in Canada, 1964

Prague protesters surround Soviet tanks in central Prague during the first day of
Soviet-led invasion, August 21, 1968. Photo by Libor Hajský

PART TWO

Chapter 6

IT HAD BEEN SIX YEARS. MY FIRST VISIT HAD BEEN A QUICK touch-down, a thrilling episode in a flight through Europe. This time I was coming as an exile searching for home.

At the Czech consulate office, I rejoiced to see the red, white and blue flag flying above the door, the lions on the coat of arms inside. When the surly middle-aged woman behind the wicket spoke to me in my own language, I was moved to tears.

"I want to go to Prague," I said in English. "I need a visa."

"*Vizum?*" Her eyes were cold. I nodded. "*Pas,*" she barked.

I was grateful as always to have a Canadian passport.

"*Na jak dlouho?*" she asked. For how long?

"*Čtyři týdny,*" I ventured. Four weeks. She disappeared.

I'd heard the consulate in Berlin was a good place to apply for a visa to Czechoslovakia, as it was one of the few consulates with the authority to issue visas without notifying police headquarters in Prague, which if contacted could turn me down. I'd read restrictions had been tightened since the invasion of '68. I had no idea what I'd do then. I waited.

The woman reappeared with my passport. I was weak with relief when she opened it and showed me the visa stamped inside. Happily I exchanged the required seven dollars per day for Czech crowns and ran out of the building. The next morning I was on a train to Prague.

The Czech train, rusty, the seats worn, the windows opaque with grime, chugged its way to the border. There we waited while two grim policemen strolled down the aisle, checking the few passengers' documents. Eventually we were moving again. Hungrily I stared as the rolling hills, the woods, the towns and villages of Czechoslovakia flashed by. A few hours later we pulled into Hlavní Nádraží, the main train station in the centre of Prague.

Once again, the glorious Prague in my imagination was not the Prague I saw. The station was dingy – broken tiles on the walls, overflowing garbage containers, the smell of urine. I put my bag in a locker and walked out into the streets.

The city had deteriorated even further. Stucco still falling from facades, pedestrians picking their way over treacherous sidewalks, old cars rattling over roads pitted with missing cobblestones.

But I was in Prague. Thrilled to hear Czech all around me, I walked around the city, sounding out the names of streets and shop signs, practising the feel of the language. Despite the dirt and neglect, beauty was there in the bones of the city, the architecture and design laid out centuries before – the wide avenues and the squares, each with a church at its centre.

I loved the atmosphere of Prague, the cool scent of ancient stones and that dark, pungent aroma of smoke and soot. I gloried in the grand Renaissance buildings of the Old Town, the arched passageways, the twisting lanes and jumble of houses in the Little Quarter. The majestic river, the swans, the fourteenth-century Charles Bridge with its looming statues, black against the sky.

But the mood in the streets was heavy; a pall of hopelessness lay over the passersby. Back before '68, restrictions had been easing and hope was blossoming. With Prague Spring quashed, an even more oppressive era had begun, with a process that with bitter irony was called "normalization" by the harsh Soviet-backed regime. I could feel it all around me.

It was painful looking at these fellow Czechs of mine, despair in their expressions, their posture. How many defeats can a human being endure? How many cycles of hope ignited, then dashed? Just as I had done before, I found myself staring into people's faces, trying to make a connection. Those whose eyes I did happened to catch turned quickly away. I felt like Pollyanna, stumbling upon a scene of bewildering tragedy.

I found a small *pension* close to the centre and moved in. My plan: to find a flat and a job, to study Czech, and reunite with my Prague family. Home at last.

I looked for newspapers advertising apartments for rent. There were none. I went to Čedok, the only travel agency.

"Where can I find a listing of flats to rent?" I asked the severe-looking woman at the counter in my tentative Czech. Apparently I had asked something outrageous.

"There are no flats to rent," she informed me, her lips curled into a sneer.

"How do people live then?" I asked.

"Citizens have flats already," she snapped, "and foreigners stay in hotels or *pensions*."

I walked out, stymied.

I had a friend, a Canadian named Paul Wilson, who had come to Prague, fallen in love with it and stayed. He'd married a Czech woman and, having learned Czech fluently, worked as a translator. I'd met Paul a few years earlier through mutual friends, when he'd come to Canada to visit his parents. He was a burly man with longish hair, a ginger moustache and beard, and an easy laugh. I'd invited him to Chinook, our family cottage, where we all had a wonderful time sitting around the campfire, drinking, singing Czech and Canadian folk songs, Paul telling us stories of his life in Prague.

"I want to live there too, one day," I'd said to him.

"Give me a call if you ever come," he said and wrote his phone number down for me. It had seemed like a distant dream – yet here I was.

"You made it! Come to U Svítáků," he said. "We're there every Tuesday, Thursday and Saturday. Ask anyone, they'll know where it is."

"I'll be there. This Tuesday," I said. U Svítáků, after the practice of naming pubs and restaurants with the preposition U, meaning At. At Sviták's.

I spent the rest of that first day wandering around, elation alternating with rage. I climbed up Nerudova Street to the castle and looked out over the sea of clay rooftops, the chimney pots, the thousands of church spires, and fell in love with the city all over again. I walked down the castle stairs to the Little Quarter, furious at everything that had been stolen from me. All this beauty had been my birthright. They'd wreaked havoc on it, allowing one of the most beautiful cities in the world to fall into ruin, and subjecting my fellow Czechs to a despair that took them beyond my reach. Could I, who had never experienced what they had lived through, ever be more than a visitor here, a stranger among my own people?

The next day I set out to visit my Uncle Paul and Aunt Růža. I'd had no contact with them in six years.

Once again I pushed open the heavy street door to Jugoslávská 11. Again I was enveloped by that evocative smell of coal, soot, beer, and ancient stone as I climbed the stairs to the second floor and stood outside the door bearing my grandfather's name. I rang the bell and again heard the shuffle of footsteps, keys inserted into one lock after another. And then Uncle Paul and I were in each other's arms, tearful, grateful. Růža stood on her tiptoes and hugged me. The red arm chair by the coal stove was empty now. My grandfather had died in 1970, two years before. Again I sat with my beloved family at the table in the small anteroom, catching up and talking about the disaster that had befallen the country shortly after my last visit.

The next evening, I walked into U Svítáků, which was full and rowdy, and found Paul sitting at a large table surrounded by friends. We hugged and he introduced me. Men, women, Czechs, expats. A waiter brought a stein of beer. The conversation was rollicking, intelligent, angry, anarchist.

"They found out where our next gig was and they've shut the place down," someone said. "Brought the manager in for questioning, the assholes."

"Have you heard of the Plastic People of the Universe?" Paul asked me. I hadn't. "A rock band. Started in 1968, right after the invasion. Definitely underground. Fantastic musicians. I was brought in to teach them English lyrics and now I'm the lead singer," he laughed. "Rock is illegal here, and we're constantly being shut down and occasionally arrested. But the kids love us. They need us."

He turned to his friends. "Let's plan another. This time dead quiet. No leaflets, only word of mouth."

"Let me know," I said. "I'd love to come."

"Sure."

"Paul, I need a place to live. How do I rent a flat?"

Paul snorted. "You don't. There's an incredible housing shortage. People are crammed together. It's bizarre. So many people left the country in ´48 and then again after ´68, you'd think there'd be all kinds of empty apartments. But there's nothing. Young people get married, have kids and have to stay with their parents, often with grandparents as well. Space is allocated by the metre for ordinary folks. But let's see what we can do."

He turned to his friends around the table. "Helen here needs a place to live. Any ideas?"

That's how I ended up crashing for two weeks with Jakub Kaše and his wife in a flat on Pařížská. Their daughter was away and they offered me her room. Tree-lined Paris Street was one of the loveliest streets in Prague, running from Old Town Square to the Vltava River. Once a bustling, crowded Jewish quarter, Jakub told me, it had been razed at the end of the nineteenth century and replaced with elegant five-storey Renaissance-style apartment buildings with luxury shops at street level. It was a study in contrasts now between the grandeur that had been and the harshness of communist life. Like all of Prague, the exterior of Jakub's building was shabby and black with soot. But inside, a graceful staircase curved up encircling a central hall, its balustrade finely wrought ironwork. A dazzling stained glass atrium arched overhead, filtering golden light to the floors below.

Through Paul and his group at U Svítáků, whom I joined regularly, I was discovering how things happened in Prague. Everything was done through contacts. Few people had telephones; they were expensive, there was a long waiting list to have one installed, and a person's political status determined whether a phone was even approved. A circle of friends was critical, and everything happened in pubs. The entire culture revolved around pubs. Groups had their favourites, where tables were reserved for them on specific evenings. Friends gathered there to catch up with one another, exchange news, pass on tips and solicit help.

————

In the meantime, I continued my search for my family. My father had rarely spoken of his family, though he'd mentioned his younger brother Otto, and had given me his phone number. I called him and was invited to their apartment for dinner. He was the very opposite of my aesthete father. Dark-haired, swarthy, with bushy eyebrows, short and a bit overweight, he was jovial and welcoming. His wife was a doctor, quiet and pale in his shadow. I met their two teenage sons, my cousins. At subsequent dinners and outings, I was to meet my father's mother, my other grandmother, whom we called Babička na Smíchově. I had no idea if my father and she had been in touch all those years. Though I was never to become as close to Otto and his family as I was to Uncle Paul and Aunt Růža, all the same I felt blessed with family, with people to visit and call on.

I never found out what Otto did for a living. I saw him as a character who knew how to operate in a corrupt system, who finds ways and means. Not that he was a communist; he was as opposed to them as any dissident.

"There's so much corruption and mismanagement that people can't count on the most basic things here," he railed over dinner that first evening. "The word goes out the corner grocery store is getting a shipment of tomatoes and people go out at dawn and stand in line-ups three blocks long! The tomatoes arrive and there's enough for the first dozen people. The rest shuffle on home, the poor schmucks. This in what was one of the most prosperous democracies in Europe! Can you imagine what incompetence and stupidity can accomplish a disaster like that, and in such a short time?" He paused to take a gulp of his beer. "Some factories and farms are still operating, of course, though at a snail's pace. What incentive is there to work? It's the Soviets, too. They're bleeding us dry. We ship tractors and tanks and get shipments of cabbages in return."

Driving me back to Pařížská that evening, he said, "By the way, if you need dollars exchanged, I'm happy to help you out."

Uncle Otto became my black market contact. We'd meet at the Slavia Café and over coffee and conversation, I'd slip him a hundred dollars and instead of the official exchange rate of seven crowns per Canadian dollar, he'd pass me three thousand crowns, thirty crowns to the dollar. I had more money than I knew what to do with – especially since there was so little to buy.

The black market was illegal but all-pervasive. Hard currency was necessary for anyone wanting to leave the country, legally or illegally, or to buy goods at the Tuzex stores, goods that weren't available for Czech crowns – "luxury goods" like radios and jeans. As I walked around Prague, people would regularly sidle up to me and mutter, "Exchange money?" I'd shake my head. My uncle was my source.

Then there was the mystery of my other half-brother in Prague, Rudy's older brother, my father's first-born. No one mentioned this other brother while I was growing up. There were family secrets I came to understand were taboo. Hints and whispers, allusions, names overheard – Malý Pavel, Erika, Valerie – a sudden silence when I entered the room, mysteries to unravel, mysteries created by my parents' silence. Who were these shadowy figures? I would beg my mother to tell. She'd squirm and turn away.

"Why won't you and Dad tell me about them?" I demanded.

"Don't ask," she said. "It isn't pretty."

What did I care about pretty? I wanted the *truth*.

As a young child, I'd been puzzled that Irene's last name was different than ours. It was Irene who told me her father and our mother had divorced. Her father still lived in Prague, she had left him behind and wasn't allowed to mention him. My mother didn't tell me she'd been married before or that my father wasn't Irene's father. Did they believe divorce was shameful, even though both of them had divorced, my father twice?

Irene became the source of much of the forbidden information my parents had kept from me. There were some terrible stories. When my mother and Irene's father divorced, Irene lived with her and her grandparents. When Irene was seven, her father kidnapped her from school and drove her out to an orphanage far from Prague, where he left her, lying to the nuns, telling them her mother had died and he wasn't able to take care of her. It took my mother, with the help of Uncle Paul, an entire year to find her, a year of frantic, heartbroken searching.

Irene told me my father had hated her and when he married my mother, he refused to let Irene come live with them. She lived with my mother's parents for over a year before he grudgingly relented, and then she had to abide by much stricter rules than those for Peter and me. She told me of his coldness and cruelty towards her, the ugly names he called her. Back in 1948, she had indeed overheard him saying he would not help her escape, so she'd fled on her own, a teenager of seventeen. I was horrified to hear these things about my father.

––––––––––

One day at home in Canada, rooting around in a suitcase full of pictures, I'd found an old sepia photo of a young girl at a funeral surrounded by people in black. Examining the photo closely, I recognized my father at the back, not looking at her. Something about her haunted me, her wistful, beautiful young face, the penetrating eyes. I brooded over the mystery of who she could be, and whose funeral it was.

It was years later before I found out. The funeral was Valerie's, my father's younger sister. She had suffered from severe depression and was addicted to cocaine. Her husband, a doctor, had actually prescribed the cocaine for her, hoping to relieve her depression. It didn't and she committed suicide. My aunt.

I discovered that the wistful young girl in the photo was Erika, my father's daughter from his second marriage, whom he'd left behind when we escaped. My father had another daughter and had kept it secret from me! My half-sister, sixteen years old when we left.

All those years, I'd been wrapped in cotton wool and denied the truth. With every piece of information, our exile took on added dimensions. How terrible for him to have had to leave her; how terrible for her to have lost her father. I wondered how he could have had the strength. Yet if he'd told his ex-wife of our planned escape, she might have informed on him.

Over time I learned he had not abandoned Erika; in fact he had been in contact a great deal. Erika, in her twenties, working as a lab technician, had become ill with a mysterious illness that left her unable to walk and in constant pain. Her young husband was a doctor, yet no diagnosis or cure could be found. From Canada, my father entreated her to apply for an exit visa, offering to pay all her expenses to bring her to Canada for treatment, or even to get her to Cuba, where Czech citizens were sometimes permitted to holiday. He would arrange for specialists. An exit visa was denied no matter how often he tried. One day when Erika was thirty-four and no one was home, she turned on the gas in their apartment and committed suicide. Her mother, who lived with them, found her. I was twenty-three that year, had graduated from university and just started my job with the Film Board.

I was dumbfounded that these dramatic family events could have been happening without my parents speaking of them. There was tragedy in our history as well as love and loss, and in Canada we had lived as though our family in Prague didn't matter. I felt robbed. This was my family; they belonged to me too, and their suffering was part of our lives, connected to us, to our flight to Canada.

Thinking of these things as I walked around Prague in 1972, I realized most of this was history. Valerie was gone, Erika was gone. Irene's father was of no interest to me. But my father's eldest son, Malý Pavel, was alive and I was determined to find him. Over time I'd gleaned enough to know he was an idealistic twenty-one when we left, an ardent communist, editor of *Rudé Právo*, the official communist newspaper in the forties. I'd also learned that after we escaped in 1948, he was fired and sent to work in the coal mines – for not having reported our escape, though he had no prior knowledge of it, and for having a father in the West. I understood my father had disowned him. How else to explain his utter silence on the subject of his own son? Politics had made them enemies.

————

I wanted to find him now. Where to begin? His name wasn't in the phone book; if he had a phone, it was unlisted. I was told I had to go through official channels, through the Ministry of the Interior. I worried whether my search might have repercussions for him still. Hoping that would not happen, I made my request at the ministry and was given an address on Letná Street, on the other side of the river.

I found his building and there was his name on the panel by the front door: Pavel Notzl. My father's name. I pushed the buzzer; an answering buzz allowed me to push the street door open. A few moments later, a girl stood holding open the door of an apartment on the main floor.

"Do you speak English?" I asked her. Eyes wide, she shook her head.

"I'm Helen from Canada," I said in my halting Czech. "Your father is my brother."

"*Je!*" she exclaimed, delight irradiating her face. "*Moje teta! Prosím, pojd'te dál!*" Oh! My aunt! Please come in!

We sat in the narrow entrance hall that was also her bedroom. Her parents were at work, but would be home soon, she told me. We smiled at one another. She was friendly, curious, intelligent and very pretty. I had found a niece, whose name was Helena, the same as mine.

"We've met once before," she ventured. I didn't understand. How was that possible?

"Your father invited me to your cottage, Chinook, it was called, some years ago. I was staying with my Uncle Rudy, and your father invited me for the weekend."

Vaguely I remembered that interloper who had upset me.

"You paid no attention to me," she added, smiling shyly. "You were with your boyfriend. I was sad about that. I admired you from afar."

"I'm so sorry. No one told me who you were!" I exclaimed. So my father had been in touch with Rudy after all and with his family in Prague, and had kept it secret from us, his children in Canada. Or simply hadn't mentioned it.

When we heard a key in the lock, Helena leapt up and ran to the door. "Look who's here! Your sister from Canada!"

Malý Pavel was the image of my father. He was tall and slim with broad shoulders, a receding hairline, a narrow aristocratic face and expressive hands. His wife, whose name was also Helena, was his opposite – plump, effusive, with a round, florid face and a warm smile. Malý Pavel offered his hand, flushed and was awkward – yet pleased – when I hugged him, just like my father, while Helena reached out and enfolded me in her arms.

They insisted I stay for dinner. There we were, the Notzl clan: three Helen Notzls in one room and Pavel Notzl, my father's namesake. Helena Sr. was a happy soul. Malý Pavel was reserved and deep, an intellectual. We didn't talk politics – I sensed the topic was avoided here. Malý Pavel spoke some English, so our conversation was a mix of Czech and English, my attempts at Czech frustrating me at times, so I turned to him to translate as best he could. I gave them news of my Canadian family: parents well, Peter working for Imperial Oil, married to Jane, a teacher, Tom a lawyer, Irene with three grown children, divorced, working as sales manager for *Canadian Business* magazine.

Malý Pavel was an engineer but had a menial job in an office, still held back, it turned out, because of having family in the west. His wife Helena was a clerk with Czech Television, and young Helena was at university. She'd wanted to be a doctor but had been refused admission to this prestigious profession, again because of us, and was working towards a degree in dentistry instead.

"I'm so sorry," I said.

Malý Pavel shrugged. "He had to leave. It was too dangerous for him."

"Did you know we were going to leave?" I ventured.

"No," he said. "They didn't tell anyone – wisely. It would have put me in a terrible position." His ideals versus his love for his father, a terrible choice indeed.

"You didn't consider coming too?" I asked again, knowing I was treading on fragile ground.

"No," he replied. "Living in the West didn't interest me."

"Haven't you found it difficult living here?"

He hesitated. "There have been sacrifices asked of us, but it has been worth it. We are working towards something important in the world. We have to accept that radical change is difficult but necessary."

"Do you miss your father – our father? I missed my family here very much."

He looked away. "He had to leave. I had to stay." He shrugged. "He can't come back and I can't leave."

"We've had a good life," Helena Sr. put in. "We love each other, we have our home, a wonderful daughter. What more could we ask?"

"I hope it won't cause you any trouble, my being here," I said. "Is there a chance any of you will be hurt by my presence here?"

"Not at all," Malý Pavel said.

"I want to live here," I told them. "I want to become fluent in Czech, to find a job. I want to figure out where I belong."

"Maybe you belong here," Helena Sr. smiled. Tears sprang to my eyes.

"It's been very confusing," I said. "My mother isn't happy. All my life she's pined for home and filled my head with stories of Prague, how happy she was here. My father's the opposite. He's done well in Canada and is furious at what's happened to this country and refuses to ever come back. He seems to have let go so easily. He's against my being here and is afraid for me. I've done well in Canada too. Yet all my life I've dreamed of coming back. I have to figure it out."

"You will figure it out," Malý Pavel said. "You had to come and find out for yourself. It's wonderful that you're here. Finally I get to know my sister." He gave me a rare smile. "You must get a residence permit. You can't do anything without one and when your visa expires, you'll have to leave."

"That's my next challenge. Bartolomějská," I said, naming the street where the police headquarters was located. "It's the police that issue residence permits, right?"

"They'll want to know what you plan to do here, so you must think about that and be able to answer."

"I want to be a full-fledged citizen."

"Give it a try," he said. "And welcome back."

"Come often!" Helena Sr. called as I kissed them goodnight at the street door. Another wonderful family, I marvelled, as I skipped down the street.

Chapter 7

"GETTING YOUR RESIDENCE PERMIT," PAUL WILSON TOLD ME, "is a Catch-22 situation: you're more likely to be issued one if you can show you'll be a student or if you've been offered a job."

So before I summoned the courage to open one of those doors on Bartolomějská Street, I researched. I visited Charles University, the Ministry of Education, and the Pedagogic Institute, where I was shunted from one department to another. People seemed unsure how to proceed. It was clear they hadn't encountered a situation like mine before. I kept hearing the same thing: We can't offer you anything without a residence permit.

I looked into work opportunities such as teaching English or translating. Same result: We could definitely use your help but can't even consider hiring you until you have a residence permit.

Bartolomějská Street was a curving street in the Old Town, with narrow sidewalks and missing cobblestones. The entire street, both sides, consisted of police buildings, grim structures with sightless, opaque windows protected by iron bars. Unsure which building I needed, I selected one at random and pushed open its heavy metal-studded door. I was immediately accosted by a guard who grasped my arm and shoved me back out on the sidewalk. *"Povolení k pobytu!"* I cried out. A residence permit.

"*Číslo 14*," he barked, pointing across the street. I had a sense that terrible things happened behind those blind windows.

Crossing the street to number 14, I pulled open the door. A grey-haired porter with watery eyes sat behind a barred window.

"*Dobrý den*," I said. Good day.

"What do you want?" he asked.

"A residence permit."

He raised his eyebrows, pursed his lips and regarded me. Finally he held out his hand. "*Pas!*" Passport. He opened it. Born in Prague. 1944. He looked up, his eyes narrowing as he looked me over. He went back to my passport, studied it page by page. England, France, Italy, Austria, Germany, Spain. He took his time.

"*Moment*," he said, finally, picked up the phone and spoke in rapid Czech. I waited. He ignored me. After a long time, a door behind him opened. He got up and handed over my passport. I stood. The porter turned the pages of a newspaper. Finally a door to the interior opened and a uniformed policeman with dark, greasy hair combed straight back and a pock-marked face jerked his head to beckon me inside. I followed him through another door that opened onto a long, narrow corridor. On one side stretched a row of identical unmarked closed doors. Facing them against the opposite wall was a long row of tubular metal chairs with worn orange plastic seats.

"Wait here," he said.

I sat there for a long time. The empty walls were a dirty yellow, the floor was grey linoleum, worn down to the burlap backing in front of each chair by many anxious feet. I should have brought a book, I thought. Muffled voices came from behind the doors.

At last one of the doors swung open. A tall, thin man with a beak nose gave me a curt nod and held the door. I entered a small office dominated by a chipped wooden desk and a large metal filing cabinet. At his bidding I sat down on one of the hard chairs facing the desk. He took his seat and opened my passport that lay on the desk in front of him. In silence he contemplated it, turning the pages. My hands were cold and a rivulet of sweat trickled down my back. At last he looked up.

"So you want a residence permit. Why?"

"Do you speak English?" I asked. He shook his head dismissively.

I began in my halting Czech, "I was born here—"

"I see that," he cut in.

I tried my best, stumbling through my tentative and grammatically incorrect Czech. "I want to speak Czech well. I'd like to live and work here." I tried not to show my anxiety, to look innocent and persuasive. I wanted so desperately to stay, and he held all the power.

"What work would you do?" he asked.

"I could teach English," I said. "Or work as a translator once my Czech is better. I understand Czech better than I speak it."

"What work did you do in Canada?"

I couldn't describe my work with the National Film Board. "Film," was all I could manage. He pursed his lips and nodded slowly.

"Wait here," he said after a moment or two. He disappeared through one of the doors to an adjoining room. Many muffled words were exchanged on the other side of the door. Eventually he returned, a sheaf of paper in his hand. Sitting down, he pushed the papers towards me.

"You must fill in these forms and bring them back completely filled in."

I beamed at him. "Thank you very much!"

"No, no. We need this information before we can make any decision. Come back when you have filled them in." He stood up. Getting to my feet, I shoved them into my purse.

"*Na shledanou,*" I said. Goodbye. And the door shut firmly behind me. I didn't realize I'd been holding my breath until I was back on the sidewalk, out in the fresh air.

————

The forms were long and asked a great many questions, some standard ones but many others that surprised me – the names of my friends, what organizations I belonged to, the names of all my family members, their occupations, the organizations they belonged to, their political affiliations, the names of their friends and associates. I filled them in as best I could, leaving out everything I thought might be sensitive or damaging to anyone. Paul Wilson translated it for me, made a few suggestions, what to add, what to leave out, to make it more convincing. Within three days, I was back, handing the envelope to the same porter, then sitting again on one of those orange plastic chairs, waiting for a door to open. Again the interminable wait, alone in that blind, empty corridor. Again I'd forgotten to bring a book.

Another shabby office. This time there were two men, both in uniform, neither of whom I'd seen before. The older man with very short, iron-grey hair and pale eyes contemplated me blankly, while the younger man stood by the window flipping through my sheaf of papers. He tossed them on the desk, where they landed with a sharp slap. "This is not what we expected," sneered the older man. "It's useless."

"What? I filled in everything!"

"We are not stupid. We know who your parents are. We have thick files on them. We know all about your father. A raving capitalist. A Nazi collaborator. An enemy of the people who deserted his country. He left illegally. If he tried to come back, he could be arrested. A traitor. And that applies to you too. Your leaving the country was against the law. I read no apology here." He slapped the pages in front of him and sat back in his chair.

I could feel the blood leave my face. My father, who'd been summoned to testify against the Nazis at the Nuremburg trials, labelled a Nazi collaborator. I was speechless with outrage.

"So why should we let you into the country?" he drawled. "How are we to know you're any different than your father?"

I had to control myself. I used the only tool I had – being pretty and young, and in men's eyes, naive.

"I don't know anything about that," I said. "I'm not interested in politics. I want to live here for a while to learn about it. To get to know the country where I was born."

They gazed at me, derisive, skeptical, as though I'd said something hopelessly sentimental.

"I was four years old!" I cried.

The older man drummed his fingers on the desk. They exchanged glances. The other man shrugged, looking bored.

"Tell you what," said the older man. "We'll give you another chance. Write up a *životopis*. A *curriculum vitae*. A full declaration of your life. Your thoughts, your opinions, your complete personal history. What you studied. All the groups you belonged to. All your connections, especially to the Czech community in Canada. And we need more about your parents. What work they do, who their friends are. We need a full disclosure." He stood up. "Otherwise, this is worthless."

I stumbled into the street, angry, frightened, and determined. They would not win. Back in my room, I laboured over that document. Wrote and rewrote it, struggling to get just the right tone, filling it with a great deal of information but nothing they could use against me or anyone else. A tone of openness and naive trust, a great flow of words, a mountain of information, but all of it innocent. Brownies and Girl Guides, the schools I went to, the subjects I liked and didn't like, my summers at camp, our cottage in Haliburton, learning to drive, studying French at Laval summer school during high school, my camping trips, playing hockey and basketball for Queen's University, my projects at the National Film Board, living in Ibiza.

I stressed my independence, overdid my distance from my parents. Emphasized how little they had spoken of the past, never expressing their opinions, insisting on leaving the past behind in order to start a new life. As though I'd never heard my parents talking, never heard my father's rage, my mother's heartbreak and anguish. As though I didn't know these men were the scum of the earth, thieves and criminals who had stolen everything from us, from me.

A week later I was back in that stark yellow corridor, sitting on an orange plastic chair again, in a cold sweat, awaiting my fate. Kafka's stories came to my mind; the sense of unknown threat, vague horror, and the utter absurdity of it all.

A door opened. The same two men, the same office. I sat across from them, waiting. My papers were in front of the older man, who again sat at his desk, turning the pages. Could it be he looked pleased? The other man stood looking out the window.

"This is better," the older man nodded, a faint smile on his lips. He turned more pages, which rustled in the silent room.

"I've been to the Prague Language School and they told me they could use my English teaching skills," I said. "I've also been to Rapid and Strojimport, to offer translation work. They said they would hire me if I had a residence permit."

"*Moment,*" said the older man, and with a gesture of his head asked the other man to follow him into the adjoining room. After an eternity they returned, resuming their places. The older man did the talking.

"These documents tell us there could be a serious problem here. We're afraid that you might end up moving in questionable circles. You probably don't realize you have to be very careful whom you associate with in this country." He paused. I waited. He continued. "If we grant you a residence permit, it's our job to make sure you don't fall into the wrong hands." I looked at him blankly.

"If we issue you a residence permit," he went on, "there is a condition we need you to abide by. We would ask you to meet with us regularly, perhaps once a month, to let us know how you're getting on. For your own safety and well-being."

"Meet with you?" I asked.

"Yes. Meet with us and let us know how you're doing. We'd want to know who you are in contact with, what they do, anything relevant or out of the ordinary they said or did. Who their friends and associates are. To make sure you're all right."

I stared, looking from one to the other. "I don't understand. I can take care of myself."

The older man shrugged impatiently. The other turned from the window and faced me, scowling.

"Look," the older man tried again. "You have worked in film. You have a philosophy degree. You want to teach English. You could be drawn into circles of writers and other such people. These are people we are interested in. We want to know what they are doing. What activities they are involved in. Some are honest and honourable, of course, and have our full approval. But some of these cadres may be enemies of the state. We need to make sure you don't get involved in any illegal activities."

"I ... I ... I don't ... I won't do anything illegal," I stammered.

"We are simply asking you to keep us informed of your activities and the people you meet. Under these conditions, we might consider granting you a residence permit, despite your unsavoury family history."

Was I hearing what I thought I was hearing? How could I respond, if my staying depended on becoming a spy? When I answered, the words choked in my throat. "You are asking me to report to you on people who might become friends, employers, colleagues. To inform on them. Is that right?"

They looked affronted. "No, not at all. You are mistaken. We are expressing concern for your welfare as well as acting for the good of the state. If you want to live here, that is what is required."

I stared at them. "I ... I don't think I could do that."

Their eyes were hard. The older man stood up. "This interview is over. You insist on misunderstanding. You could fall into the wrong hands and not know it. Dangerous hands. We'll give you some time to think it over. Consider whether you want that residence permit or not." He strode towards the door. "We'll keep your papers for now." Adding, "We'll be in touch."

Four days later a plain white postcard arrived in my mailbox. "Present yourself at Bartolomějská 14 on Monday, February 12, 1972 at 10:00 a.m." I flew to U Svítáků that evening and found Paul Wilson.

"People live in dread of these cards," he told me. "They keep the appointment and sometimes are never seen again. They disappear and their family has no recourse." Was he joking? "But not you. Not with a Canadian passport. They'll either throw you out or give you the permit."

I told him what they had asked of me in exchange. Paul grimaced. "That's how they operate. Anyone they have something on, the smallest infraction, often trumped up, or anyone who needs something, is vulnerable. The police force them to become informers. If the person doesn't agree, they can arrange for him to lose his job, or prevent his kids from getting into the profession or job they want. He might get a notice he has to move to a smaller flat, or they can move another family in, deciding his family has more space than they're entitled to. They control everything and want to know everything. That's why nobody trusts anyone here. You never know who's an informer. A group like ours is the only place we can speak freely."

"What should I do?" I asked.

"You have to go," Paul advised. "See what happens. Play dumb. Play earnest and innocent. At worst you'll have to leave when your tourist visa expires."

Once again I pulled open that heavy street door, was taken into that long empty hall and sat alone, shivering. My future lay in the hands of the men behind those doors, men who were asking the impossible of me. I sat trying to plan what to say but coming up with nothing. Could I do it? Could I agree and then not tell them anything?

After an hour, one door opened abruptly. A tall bald man I hadn't seen before gestured for me to enter. He was wearing the usual dark green police uniform but with more stripes. Another stark room just like the others. A file lay on the desk. He pointed to the chair across from him as he sat down, opened the file, and nodded slowly as he flipped through the pages. Finally he looked across at me.

"I hope you have thought about our offer and our request."

"Not really," I said after a moment of awkward silence.

"What do you mean?"

"I don't really know what I'm supposed to be thinking about. I'm hoping to receive a residence permit and I don't understand why it is so difficult to get one."

He glared at me and said, almost shouting, emphasizing each word, as though he were speaking to an imbecile, "It is not difficult. We were very clear about our expectations. You were to come back with a decision. If you do not comply, you cannot stay here. Do you understand?"

What could I say? I had to have the permit. I simply nodded.

"Then will you agree?"

I hesitated, then shook my head.'

His fist banged down on the desk. I jumped.

"Já jsem Češka," I ventured. I am Czech. "Why wouldn't I be able to stay here for a while?"

It was his turn to stare at me. I continued. "I don't need help and I don't want to talk about people I might meet." Innocent. Naive, I hoped.

"Of course you can stay here, being Czech, but you have to comply with the rules now. I can see you need to think about this further." He went to the door.

Gathering my courage, I asked as I rose, "Would it be possible for you to extend my visa, while I do that?"

He considered, then nodded. He scribbled a note in my passport and returned it to me. "We will contact you."

At best I had bought myself more time, but my quest seemed mired in quicksand.

⧛ Chapter 8

IN BETWEEN VISITS TO THE POLICE STATION, I CONTINUED to follow up leads given to me by Paul and his friends and the Canadian consulate. One name led to another and I did the rounds of various faculties at the university, numerous ministries and a number of companies that did business outside the country and might need a translator. I was often well received, but everything depended on that residence permit. No one dared admit me or hire me without that document from the police.

At the pub one evening, Jakub came over and with a rueful face informed me that his daughter was coming home from brigade work and would need her room. Paul put the word out again to the group. One of them, Leoš, had a photographer friend who'd been allocated a small studio he wasn't using. "I'll ask him," Leoš had said, "and let you know in a couple of days."

I came that evening full of hope and apprehension. So much of my life here depended on others. Leoš arrived smiling, holding out a chain with two keys dangling from it. He wrote down the address: U Lužického Semináře 19, Malá Strana. "Go have a look," he said, "and if you want it, it's yours – for the time being. But he told me to warn you, it's tiny and filthy. A cell, really."

I crossed Charles Bridge early the next morning, the grim statues watching me as I passed, the castle walls stretching across the hilltop above. Street map in hand, I made my way through the twisting lanes and high walls of the Little Quarter, where an open gate could suddenly reveal an expansive park. I followed the narrow street toward Klárov, a small square close to the river, and there was number 19. A smaller door was carved into a pair of larger wooden gates. Shakily I inserted the heavy old-fashioned key and turned. The door swung open onto a cement courtyard. It was a small two-storey building with the second floor balcony encircling the courtyard. A few bicycles leaned against the railings, and laundry hung from clotheslines. On the ground floor, a row of garbage cans lined one wall. At the back, someone had created a lush garden, a burst of green in an otherwise bleak courtyard.

Immediately to my left was a brown-painted single door with the number 1 on it. I put the smaller key in the lock and the door opened. A musty smell hit me from out of the darkness. I groped for a light switch. A dim single bulb hung from the ceiling, revealing a tiny, dank room with trash in the corners and cobwebs hanging from the ceiling. I shuddered. A wide, low bench stretched along one wall, and a counter with a sink and two faucets was affixed to another. Once upon a time this may have been a storage room for the building's caretaker.

I stumbled across the cluttered floor, opened the double windows and threw open the shutters. Sunlight and fresh air poured in. I was looking directly out onto the street, its cobblestones and passersby, and the river sparkled between two buildings across the street. Yes. I would make this my home.

Exploring further, I discovered the WC was off the hallway at the back of the courtyard, shared by several tenants. A toilet.

No bath or shower. For that, I was to find the public baths at the foot of Charles Bridge on the other side of the river.

I bought a broom, a sponge and a pail and scrubbed the room thoroughly. I pasted my name beside the bell by the street door. I bought a foam mattress the width of the bench, some bedding, a chair, a kettle and a hotplate, a few dishes and some cutlery, got my things from Jakub's and settled in. Poking around my new digs, I looked into the garden at the back of the courtyard. No one seemed to be home. I marvelled at the trouble someone had gone to, so rare in Prague, to create this garden. Runner beans had been planted and ran up strings that stretched from the ground diagonally to the wall, creating a bright green canopy dotted with red flowers. Underneath in the filtered light were many varieties of flowers and plants, and among them, cement benches and small statues. An oasis of beauty lovingly created.

I pinched myself – to have a place in Prague that was all my own, even temporarily. I adored the Little Quarter, its gas lit streets, its houses crowded together below the towering castle. As was required, I notified the police of my new address.

Shortly after I moved in there was a knock on my door. An older man, maybe 45 – it was hard to tell ages in Czechoslovakia. I'd seen few good-looking middle-aged men or women. Good-looking young people aged quickly; people looked wrecked by the time they were forty. This fellow looked wrecked. He bowed a little and introduced himself as Mirek Sadovský, my neighbour who lived at the back of the court-yard. The one with the garden.

He was short and wiry with thinning grey hair, a stooped, apologetic way of standing and an ingratiating look on his face.

"Welcome to the building," he said in Czech, and he invited me over for a coffee.

I'd only received one letter from my husband John in England, a cool letter letting me know he had settled in, was working with Gerhardt, and though he was sad and missed me, he thought our separation was for the best. I'd sent him a letter urging him to come visit me in Prague. I missed him terribly and would have been overjoyed to have a visit from him. He hadn't replied to my invitation. Much as I valued my visits to Uncle Paul and Růža, to Malý Pavel and his family, and much as I enjoyed the camaraderie of pub nights with Paul Wilson and his friends, I was lonely. I hesitated. "Just a coffee, that's all," he insisted. Okay, I said.

His room was a studio, and it was dazzling. He was a designer and creator of light fixtures. Lights of all shapes and sizes filled the room, lamps of the most original design, all in various stages of completion. He handed me a mug of the strong Turkish brew that I'd learned was how Czechs drank their coffee and he took me around, showing me lights made of all sorts of material, some bought, most found. He was a creative scavenger. Jumbles of tangled metal tubes with tiny bulbs at the end of each one. White canvas soaked in shellac and stretched to harden over wire frames. He worked on his own, he told me, always on the lookout for commissions. He led me out to show me his garden, much of it decorated with found objects he'd brought home. Every corner of his room and garden was filled with something he'd found or made or was in the process of making. He was bursting with creativity. Yet he seemed a sad man, lonely, struggling to make a living.

Mirek and I became friends. We'd sit together at the Two Hearts pub across the street or take the train out into the countryside, to Chuchle, to pick mushrooms. He taught me where to look for Wenceslas mushrooms with their curving stems and fuzzy brown caps growing in clusters from old tree stumps. He'd invite me over for dinner and we'd sit on floor cushions, dining on a whole boiled chicken he'd cooked on a hotplate beside us on the floor. He wooed me with an urgent and humble persistence. He was kind and he was there, and so we became lovers. He was passionate and hungry and so was I. I didn't love him but I was glad to have his companionship. We met almost every day.

———

Soon another white card arrived for me. This one was different. "Please come to the Palace Hotel dining room on Tuesday, March 13, 1972 at 5:00 p.m." The return address was the same: the police station.

The Palace Hotel, I discovered, was a luxury hotel, a place ordinary citizens would never enter and could not afford. I stood at the entrance to the dining room. Gleaming white tablecloths and brocade drapes at the windows. Mostly men in dark suits. So ... ranking communists took care of themselves well, despite the poverty and ugliness everywhere else.

A youngish man sitting alone at a table stood, waved and came towards me, his hand outstretched. "Miss Notzl? How nice of you to come. Please join me." He ushered me to his table, drew back the chair for me. "My name is Zdeněk and I'm delighted to meet you." I gave him a wan smile. What was this?

Zdeněk was tall, slim and very handsome and probably just a few years older than I. "Allow me to offer you some champagne," he said and beckoned to a hovering waiter. The champagne was poured and Zdeněk held out his glass. "*Na zdraví*," he toasted me. To your health. I took a sip and waited. "Helen – may I call you Helen? I do understand your great desire to live here," he said, sitting back in his chair. "It's a wonderful country. So rich in history, in culture, going back to the kings of Bohemia. But as you may not know, there is a great experiment taking place here. An experiment to see if we can create a fair society, a society of equality for everyone. For the working people, not just the elite. It is unfortunate that some people don't understand our glorious aims. They refuse to participate. They are, in fact, destructive. They could ruin everything and cause our noble aim to fail. Please understand. We must be vigilant to ensure that doesn't happen." He took a sip of his champagne and smiled at me. I downed my glass. He summoned the waiter, and when our glasses were topped up, he continued.

"We have to be very careful about who we allow to participate in this great experiment. We like you. We understand and admire your wanting to come here and be part of it. But you must understand we cannot allow you to be led astray by undesirable elements. You have much to learn and we – I, in fact – would be delighted to be your friend, to teach you and help you learn everything you have come to learn about life in the Czechoslovak Socialist Republic." He took another sip of his champagne.

I thought about my father's escape, the prison he would have been rotting in – if they hadn't murdered him outright. I thought about my brother Peter and me working on an assembly line, denied an education because our father had been a bank director. About my mother risking herself and her two small children getting shot by border guards because we didn't choose to participate in the glorious experiment Zdeněk described. I thought about Stalin and the purges, the mock trials, the murder and disappearance of countless innocent people, the thousands of imprisoned, tortured and executed people innocent of any crime. The postcard summons in the mail, the knocking on the door at night. I thought about 1968 and the tanks rolling in to extinguish the ray of hope that had begun to dawn.

"I'm hoping you will give me the pleasure of joining me for dinner," Zdeněk said, "and we can discuss all this further."

"Actually," I stammered, "I have to go now, I have plans for dinner already." I stood, snatching my jacket from the back of my chair. Zdeněk, surprised, half rose. "Please think about what I've told you. Let's see one another soon," he called out as I blundered towards the entrance.

There was nothing anyone could do. Paul and his friends at the pub nodded sympathetically. Uncle Paul and Růža shook their heads. "*Gauneři*," my uncle swore. Bastards. "*Dej si pozor*," my aunt warned, frightened for me. Be careful. Mirek and I sat at the Two Hearts and drank stein after stein of beer while he cursed and raged at the system, at life, at everything.

Another postcard arrived. A summons to the police station. No champagne this time and no handsome charmer. I was angry and resigned. How much longer could this go on? They would hound me until I gave up, my resistance worn down. I wanted so badly to stay. It was clear I'd be able to study, to find work if I did stay. I had found family that I treasured, friends and a lover. I wanted this life. I wanted to stroll along the banks of the river, drinking in the beauty around me. I wanted to explore the tangle of streets and lanes, to stop and have a coffee or a beer and sit and listen to Czech. I raged at their power over me, their ability to throw me out of my own country. I raged at everything they had done to ruin my country, and I yearned to reclaim what was left of it. How could I leave now?

As before, after another long wait, I was brought into one of those interrogation rooms. Two men I'd seen before sat there, one of them the more senior and more decorated one. My file sat on the desk. I noticed it was a good deal fatter.

The older one began. "I think we have given you enough time to make the right decision. You are being foolish and stubborn. We have wasted a great deal of time and resources on you. Surely you don't need more time."

The other one broke in, moving forward and leaning one arm on the desk. "Think of how much you want to be here. You can have everything you are after: work, a place to stay, a nice life in a city you love. How disappointing to have to leave and return home, without achieving what you came here to do. It's not a lot we are asking of you. It's very easy, only taking a few minutes of your time each month. Surely being allowed to stay here is worth such a small task. And you understand, you would be helping this country, a country you claim to love so much."

My heart was pounding so hard I was sure they could hear it. I was silent for a long time. Finally I mustered my courage.

"Look," I said. "We could keep doing this. I could keep coming here, or wherever, you could keep trying to talk me into agreeing to what you are asking of me. I am not going to agree. Please understand. It is not political. I would not agree to it in Canada, I will not agree to it here. Yes, I want very much to be here. I would add something by my being here. But if I have to do what you ask in order to get a residence permit, then I guess I won't get one. I'm very sorry. It's your decision, not mine." I stood and on shaky legs left the room, shutting the door behind me.

I spent the next few days wandering around, practising saying goodbye. Four days later, there was an envelope in my mailbox. It was my residence permit.

I ran to U Svítáků that evening, brandishing it aloft. Paul and his friends burst into applause and bought me rounds of beer. The next day I went to visit my uncle and aunt, bringing with me a bottle of champagne from the Tuzex store, and we laughed and cried and celebrated. I did the same at Malý Pavel's. We could continue being a family. I sent a telegram to my parents.

"Finally received my residence permit STOP Now I can study and work STOP Everything going well STOP Will write soon STOP"

A telegram from my father came back the next day:

"Congratulations STOP Please be careful STOP Still worried and miss you STOP"

Going back to Canada was the last thing on my mind. It was this home I was intent on creating. I sat down and wrote them a letter full of reassurance and a promise to visit soon.

———

I enrolled in Czech classes at Charles University and did the rounds to the agencies that had expressed an interest in hiring me as a translator. Paul Wilson suggested I try Artia Publishing for whom he did some work. Artia's specialty was producing illustrated children's books for export. The text was relatively simple, as the books were primarily vehicles for the magnificent artwork. They hired me immediately and gave me my first assignment, a fairy tale to translate into English. My Czech-English dictionary, my Czech classes and Malý Pavel would be on hand to help me.

I set up my portable typewriter on the bench which doubled as my desk, flung open my window and set to work. The story was an easy one, yet I was discovering there were nuances to translating, determining when to translate literally and when to focus on communicating the flavour or a subtlety which might require a better choice of words or phrasing. I loved moving from Czech to English and back again. It confirmed something I'd long felt: the complexity, richness and musicality of the Czech language compared to the sparseness and rigour of English.

My days took on a homey routine. I'd work at my typewriter for a few hours, then take a break to explore my neighbour-hood – the walled park just around the corner, Malostranské Náměstí, Little Quarter Square, with its magnificent St. Nicholas Church, Kampa Island. Sometimes Mirek and I would meet at the pub across the street and walk together. I shopped for provisions in the square. Malostranská Kavárna, the Little Quarter Café, became my regular haunt, and I'd often take my work there. Tram 22, which stopped right in front, would take me to my aunt and uncle's across the river on Jugoslávská in one direction and to Malý Pavel's in the opposite.

Mirek turned out to be a heavy drinker. It seemed everyone in Prague drank, or most of the men. Pubs were everywhere, often several per city block; they opened early and were full much of the day. Pubs were the heart of Czech social life, but again, mostly for men, who sat with their male friends in the evenings, hour upon hour, then headed home to wife and family. But it turned out Mirek was a chronic drinker, who disappeared on binges for days at a time and then showed up ruined, his face crumpled and sallow, his clothes and hair filthy. We'd make dates and he'd let me down, disappearing and surfacing days later. I never knew where he'd gone and how long his benders would last. I'd be disgusted and furious; then I pitied him and we'd reconcile. Like everyone else in the country, he had a history, no doubt a tragic one. I knew nothing about his life, whether he'd been married or had children. He wouldn't talk about those things, and he was a loner. I never met anyone through him.

One weekend we were supposed to meet to go to Chuchle. I waited at the train station. He didn't show up, so I went by myself. I found a beautiful cluster of Wenceslas mushrooms and left them hanging in a bag on the handle of his door. It was two days before he found them.

After I'd lived in the studio for about a month, Leoš arrived at U Svítáků and broke the bad news. His photographer friend would need his studio back at some point. Once again, I had to find a place to live. A huge setback. Again it was put to the group, but no one had any ideas. As I sat with Mirek at the Two Hearts, I told him I had to move. He was as upset as I was.

"You can't move," he said. "Where would you go? To some *pension* somewhere?"

I shrugged, frightened. "That's what the police suggested back when I asked them. That's what foreigners are expected to do."

"No. You're not a foreigner."

———

A week later, Mirek stood at my door. "Come with me." We headed towards Charles Bridge, past Mostecká Street, passing a magnificent palace with a row of dark statues across the roofline. "Nostitz Palace," Mirek informed me, "now housing a ministry." We continued down a narrow cobblestoned street. Gaslights hung on the stucco walls on either side. Halfway down, on the left, was a wall and a gate. Mirek took a set of keys from his pocket and opened the gate. It led through a courtyard to a two-storey building.

All this time, Mirek had said nothing, but there was a grin on his face.

"Follow me," he said. He led me to a door to our right, selected a key and unlocked the door. We were in a large room with two double windows that looked out onto a narrow garden. Beyond the garden were trees – Kampa Park – and the river. The sunlight streamed in.

I turned to stare at him. "It's yours if you want it," he said.

"This is the most beautiful part of Prague!" I exclaimed. "On a river, and in Malá Strana. Is it yours?"

"It is now."

"However did you get it?" Where did people go to claim a studio or a bit of extra space?

"I went and demanded a studio. Told them I couldn't make a living doing what I do, living and working in one room. This was vacant so they let me have it – after a lot of persuading." He looked away. "You'll have a nice view of the river," he said, walking over to the windows, then turning back to me. "Do you like it?"

"It's fantastic," I said, "but I don't know if I can accept it."

"Why not?"

"I could only take it on one condition. No strings. I'll pay the rent and utilities. It will be my place, not our place. Not a place for us to be together or for you to come and see me whenever you want. I will be your tenant." He agreed immediately and handed me the keys.

"Let me show you one more thing." He led me back out into the hall, pointed to a door beside mine. "That's the toilet," he said, "but here's what I want to show you." Another door led to a narrow passageway to the garden, and a path continued to a terrace, from which a set of steep stone steps ended at the small fast-flowing river.

"The garden and terrace are yours too, since there are no other tenants on the ground floor," he said. Over and over I thanked him, unable to believe his kindness and my good fortune.

Mirek helped me move my few belongings, lugging them with me through the streets of Malá Strana. Finally there on my own, I cleaned the room and whitewashed the walls. I bought a wardrobe and stood it so that it separated the sink from the rest of the room, creating a bit of a washroom. From Uncle Paul I got several small Persian rugs that had belonged to my mother and had been stacked on his grand piano. I picked up a low wooden bedframe, stained it black and covered my foam mattress with a pink and black Indian cotton bedspread. I bought lumber and built a sturdy low coffee table, stained it black and placed it next to the bed. I found a used wooden table, painted it black. Mirek donated an antique cabinet with a mirrored interior and a light inside, to hang between the two windows. I hung blinds in the windows. It felt like home, at last.

Nosticova Street was one of the most charming streets in Prague. At the end of the garden was the Čertovka – the Devil's Channel – a narrow arm of the Vltava River, encircling the island of Kampa. I sat on my terrace and watched mothers pushing prams, couples strolling arm in arm, and old men sitting on benches in the sun, reading newspapers. Dogs frolicked. My very own place, in the very heart of Prague.

The room was heated, like everywhere else, with a small coal-burning stove in the corner. Coal was delivered to a coal cellar outside my room and I'd carry it in, a pail at a time. The room warmed up quickly. The stovetop doubled as an extra hotplate for cooking. A desk lamp curved over my typewriter on the table where I did my translating. There was no fridge – they were rare in Prague – so I shopped every day or two at the small shops on Malostranské Náměstí for my bread and cheese, eggs, coffee and wine, and when they were available, an apple, a peach.

I didn't get to know any other tenants. On the few occasions when I met anyone in the hall or courtyard, we'd mumble *Dobrý den*. They eyed me with suspicion. And I guarded my room jealously to myself. I met Mirek in pubs or at his place.

There were nights when we'd agreed to meet and he wouldn't show up. I'd arrive, sit by myself and then leave, the barman shrugging as I passed him. One day Mirek proposed taking the train to the countryside and having a picnic. I prepared the food and rang the bell outside his street door. No answer. I waited. Perhaps he'd gone out to shop for a few things. I waited. Someone came out of the house and I slipped into the courtyard. I knocked on his door, then looked in his window. No one home. I sat in his garden, waiting. I waited an hour and then I went home.

Three days later he rang my bell. I didn't answer. He let himself into the courtyard and knocked on my door. I ignored it.

"*Helenko,*" he whispered through the door. "It's me." I sat at my desk, silent. "Please, open the door."

No. "*Helenko!* I'm very sorry. Please forgive me."

My heart was a stone. He banged on the door, called my name over and over, louder each time.

"Be quiet!" I whispered hoarsely through the door. "Go away! I don't want to see you."

"Please, let me in, I must see you!"

I softened. I knew he was an unhappy man. Kind, I thought, and I owed him a lot. I opened the door. He looked dreadful: dirty, dishevelled, dark circles under his red eyes. He stepped inside, a picture of abject apology. His entreaties continued and he reached out his arms to me. I stepped back. He smelled hideous. I accepted his apology but asked him to leave.

"I hate to see you when you're like this," I said.

"Can we meet tomorrow? Please? At the Two Hearts?" He was abject. "Please. We have to talk. I'm so sorry," he begged. Reluctantly I nodded. "But please go now."

He turned, humble and grateful, and left.

We met and it was awful. I felt sorry for him. When he was sober he was a good friend who eased my loneliness, but this was too hard. I hated to have anything to do with such a man. He vowed he would stop. I didn't believe him.

He came to my door unexpectedly a couple of evenings later. When I opened the door, there he stood with that sorry, hang-dog look, and the moment he opened his mouth, I knew he was drunk again. I slammed the door in his face. He knocked, pleading for me to open it. I refused. "Go away,"

I said. "I can't do this." He knocked on the door, knocked and knocked, calling my name, begging me to open the door. I went and sat at my desk, silent, waiting for him to give up. He got louder, bashing at the door, crying out for me to open it.

I heard footsteps coming down the stairs and suddenly a man's angry voice. "For God's sake, quit that yelling and banging! You're insane! You're disturbing the whole building!"

"*Do prdele,*" Mirek swore back.

"Get out of here!" the man shouted. "You're creating a scandal!"

What was I going to do?

Chapter 9

IT WAS OCTOBER, I'D BEEN IN PRAGUE EIGHT MONTHS. AFTER I'd handed in my first story, the editors at Artia were pleased and gave me two more. The illustrations were beautiful and gave me a clear sense of what we were aiming for. I set to work.

Late one evening, I got up from my desk and stretched. I needed to get out, walk in the night air, rejoin the world. I grabbed my jacket and strode through the dark courtyard to the front door, locking it behind me. The night was cold and clear, the sky full of stars. My footsteps echoed down the narrow, silent street. Gas lamps cast dim pools of light. I passed the gate to the park and could hear the murmur of the river. I crossed Maltézské Náměstí, its fountain silent, and on through the dark streets to my square, Malostranské Náměstí.

I'd taken to frequenting U Glaubicŭ, one of the pubs on the square, and had made some friends there, but it was late and the pub was closed and shuttered. Further on was Rubín, a wine cellar and jazz club that stayed open late. That too had become my local over the past weeks. The bartender was friendly and I'd sit at the small bar and chat with him.

The courtyard was dark and I felt my way down the narrow, curving stone steps and entered the cellar. A quiet night. Two couples sat at low tables. No jazz band in the small theatre beyond the bar, just a blues vocalist singing quietly over the speakers. I took one of the three stools at the bar and ordered a glass of wine. It was good to be out.

Suddenly loud voices, gales of laughter and a rush of foot-steps cascaded down the stairway, and a party of young men and women burst into the room and surrounded the bar. Good-looking, rosy-cheeked from the cold, they were dressed in jeans and dark jackets, and radiated health and good spirits. They milled around the bar, ordering drinks, calling and joking with the bartender, who knew them by name. Some of them acknowledged me with a nod or an "Ahoj," then carried on their conversations. I sipped my wine, feeling my aloneness keenly.

I watched them out of the corner of my eye, listening to their rollicking camaraderie, trying to follow their Czech. I consid-ered paying my bill and leaving. Instead I ordered another glass of wine.

Then there was a voice near me. A male voice. "Ahoj," he said. I turned. The first things I noticed were his dark brown eyes and the tilt of his head as he moved towards me. His friends got out of the way. He was tall, solid. He had light brown hair, a ginger moustache and a ruddy complexion. He wore jeans, a soft brown sweater and a green American army jacket.

"Ahoj," I answered.

"How are you?" in Czech.

"Good. You?" I could still pass for Czech at this level of conversation.

He smiled. "Good, now." Pause. "I've never seen you here before," he said.

"I come here now and then," I said. "I live nearby."

He looked at me more closely. "Where are you from?"

"Canada."

"You're kidding."

"No."

"No really. You're joking."

I laughed. "It's true. I was born here, but grew up in Canada. I've come back."

He gazed at me. Took a drink of his beer.

"What's your name?"

"Helen," I said. "*Helena*." My Czech name. He told me his. Karel. Karel Zavadil.

"Helena from Canada," he repeated, shaking his head. "Have you heard the expression *To je Kanada?*"

"No."

"It's a way of saying something is perfect. Beautiful. A weekend in the country with good friends: *To je Kanada*. One of us ..." he nodded toward his friends, "getting permission to mount an exhibition and selling some of our work: *To je Kanada*. Pulling off an *akce* – a happening – lots of people showing up and everything running smoothly: *To je Kanada*. That's what Canada means to us in this godforsaken country." I didn't understand some of his references but I gave him a look that said I agreed with what he said.

He wanted to know everything. "How long have you been here?" I told him.

"How long are you staying?"

"I don't know – as long as it feels right."

"What are you doing while you're here?" I told him: taking Czech classes, translating, teaching English privately, reuniting with family.

"You?" I asked him.

"I'm a painter. I teach at the Academy of Fine Arts." Oh my God. "These degenerate friends of mine ..." he swung his arm to indicate the group he'd come in with, "are all artists of one kind or another. Friends since university. We call ourselves the *Spolek Pohodlí*. Some of us are also members of *Zlatá Praha*, another group of artists and reprobates that hang out together." I figured *Spolek Pohodlí* meant something like the Comfort Club, but I was sure there were nuances there I didn't get. *Zlatá Praha* – Golden Prague. There was irony in both names, I was sure.

"What about you?" he asked me. "Where do you go? Who do you hang out with?" – as though this was the defining thing. I mentioned Paul Wilson's group at U Svítáků, and the friends I'd made at U Glaubicŭ.

He frowned and shook his head, taking another swig of beer. "Those are no good." I was taken aback. Condescending, I thought. Arrogant. I downed the rest of my wine.

"You need better groups than that," he continued. I was silent.

"The thing is, the way this country is, there's nothing good happening. Absolutely nothing. So we band together to create our own *akce*. We couldn't stand it otherwise."

"What sort *of akce*?" Happenings.

He shrugged. "All sorts. You have to know where to go. U Glaubicŭ is nowhere. You're wasting your time. We meet at U Bonaparta, on Nerudova every Wednesday and Friday. And Zlatá Praha meets at U Tygra on Sundays. People like the writers Hrabal and Jiří Mucha sit with us sometimes. That's where the action is." I nodded. If only.

"Coming, Karel?" One of the women in the group put her arm around Karel's shoulder. His friends were paying their bills, putting their coats on.

"What's your address? What number on Nosticova?"

"Two," I said.

"See you." And he was gone.

Rubín was silent again. I paid my bill and walked the dark, empty streets home. I didn't think I'd have the courage to show up at U Bonaparta one of those evenings, but I knew come Wednesday I'd be thinking of it.

I did go to Rubín again, hoping they might show up, but they didn't. Wednesday came; I didn't go to U Bonaparta. I wasn't sure I liked him anyway, I told myself.

A few days later I found a note in my mailbox. "Be at the main entrance to the Academy of Fine Arts at 16:00 on Tuesday. Karel." The peremptory tone of the note annoyed me. Was he a man used to ordering others – women – around?

At U Glaubiců I asked a waiter where the Academy of Fine Arts was, located it on my map and set out by tram. Up on Letná hill, across the river. Getting off too soon, I had to walk several long blocks before I found it, but I was on time. An expansive, imposing building. Warily I climbed the wide steps, took a deep breath and pulled open the door. I was in a huge, echoing, empty atrium. In a cubicle at one end sat a porter. I didn't remember Karel's last name. I waited a while, debating whether to leave. I gave it five more minutes. Just as I was turning to leave, a door slammed above, quick footsteps thudded on the floor and there was Karel taking the stairs two at a time, one hand sliding down the wide banister. He wore the same jeans and jacket he'd had on before.

"So sorry!" he called out. "A student had a problem." He stood beside me, grinning. "I'm glad you've come. I thought you might be interested in seeing the Academy."

"Oh. Yes, I am," I said.

"Come then."

I felt another twinge of irritation at his presumption, but I followed him as he led me through the wide halls, so at home in this magnificent environment. We entered large empty studios, their floor-to-ceiling windows flooding the rooms with warm afternoon light. Everywhere the delicious smell of paint, linseed oil, turpentine; rooms full of easels, canvasses, pots of brushes, inks, pastels. He described the classes and the subjects he taught. We went from one room to another.

In one large studio, he stood at an easel, flipping through a series of pen and ink drawings, the work of one of his good students. "One of the few," he said. He was describing to me what he saw in each one, its merits, where the student could make improvements. I was suddenly overcome by a wave of admiration and gratitude – and desire. How fortunate I was to be there. I wanted this beautiful man. I wished I could be a part of this life.

"Now I want you to come and meet my friend, Pepík Hampl," he said. He led the way to an office down the hall where a thin, older man with a black beard and twinkling eyes sat behind a desk piled high with papers. "One of the best graphic artists in the country," Karel said. "My new friend from Canada. And a Czech." We shook hands, his handshake warm, firm.

Pepík drew a bottle of Slivovice, a fiery plum brandy, from the bottom drawer of his desk. He ushered us to three worn chairs around a low coffee table; they put their feet up on the table, I followed suit, and we drank.

"The Academy is beautiful," I said. "I'm happy to have seen it."

"Physically, yes," Pepík said, "but in this environment, nothing worthwhile is created. If we could only get good students, kids with talent. If only they were allowed to create works of some significance."

"There are a few, but the majority are mediocre," Karel agreed. "The stupidity of functionaries, the idiots in charge of things in the various ministries, whose job is to prevent anything meaningful from happening. Anything new is forbidden – seen as a sign of Western decadence."

They railed at the system. Roadblocks at every turn. Students without talent, there because their parents were well placed in the Communist party. "Good students, real students who are passionate about art, don't stand a chance," Pepík grumbled, refilling our glasses.

"It's not apathy," Karel said. "I wish it was, then something could be done about it. The idiots in charge are actually enemies of anything artistic, fine or beautiful. They loathe culture. It's foreign to them. The only art they want is propaganda. Proud factory workers turning out tractors, joyful peasants dragging home sheaves of wheat. Anything else scares them."

He turned to me. "Can you imagine? There's a panel of 'experts' who decide who can exhibit in a gallery and who can't. What do they know about art? Not a damn thing! Their criteria? Whether the artist's – and I use that word loosely – family are members of the party. And whether the subject matter glorifies this workers' paradise. It's disgusting!"

"Can either of you exhibit?" I asked.

They laughed ruefully. "We don't paint that kind of crap," Pepík said. "Karel qualifies with the first criterion, however."

Karel winced. "His father's high up in the Party. Obviously they don't get along."

"Let's not get into that. What we do is exhibit for one another," Karel said. "That's one of the main reasons for groups like Spolek Pohodlí and Zlatá Praha. None of us are willing to produce the kind of garbage they consider acceptable. We're artists who don't exhibit, writers who don't publish. We organize our own exhibitions. Writers make copies and pass them around. It's the only thing that keeps us going. That's what good writers – those who haven't got the hell out of here – are doing. Or just writing, shoving it into a drawer, hoping maybe someday..."

"Not likely in our lifetime," Pepík muttered, "the way things are going."

"You Westerners have no idea," Karel turned to me. "You're so naive. And you don't know how lucky you are. You take so much for granted."

"Wait a minute," I cried. "What I do know is that my family had to escape, risking being shot at the border. Just for wanting to leave! This country – *my* country – was stolen from me. I had to grow up in a foreign country where I have felt alien all my life. My own family torn apart and my family here punished on account of us leaving. I've had to live with that." At least that's what I tried to say.

"You have been free to go where you want, do what you want," Karel said. "I have no idea what that's like. Can you even imagine it? I've never been anywhere but here. Someone else decided for me that I'm not allowed. I'm a prisoner here! And you blow in here just because you feel like it!"

I stared at him.

"You didn't grow up afraid," he said. "Afraid of everything. Unable to trust anyone, not even your own parents, or parents their own children. You didn't grow up with atrocities happening all around you, disappearances, innocent people rotting in jail for decades – even though their accusers know damn well they're innocent. Imagine your every move watched. Every friend and neighbour a potential informer. You Westerners have *no idea* what that's like."

We sat still and quiet, the three of us. I thought about those visits to the police station. They'd been asking me to spy. I could be collecting data on these two right now, having accepted an agreement that had bought me my residence permit. How could they be sure I hadn't said yes? Uncle Paul's years in a concentration camp because of a neighbour's lies. Envy, suspicion and wishing one another harm must run deep in this environment, I thought. Was it naiveté that in Canada I'd prided myself on trusting everyone until I learned otherwise? It was one of my values. I'd deliberately put myself in situations where trust was essential – and I'd never been proven wrong. Hitchhiking to the cottage. Allowing a stranger to help me when my car broke down on the 401, getting into his car and letting him take me to the nearest service station. Taking a bus to Port Severn, renting a canoe and paddling by myself among the islands of Georgian Bay, my sleeping bag rolled out under the stars, a small fire beside me; docking and hitchhiking to the nearest town and pub when I was lonely. I had taken for granted that I would be safe, that people were kind and to be trusted. That was Canada in the sixties. Or at least my experience of it.

"You're right," I said to Karel. "I grew up far away from all that. I grew up with freedom. Also with loss, grieving for everything we'd left behind. But not with fear."

He'd subsided. "You're very lucky."

"I know."

We drank.

"Once I belonged here," I said. "I don't know if I can ever belong here again."

"I don't know why you'd want to belong here, under these conditions," Karel said. "What they've made of this country is a disaster. But we do the best we can."

Pepík stood up. "Time to go, ladies and gentlemen," he said.

Karel walked me to the door of the Academy. "Come to U Bonaparta some Wednesday or Friday. Please come."

I sat in the tram going back to Nosticova, looking anew at the heavy, unsmiling people around me. No doubt every one of them had been scarred by tragedy in one way or another.

———

Mirek came to my door the next day and I agreed to go to the Two Hearts with him. My dilemma weighed on me. I didn't want to see him anymore. Yet I lived in that beautiful room thanks to him. True, our agreement stipulated that I was a tenant, no strings. Yet he would never have found it for me if it weren't for our relationship, I was sure. And I felt sorry for him, a good soul destroyed.

I toyed with my coaster as we sat across from one another in the smoky pub.

"There's something I need to tell you, Mirek," I began. He turned those sad eyes on me. "I can't continue. I need to break it off between us. I hate your drinking, I hate you disappearing on me and coming back so ruined. I can't do it anymore."

He promised me he'd stop, that he'd never go on a bender again. He begged me to change my mind. He told me he loved me. I was moved, but adamant. "I'm sorry," I said.

"Let me prove it to you," he urged. "Give me another chance. I'll show you."

"We'll just be friends, then," I said. "Back to being friends. And we'll see." He was relieved and heartened, and he took my hand gratefully as we parted.

The following Wednesday I climbed steep, cobblestoned Nerudova Street, the ancient buildings looming on either side. Halfway up, there it was – U Bonaparta. I stood across the street, watching people come and go. A blast of sound filled the quiet street whenever the door opened. I hesitated, my heart in my mouth. As though my future depended on what happened next. I paced up and down for a while; I couldn't do it. I walked further up Nerudova, up to the very top, where it opened out into Hradčanské Náměstí, the castle square, the high wrought iron gates to the castle courtyard in front of me.

I leaned on the parapet and looked out over the city, the dark green of its many parks, the wide, meandering river. A young couple passed me, whispering, their heads together, their arms entwined. My feeling of longing choked me. I turned and slowly went back down the steep street and pushed open the door. A wave of noise; laughter, a hubbub of talk, shouts, the clink and thud of beer mugs, clouds of smoke. Mostly men. A few women. Every eye turned toward me, a stranger.

I walked past the tap where a fat man in a grungy apron was filling a tray of glass steins, creamy foam spilling onto the tray. Intensely self-conscious, I walked to the last room and back again, looking at each group, looking for Karel, not finding him. I passed the barman again and walked to the front, where a partition hid several tables. There sat a group of young people. I searched among them for Karel and found him. When he saw me, he jumped up and came towards me, his face breaking into a wide smile. He reached for my hand, held it.

"This is Helena," he said to his friends. They regarded me. "She's okay. She's from Canada. But Czech." Hands were raised in greeting, nods, calls of *Ahoj*. I recognized some of them from Rubín. I sat down on the bench beside Karel, and his friends resumed their conversations. Karel filled me in. "That imp-like fellow is Pepa Steklý," indicating a short, red-haired older man with a round face and a full carrot-coloured beard. "He's an art restorer, the best in the country. He restores artifacts and treasures, mostly in churches and ancient buildings."

A handsome couple sat beside him. "That's Milan Kohout, graphic artist, and Jana, also an artist. They do the notices and invitations to our various happenings. And that reprobate beside her is Milan Udržal, a painter." Tall, with dark, deep-set eyes, long, wavy black hair and a black beard. "And over there is Honza Bartoš, sculptor." Clean-shaven, tall, with short, sandy-coloured hair, he wore a beige military uniform. "He's doing his patriotic duty, his obligatory stint in the army. So he works in a spacious, luxurious studio, unlike the rest of us," Karel taunted him. His friends laughed. Honza, red-faced, sent me a crooked smile. He did look out of place among the others. The barman plunked a stein of beer in front of each of us and, scooping up the empties, penciled a stroke on each of the scraps of paper on the table. Karel indicated I should be put on his tab.

"So you get to meet the Spolek Pohodlí," Karel said. "This is how we survive the system and create a life for ourselves.

We help one another, like passing on commissions we hear about. Take Pepa here – not much money being devoted to church restoration these days. So when there's a rumour about a palace or a villa some communist has taken a liking to and is restoring, we let him know."

"Much as it pains me to work for those bastards," Pepa snorted, "living in the lap of luxury, everything stolen – excuse me, *expropriated* – from the rightful owners."

"And then there are true communists, like my parents," said Karel, "idiot idealists who actually believe all that bullshit propaganda. The flat's full of pictures of Stalin, whom they love, and Gottwald, the Czech traitor who sold us out to the Soviets. And posters. '*Bez práce nejsou koláče.*' '*Kdo nepracuje, at' nejí.*' Without work, no cake; those who don't work, don't eat. Crap like that. Living in that damp, musty apartment. Why? Sacrificing themselves for the cause – 'Because no one else wanted it!' my mother told me proudly when I wondered why they had accepted such a flat."

"And gave you the best room in it for your studio," someone said.

"True," Karel nodded, "but like all of us, I'd prefer my own place. We all live like mice in our burrows, crammed together, instead of having something adequate, something that inspires us. Screw them," he said. "Screw every one of those assholes." He took a long pull at his beer. "How are the plans for your *vernissage* coming along, Udržal?"

"I've done my part – the works are ready for the big show," he replied wryly.

Karel turned to me. "He does great work. A tragedy so few people can see it. Our exhibitions are very exclusive – in basements and backyards."

"The graphics for the notices are done," Jana interjected. "I'll bring them next time."

"They're great," Milan said. "She's kept them a little less provocative this time." They laughed.

The conversation carried on for hours, irreverent, angry, rollicking, and the beers kept coming. My head was swimming. I didn't know if it was the beer, what was happening around me, or the man sitting next to me. He sat forward, passionately involved, clearly a leader among his friends, funny, intense, self-assured. I saw the respect and admiration the group felt for him. How did I manage to be sitting here among this group of wild and talented Bohemians, the true Bohemians, welcomed in, privy to their laughter and their despair, in the company of this glorious man?

I added a word or two, but my Czech wasn't up to their level of discourse. The Czech I knew was the language I'd heard my parents speaking, the vocabulary domestic and out of date. Karel and his friends were speaking a different Czech – fast, clever, intellectual, and peppered with slang I didn't know. I felt inadequate, struck dumb. How limited I was in my ability to express myself. How could Karel and his friends have any sense of who I was?

Karel was talking to me. "Will you come?" I woke up.

"The roller skating race," he said. I stared at him. "Our next *akce*. A roller skating race across Charles Bridge next Sunday. Over the cobblestones." He smiled. "One of those things we do to keep ourselves sane – or maybe insane. Why don't you come?"

"I'll try," I said. I certainly would.

People began to get up, say their farewells and drift out. "Can I walk you home?" Karel asked. I nodded.

We went out into the dark night, the sky black but full of stars. Side by side down Nerudova to Malostranské Náměstí, across the square, quiet now, and into the small lanes leading to my street.

"Tell me more about yourself," Karel asked. "I don't know anything about you."

"If only you spoke English!" I said.

"I wish I did too. If you're over fifty, you speak German; if you're our age, you speak Russian. English was never allowed to be taught the whole time I was in school."

I struggled to tell him, again cursing my limited Czech. I had no idea what impression my words created, whether they had any connection with what I intended and who I was. I told him about my bank director father, I told him the story I'd heard so many times, the story of our escape. About growing up in Canada, my longing to return. My father's success, my mother's yearning for home. The rediscovery of my family. My half-brother, Malý Pavel, a communist. "And yet I love him," I exclaimed, "He's a good man, kind to me and very bright!"

We walked along in silence.

"Is there anyone?" Karel suddenly asked. "A man in your life?"

I hesitated. "I'm married." He stopped in his tracks. The look he gave me was stricken. "But separated!" I added, groping for the word. "He's living in England now. We were only married one year. I ended it. We couldn't agree on our life." I couldn't say more. Karel resumed walking. Our footsteps echoed through the silent streets until we stood facing each other at the door to my courtyard.

"Do come on Saturday, two o'clock, the Kampa end of Charles Bridge." He reached up, lightly stroked my cheek with the back of his hand, turned and strode away. I closed the door and leaned against it, listening as the sound of his footsteps faded down the silent street.

Chapter 10

AT A QUARTER TO TWO THE FOLLOWING SUNDAY, I HURRIED down Nosticova, across the low bridge over the Čertovka and onto Kampa island. As I climbed the wide steps up to Charles Bridge, I saw a knot of young people milling around at the foot of the bridge. Passersby were detouring around them with resentful glances and hurrying on. I approached with trepidation. Milan and Jana waved, Pepa shook my hand. He had on a First World War leather pilot's helmet and leather shorts. I looked around for Karel. "He's coming," Jana assured me. A much older man with a trim white beard – he must have been seventy – wearing shorts and a tank top that emphasized his skinny white arms and shoulders, was stretching, touching his toes and performing a rapid series of jumping jacks. He wore a racer's sign on his chest, which read *Pozor! Začíná Závod!* Attention! The Race is Starting!"

Karel hurried towards us, a pair of roller skates swinging from one hand. He threw me a wide grin and a wave, sat down on a curb and affixed the skates to his shoes. Suddenly he was even taller as he staggered over to me. He gave me a quick hug. "Ready, Jarda?" he asked the older man in the shorts and tank top, who gave a grave, official nod.

Jarda bent over into a runner's starting position. Karel took a starter's pistol from his pocket, aimed it into the air and fired. Jarda took off like a shot and scampered across the bridge, dodging people and shouting *"Pozor! Pozor!"* in his most officious voice. People turned, stepped aside, made way. At the far end of the bridge, Jarda turned and continued clearing the way on his return trek. Curious passersby stopped and lined the bridge, waiting.

The group assembled, ten men, four women, all in various get-ups. Afro wigs, Austrian lederhosen. Karel handed Jarda the pistol, the racers crouched into their starting position, the gun roared and the racers lurched forward, hobbling over the rough cobblestones. A crowd had gathered, laughing now, infected by the racers' laughter. Cheers went up, urging the racers on. Some tripped, fell, got up and kept going. I stood at the sidelines, clapping, delighted by this spectacle, such a contrast to the oppression of daily life. As I watched Karel and his friends, I felt a powerful yearning to be a part of this life. Maybe this was what I'd been searching for.

The racers straggled back, rosy with exertion, joyful. The crowd that had gathered clapped, called out their thanks and gradually dispersed. What else was there to do but regroup back at U Bonaparta? Karel, exuberant, put an arm around my shoulders and we traipsed through Malá Strana up the steep street. We spilled into the pub and crowded into the group's usual table. I sat there, a part of the merriment, drinking, laughing along with them, Karel sitting next to me. I was falling in love, and it frightened me. I knew so little about him. How could he be so gorgeous and yet unattached? Surely women in his circle wanted him. Might one of them sitting here be angry or heartbroken, watching us together? What troubled me even more was wondering if I could ever understand Karel or these amazing friends of his. How could I connect in any real way with their experiences and be a part of this world?

It was closing time and no one wanted to go home. *"Ke Spěváčků!"* someone yelled. Everyone downed their beer, paid up and we tumbled out the door and down the hill. "Will you come?" Karel asked me. "U Spěváčků is another one of our favourite bars that stays open late." Of course I would.

We piled into the 22 tram on the square, oblivious to other passengers' disapproving stares, and leapt out at Národní Divadlo. We made our way through the streets behind the National Theatre and through a set of velvet curtains into a narrow, dark little bar. No one sat down. We milled around the bar, a dozen conversations going on at once. Shots were ordered, shots of vodka, brandy, *Myslivecká*, *Slivovice*. Even when U Spěváčků's closing time drew near, nobody was ready to call it quits.

"Let's go back to my place!" shouted Tomáš, one of our crowd.

"You got anything to drink?" another yelled.

"We'll buy wine here!"

We trooped through the streets – the trams had stopped running long ago – and squeezed into Tomáš's flat.

"How about if I make some soup?" Tomáš's offer was greeted with cheers. Music was put on, the wine opened and the party roared on. Sometime later, an acrid, burning smell wafted through the flat. "The soup!" someone yelled.

Tomáš dashed into the kitchen and groaned. "I don't know about this," he said, handing out bowls of a dark, porridge-like substance. It didn't smell good. I let mine cool, then dipped my spoon in it and took a tentative taste. It was inedible. Karel was waiting to see my reaction.

I'd had way too much to drink. I picked up a spoonful of the stuff and went to offer it to Karel, but, suspicious, he turned away and it smeared on his cheek. We both burst out laughing. I took another spoonful and threw it at him. Someone else, watching us, took a spoonful and flung it. Soon there was soup flying everywhere. The hall runner was rolled up, a couple of bowlfuls were dumped on the parquet floor and in our socks we took turns running and sliding up and down the hall, which was slippery as a skating rink. Soup ran down the walls, the furniture, our clothes, our hair.

It was close to morning when we staggered out of poor Tomáš's flat. The group dispersed.

"I don't think we'll be invited back to his place again," I laughed, exhausted, exhilarated, drunk.

"You started all that, you know," Karel marvelled. "You're incredible."

"I am," I said.

"You're outrageous," he said.

"I am."

"I think I love you," he said.

I laughed, though my heart skipped a beat. "You're drunk," I said, "and so am I."

"Still ..."

"I am dead tired," I said.

"Let's go back to your place," he said.

I stopped and looked at him. "I can't. I'm meeting someone at Artia at 11:00. That's five hours from now. I need to go home and sleep." As much as my heart was pounding, and as much as I regretted turning him down, I didn't want another drunken lover. If we were ever to sleep together, I wanted to be more or less sober. And I wanted a whole night.

"Let me walk you home, then," he said, putting an arm around me. We walked across the bridge in the growing dawn light, across Kampa, over the footbridge to Malá Strana and down my street. Outside my door, he turned and faced me. "You sure?"

I nodded. He leaned forward and kissed me, his lips light, his moustache brushing my mouth. Then he pulled me to him and held me, and I felt the tension, the electricity in his body. My own blood raced and I felt my face burning. I wanted badly to pull him into my room and lie down beside him. But I didn't.

He let me go. "Come this Wednesday," he said.

"I will."

Wednesday finally came and again I was climbing Nerudova, oddly frightened now of seeing Karel again, so much so that I almost turned back. But no, I went in. Karel was there and I felt my face flush when I saw him. He hugged me in greeting and moved over. Naturally, there was much talk and laughter about the night at Tomáš's flat, and the usual sharing of news and the ever-present political talk.

Some hours later, Karel leaned towards me and whispered, "Let's get out of here. I've had enough of this. Let's walk." I nodded.

Out on the sidewalk, Karel took my hand. "I want to show you the Prague I love." He led me further up Nerudova, then into a dark passage down a flight of narrow, stone steps. We emerged into a jumble of little lanes, dimly lit by gas lamps, the houses on either side, some no more than one room wide, leaning in on one another. Above us a quarter moon shone in a ribbon of black. All around us was a deep silence. Most of the windows were shuttered. Here and there a light glowed dimly through curtained upper windows.

"*Helenko*," Karel said. I thrilled at his using the diminutive form of my name. We stood looking at one another. He touched my cheek, saying my name again. Then he drew me to him and I moved into his arms. We stood in the lamplit dark, discovering the feel of one another. I pressed my cheek against the soft wool of his sweater, my arms holding him close, my body full of longing.

He pulled back, his hands still clutching my arms. "You are married." Despair in his voice.

"I'm separated."

"It is over?"

"Yes."

"You sure?"

I could only nod.

He let go and we continued walking. "What about you?" I asked him.

He shook his head. "There's no one now. There was but it's over."

The tension between us grew as we wound our way down the hill until we stood outside my door. I invited him in for a coffee and unlocked the door to my room. Karel looked around.

I shoved my papers and typewriter back to make room at the table and invited Karel to sit on the only chair. I put a kettle to boil on my hotplate and spooned coffee into two cups. Neither of us spoke. We kept glancing at one another, smiling, not smiling. All of a sudden he stood up, grasped my arm and turned me to face him. Oh the sweet relief when he kissed me, the relief and the hunger. I couldn't get enough of the feel of him, the scent of him, the heft, his beautiful, strong, solid, back, the softness of his brown mohair sweater. His jeans. The powerful urgency of his mouth on mine, his hands on my back, pressing me to him.

He was beautiful naked. We lay on my narrow foam-slab bed. He was an exquisite lover, tender yet urgent. Utterly present, repeating my name over and over, like a mantra, like a prayer. And I revelled in the feel of his body and in how our bodies fit together. We couldn't get enough of one another. Made love, rested, smoked, made love again. Lay looking at one another.

He had to teach the next day. Near daybreak he kissed me, whispered, "Can we see each other later?" and when I nodded, he dressed quickly and was gone. I lay in bed full of joy, lust and wonder. Could this man and this life really be mine?

———

"I want you to come and see my studio. Would you? I'd like to show you my work," Karel said to me when we were spending a Saturday together. I leapt at the opportunity. He was an artist and I had no idea what he painted.

We took the metro to Dejvice, a residential district on the hill beyond the castle, and walked through the quiet streets. "You know I live with my parents," he said wryly. Getting a flat of his own, he went on, was impossible. His parents' flat was large and he had a separate area with a studio. "I don't have much to do with them," he said, his voice tight. "My father's a heavy in the Communist party. My mother ..." he shrugged. "We've never gotten along."

We arrived at a five-storey building on a tree-lined street. Karel unlocked the street door and we climbed the central steps to the second floor, where he unlocked one of the doors leading off the hall. A small dark vestibule, pairs of shoes and slippers on a grey mat. We faced three closed doors with opaque glass panes on the upper half. One of them opened and a small, thin, grey-haired woman in a brown housecoat peered at us, startled.

"*Ahoj, Mámo.* This is Helena," Karel introduced me.

"*Dobrý den*," I said, holding out my hand.

"*Dobrý den*," she muttered, giving my hand a feeble shake, and backed out through the door, closing it behind her. Karel gestured dismissively, and ushered me through a small anteroom into his studio.

I stood open-mouthed at what I saw. A rampage of colour. Bold, stark, powerful. Some chilling. Three large canvasses that drew me to them.

"That's a triptych," Karel said. "This one's called 'Expulsion from the Garden of Eden.' The second one I called 'Life' and the third, 'Return of the Prodigal Son.'" He stood at my elbow as I stared at them. Violent, full of pain and bewilderment. Another series of three in which faces with bared teeth faced one another. "That's called 'Conversations,'" Karel said quietly. I could only stare at them, and then at him. Who was this man? What had he lived through?

Then there were others in total contrast. Chagall-like, a figure floated serenely over an idyllic and rustic country village. Two lovers holding one another, the man looking wistfully at the woman, the woman staring unsmiling out at the viewer, a mass of stars filling the night sky behind them. Another, a rowdy scene in a pub, caricatures of peasant men around a slanting table, they and everything in the scene wonky and off-kilter. Witty, clever.

I was intimidated and speechless. They were heartbreaking but magnificently rendered, the paint applied thickly with strong, confident strokes. I didn't trust myself to know whether this was great work or not. I only knew I was deeply moved, and I suspected he was a very talented painter.

He was watching me, smoking, his arms crossed. "So what do you think?" he finally asked.

"They are beautiful." Inadequate. "Powerful," I added. Still not enough. I struggled to find the words, cursing my limited Czech. If only I could say in English what I wanted to say.

"I see you now," I said. "How much pain you carry. How much you love and aspire to beauty. How powerful your vision, insight, depth. How moved you are by what you see. How lucky you are to have the talent to translate your thoughts and feelings into such images. How tragic that you are barred from exhibiting. Yes, the rawness and honesty of these paintings would not be welcome by a regime that thrives on suppression."

Those were the words I *tried* to say. I felt handicapped and frightened that I was speaking nonsense, my sentences full of grammatical errors, trying to express complex thoughts but sounding like a child, like a fool. I think he understood, and was pleased. I walked around the studio, taking everything in, deeply moved.

Hand in hand we walked to a café across the square. "I'd like to paint your portrait," Karel said to me over coffee. "Would you be willing?"

I imagined meeting him regularly in that studio with the sunlight pouring in, spending hours on end talking or sitting quietly, being able to look at him, watching him work, watching him watching me, taking in all of each other until we were filled. Memorizing that stance of his, that serious face, those intense dark eyes, the smile he would send me now and again. "Yes," I said. "I would."

From that day on, I came to his studio once or twice a week and sat for him and watched him paint. I'd never been so happy. He wouldn't let me see the painting as it progressed. It was a large canvas, at least three feet high and two feet wide, and he used oils. I sat breathing in the lovely smell I'd encountered at the Academy, that sweet, spicy smell of oil paint, linseed oil and turpentine, Karel's paintings all around us, him serious, absorbed, and then suddenly flashing me a smile and then disappearing again into his work. He'd work for an hour or two, then put down his brush. "You've sat long enough. Let's go to the pub," and off we'd go.

———

One evening, Karel and I were coming back to my room from a walk in Kampa Park. As we crossed the courtyard, a man came out of the house and said, in Czech, "Young lady, I must tell you, that other man was here the day before yesterday and again, he was yelling and banging on your door and wouldn't stop. He ended up passing out in the corner by your door." I'd been away at Uncle Paul and Aunt Růža's cottage for the weekend. I apologized profusely, mortified.

"This can't go on," Karel said, once we were inside. I'd told him about Mirek, about the deal we'd made: no strings.

"But are you still seeing him?" he demanded.

"I've gone for a drink with him, as a friend, but I don't want to do that anymore."

"You can't go on living here," he declared.

"I don't know what else to do."

"Goddamn this country! The simplest things are made impossible and it's people like you who suffer."

There was one more incident, when Karel and I were in my room and Mirek came by. We were silent until he went away. I had to do something. The next day I went to his studio and found him home. He opened the door. I stood in the doorway and told him it was over. "I know it's difficult, me living in your studio. But until I find something else, I hope you'll let me go on living there. But please don't come around anymore. It's over between us. I'm very sorry."

He tried to change my mind, contrite, apologetic, but I was adamant. "Please, Mirek, you have to leave me alone. There's someone else now. I won't change my mind." He cried. I told him again I was sorry and left.

———

My work was going well. I received an assignment from Artia to translate a large volume of children's stories, *Velká Kniha Bájí o Strašidlech*, which I translated as *The Big Book of Ghost and Monster Stories*. Through friends I was introduced to three engineers who hired me to teach them conversational English. English was not taught in schools, only Russian. One evening each week I took a bus out to a villa one of them owned in the suburbs and we'd spend a pleasant few hours conversing over coffee. The conversations had to be bland, completely neutral. We talked about the weather, told stories about ski trips to the mountains, Christmas and other holiday traditions; the names of foods we liked. We didn't know one another well enough to trust each other with anything more.

———

Karel and I and the Spolek Pohodlí were at U Spěváčků one evening – the usual standing around the bar, drinking, talking, laughing. I went to the washroom, stopping to talk to someone along the way. When I came back, Karel was deep in conversation with a beautiful, dark-haired Czech girl. I'd seen her once or twice at U Bonaparta, early on. She hadn't come since. They stood close together. She spoke to him, imploringly, her face close to his. He responded with urgency. She put her hand on his arm. He didn't pull away. There they stood, locked in intense conversation, oblivious to everyone else in the room. I stood watching them, sipping my drink. I went over to talk to Milan and Jana, my eyes straying back to Karel and the girl. It looked like she had tears in her eyes. He stayed with her, deep in conversation, never looking up or away. It went on for what felt like forever.

I walked towards the door, passing right by them. Karel didn't acknowledge me in any way. Outside I waited, thinking he'd come after me. He didn't. I walked home alone through the dark streets. Anger masked my fear. At home, I sat at my desk and despite the late hour, opened my typewriter and tried to work. I was experimenting with my own writing, playing with a story about women suddenly realizing the power of saying no, as a unified group, women refusing to be wives and mothers anymore and bringing men and the world as we knew it to their knees.

An hour or so later, close to three in the morning, there was a tapping on the window to my back garden. I jumped. It was Karel. Through the bars, I opened the window. He stood there, dripping wet, his shoes, a pair of clogs, in his hands.

"Open your door," he said. "Let me in."

"No," I said.

He was shocked. "I've come all this way to see you. Look at me! I'm soaking."

"Too bad."

"The front door was locked. I came across the Čertovka on that cable thing." There was a cable crossing the narrow river at the end of my garden with a pole with foot pads on a pulley, like a poma ski lift, that you could step onto, hold the pole and push off to the other side of the river. "One of my shoes came off," Karel continued, "and I had to jump in to retrieve it. The other floated away and I had to chase the damn thing down the river!"

He wanted my sympathy! I could have laughed and I could have cried with relief to see him; instead I was incensed. I was afraid of the pain I felt watching him talk to the girl, afraid of how bad losing him now would feel.

"Go away," I said. "You're drunk." As though we didn't drink and get a bit drunk practically every time we met at U Bonaparta, along with everyone else. Getting drunk was a way of life in this country and with this group, and I drank right along with the rest of them.

"You're sending me away? I'm drenched and it's cold out here," he protested.

"No. I don't want to see you."

With a bewildered look on his face, he turned away from my window and left. I listened to the sound of his footsteps and the front door slammed shut. Had I just ruined everything?

He left a note in my mailbox the next evening when I was at my uncle's. "Hope to see you tomorrow at U Bonaparta." I went and he welcomed me. He had no idea why I had left and why I was angry. It took me a little time to confess my jealousy and fear.

"Who was she?" I ventured to ask him. "What does she mean to you?"

"We'd been together for over a year," he told me, "but I ended it when I met you. She came to U Spěváčků hoping I'd come back, begging me to change my mind." I gulped. "I told her I was sorry, it was over and I was in love with someone else. Meaning you."

A wave of relief flooded through me.

The story of his fall into the river, and my sending him away made the rounds, becoming hilarious. He told it at the pub, with an embellishment. He described hailing a cab to take him home and when he got out, the driver saw the dark seat beside him and said, disgusted, "For God's sake, man, why didn't you tell me? I would've stopped, you could have relieved yourself in the goddamn park!"

On Sundays, Karel's other group, Zlatá Praha – Golden Prague – would meet at U Tygra, a pub in the Old Town. This group too was made up of artists and writers, some older and more established. There I met Bohumil Hrabal, a brilliant and previously published poet. He gave me a copy of his book, *Poupata*, Flower Buds, that he signed with a dedication to me. It had been published to high acclaim but was now banned.

One evening at U Tygra, Karel introduced me to a dissident playwright, another member of Zlatá Praha. Full of laughter and rage, the playwright, a funny, sensitive, irreverent man with tousled hair and a florid face, sat with us and railed at the system with the rest. His name was Václav Havel.

One day Karel took me to Hradčanské Náměstí, the magnificent Castle Square in front of the main gates to Prague Castle. At the far end of the square, he knocked on the door of a lovely house, the name Mucha engraved on a small brass plaque beside the door. We were ushered into the antique-filled home of Jiří Mucha, a well-known writer and the son of Alphonse Mucha, the Czech artist world famous for his art nouveau decorative posters, especially those of Sarah Bernhardt. Havel, Mucha, Hrabal – these were friends of Karel's and through him, I was able to meet these important, talented yet censored members of the artist community.

Another evening Karel took me to a party in the apartment of Hana Hegerová, sometimes called the Czech Edith Piaf. I loved her from the moment I saw her. Larger than life, passionate, lusty, a gypsy-like woman with flashing black eyes and jet black hair. At the party, she was one of us, drinking, smoking, dancing. Karel and his friends revered her, yet she was friendly and approachable. And that voice! Karel had played several of her *chansons* during my sittings. Deeper, richer than Piaf's but just as tender, just as evocative, full of heartache and longing. She sang Jacques Brel songs with Czech lyrics, the French *Ne Me Quitte Pas* translated into *Lásko Prokletá*, or "Cursed Love." Later I bought several of her albums. I memorized the words to her song *Bože Můj, Já Chci Zpět* – " My God, I Want to Go Back" – and years later, after I had left and was living back in Canada, I still remembered every word and cried bitterly, full of the same longing that fills the song, playing her CD for myself, far away.

Chapter 11

ONE WEDNESDAY AT U BONAPARTA, HONZA BARTOŠ, THE
sculptor who was doing his army service, often taunted for
coming to the pub in his uniform, slid onto the bench beside
me. He was the odd man out with his brush cut and clean-
shaven face, his crisply ironed uniform, while the rest of us wore
jeans and many of the men were long-haired and moustached.

"I have a favour to ask," Honza began. "I've received a commission from the Cuban embassy to do a couple of sculptures.
Two busts, a male and a female, eventually in bronze. Would
you be willing to sit as a model for me?"

"Do you think I look Cuban?" I asked, teasing him.

"You could wear that Spanish leather hat you
wear sometimes."

Curious and flattered, I agreed.

"Wow," I said a week later when he ushered me in. "Nice
studio!" It was opulent compared to the humble studios I'd
seen, on the fifth floor of a renovated apartment building in
Old Town, large and airy with floor-to-ceiling windows.

"One of the perks of being in the army," Honza said. "I'm sure
I'll be back in a mouse hole like everybody else once my stint is
over." He led me to a high stool he'd set up facing the windows.
"Is this all right?" he asked. "Will you be comfortable there?"

"I'm fine," I said, chuckling at his solicitous queries. He seemed awkward. Though he was part of Karel's group, I'd never really warmed to him, though I couldn't say why. His joviality at the pub seemed forced. I'd put it down to shyness. While he made some coffee, I looked around. The modern version of Czech furniture, spartan and minimal. Curtains, a few prints on the walls. Impersonal. I was surprised not to see other sculptures, other works in progress. When I mentioned this, he told me he did most of his work at the Academy.

"What with my army service and teaching, there's not much time left for my own work, so I keep everything there. But I thought we'd be more comfortable here."

He put my coffee on a stool beside me and set to work. This became our routine. I came to Honza's studio once or twice a week. We chatted or sat in companionable silence. After an hour or so, if it was Wednesday or Friday, we'd go to U Bonaparta to join the rest of the group.

My Czech was improving. I was with a man I loved and thrilled to be part of this dissident artists' community. I was doing work I enjoyed and was ensconced in a family that loved me and that I loved in return. I called on Malý Pavel to help me with my translations when necessary, and several times a week I had lunch or dinner at Uncle Paul and Aunt Růža's. Life was good.

Every spring, Karel took his students on a *plein air* trip to southern Bohemia. The students spent their days sketching and painting landscapes. They lived in cabins with meals taken together in a central lodge. Karel invited me to come along. Wouldn't the students mind? I asked. Wouldn't I be in the way?

Not at all, Karel answered. Besides, it was none of their business. He'd be with them, overseeing their work, but I could come out into the countryside with them, a portable table would be brought out along with the students' easels and materials, and I could work on my writing while they painted. I leapt at the opportunity.

The sun shone down on us, the rolling hills and forests of southern Bohemia were bursting with life. We worked during the day, and in the evening, went to one of the village pubs, Karel and I returning to our own cabin afterwards. We were like a true couple, together day after day, Karel working with his students and on his own painting, I working on my translation. His students simply accepted me as Karel's girl, with every right to be there.

———

One evening as Karel and I sat in the pub, he was telling me about some of his students and their work. He mentioned one in particular named Eva, and went on to say, "She's a pretty good artist – for a girl."

His words hit a nerve. "What did you say?" I asked. He stared at me, not understanding my tone, and repeated it.

"Why shouldn't she be as good an artist as any guy?" I challenged him.

The sexism of his statement shocked me. I railed at him. He listened wide-eyed, utterly unaware of having said anything objectionable, but nodded and was thoughtful as I spoke. He ended up agreeing with me, realizing it was an unthinking and unjust bias; he actually did have a number of gifted female students.

Karel was not alone in his sexist assumptions. They were woven into the fabric of Czech society. Czechoslovakia in the

1970s was a sexist, male-dominated society. In North America, the women's movement was gaining steam. I'd been away and hadn't had a chance to participate in what was going on, but I'd heard of the work of Betty Freidan and Germaine Greer and was excited at what was happening. My beliefs were strongly feminist. All my life, I'd been hurt and angered by anything that degraded women or denied women opportunities. I'd been wounded deeply by my mother, who clearly preferred my brothers and curtailed my freedom in a way she didn't with her sons. They were free to be outside playing baseball after dinner while I was to stay back to clean up and wash the dishes.

At school, my brothers took shop, building things, learning carpentry and other interesting skills; I had to take home economics, sewing aprons and baking muffins, preparing me, I fumed, for that life of servitude that seemed to be a woman's lot. Not for me, I vowed.

I hated the idea of "women's work." At Chinook, our family cottage, my family was often angry at me for not doing my share of the cooking and cleaning. I recognized that everyone needed to contribute and was willing to do my share; but instead, I chopped wood and operated the chainsaw. Having taken classes on my own in carpentry, electricity and plumbing, I did chores like rebuilding the septic tank to my cabin and enlarging my windows overlooking the lake. I refused to learn to cook, sew or type, vowing never to be a housewife – or a secretary or nurse, the traditional roles girls were steered towards, if they were thinking of working at all. The women's movement in the West was beginning to address these issues.

In Czechoslovakia, the women's movement, if it was mentioned at all, was ridiculed or dismissed with contempt as either a joke or an outrage. News was censored, so very little of what the issues were and what was happening outside the country penetrated. People couldn't know that the nonsense being fed to them through local media about the meaning of the women's movement was just that – nonsense. Feminism was portrayed as yet another example of decadent capitalism and not to be taken seriously.

In Czech society, the work women did was devalued. It was a politic run by men, with men holding all the higher status jobs in the Communist party and in society at large. Men were head waiters and waiters in the better establishments; women were waitresses in the lowlier places. No matter where women worked, they earned a fraction of what men earned. Ironically, when women entered a profession, that profession was devalued; when women became the majority of doctors, the medical profession lost status. A waiter at the Ambassador Hotel on Wenceslas Square earned more and had a higher status than a doctor or dentist, the waiter having access to hard currency.

Socially, men gathered with one another in pubs, while women were relegated to the home, expected to come home after work to care for the children, do all the housework and cook dinner for hubby when he decided to come home from drinking with his buddies. Even the Spolek Pohodlí and Zlatá Praha, the groups I was so proud to sit with, were men's groups, welcoming women only as partners of their members.

Other aspects of life distressed me and had me wondering if I could in fact ever be truly at home here. I very much missed the courtesy with which people treated one another in Canada. People in Prague were appallingly rude. Shop clerks took great pleasure in cutting a would-be customer down to size with a curt "No. We don't have it." Tram conductors loved to wait as you sprinted to the stop and then close the doors and pull away just as you arrived, panting. Head waiters relished telling prospective diners that no tables were available, even when the room was half empty. Reserved, they'd sniff, turning away. I was disgusted at how ordinary people ingratiated themselves, practically prostrated themselves, when placing their order in a restaurant or requesting some item in a shop. The rudeness, I thought, was surely the result of the powerlessness people felt; being rude and denying others' requests were simply ways of experiencing some small measure of empowerment.

One night I was walking home alone to my room on Nosticova after an evening at Rubín. I was happy. It was a warm, soft night, late, with no one else on the street. As I crossed Maltézské Náměstí, I started to sing "Summertime," a favourite of mine. Out of nowhere a car pulled up beside me and a couple of policemen leapt out, demanding my papers. Startled, I produced my Canadian passport. They were taken aback. Half saluting, they backed away, climbed into their car and drove off. What would they have done if I hadn't had a foreign passport? I wondered. Was it illegal to sing? What had I done to draw their attention – express myself? Reveal some joie de vivre?

Other absurdities occurred in this Kafkaesque environment. One day at the Malostranská Kavárna, I was sipping my coffee and reading a book at my favourite table overlooking the square when the waiter handed me a folded scrap of paper. Surprised, I opened it. There was a sentimental love poem scrawled on it, seven or eight lines about how desirable I was. I looked up at the waiter, who gestured at a dark-haired man, maybe forty, sitting alone at a table at the other end of the café. He smiled and waved at me, spread his hands as though to say,

"What do you think?" Shaking my head, I crumpled the paper and went back to my reading. The man left soon after.

Sometime later, I was in the police station on Bartolomějská sitting on one of those orange chairs, to request a return visa for a trip outside the country. The entrance door to that long hall opened, and to my surprise, I recognized my suitor from the café. He was carrying a briefcase. Another applicant for something, I thought. But no. Casting me a cursory glance, he opened one of the doors and disappeared. I was chilled. Were they keeping an eye on me?

For the first time, I was learning what it is to live with fear, a nameless, all-pervasive fear that has no clear object. It was like a permanent condition, invisible but ever-present, like oxygen, but heavy and oppressive. It was so immanent that I was unaware of it most of the time. I only realized it on the occasions when I left the country. Each time, I experienced an enormous relief as I crossed the border, suddenly breathing more deeply, my body relaxing. When I returned, the fear gradually settled over me again.

Chapter 12

CHRISTMAS WAS COMING, CHRISTMAS OF 1973. I'D PROMISED
my mother I would come home for the holidays and decided to
come for three weeks. Karel came to the airport to see me off.

"Just make sure you come back to me," he said.

I laughed. "Of course I will."

———

"Thank God you're home," my father said when I emerged
from the arrivals gate.

As we drove along the 401, everything looked clean and
new – but raw, as though scrubbed of every patina, every
adornment. Concrete everywhere. The streets were wide and
bare, the houses small, each in the centre of its little patch of
grass, separate from one another. I found I was missing colour,
character, richness, complexity.

My parents had moved to a new home on Farmview
Crescent in North York, downsizing since it was just the two
of them now. Peter and Jane lived in Thornhill, a suburb of
Toronto, Tom was a lawyer and lived in a small apartment
in Rosedale, Irene lived in Scarborough and still worked for
Canadian Business magazine.

I stayed in my parents' guest room, feeling like a child again. They seemed more content now, but the old pattern remained, my mother claiming me and my father remaining more distant. It was as though he'd lost – or never learned – relaxed, easygoing closeness. We celebrated Christmas in the Czech tradition, on Christmas Eve, as we had all during my childhood, when it had been a magical highlight of the year for us children.

———

The women's movement caught me up like an irresistible whirlwind. I'd known something big was going on but hadn't paid much attention, other than resenting the derisive references in the Czech media. I was unprepared for how powerfully it hit me. While I'd been away a revolution had begun. Consciousness-raising was going on everywhere. The Women's Press and the Women's Bookstore had been established in Toronto. Books like *The Female Eunuch* by Germaine Greer and Betty Freidan's *The Feminine Mystique* were becoming bestsellers. The United Nations had declared 1975 International Women's Year, and Canada's Secretary of State had allocated grant funds for women's projects to be launched that year. Not a whisper of this had reached Czechoslovakia.

I connected with a group of feminists and was caught up in the excitement of what they were doing and planning: Alexa de Weil, a poet, Hadassah Ashin, a writer, Sylvia Spring, a filmmaker, and many others. One day the thought occurred to me that we women were dissidents in our own country, something I'd always felt but never articulated. Ruled by a male society that was created and structured to accommodate men. Men made the rules, and women were expected to adapt to and abide by them.

I joined groups of women discussing issues that had distressed us all our lives and were finally being spoken. I discovered I wasn't alone in the anguish I'd felt at what I saw as the systemic devaluing of women; the limited life and career options my mother had assumed would be my fate; women's voices rarely heard in politics, business or the media; men's violence and abuse, for which women were often blamed; the all-pervasive assumptions of the inferiority of the "weaker sex." We raged against the sexism we'd experienced all our lives.

"'Why are there no women musicians, filmmakers, scientists, statesmen?' people ask, as though that proved the inferiority of women. Well, we *know* why, and now we can declare it out loud!" said one woman at a meeting in a coffee house on Harbord Street one day. "It's because we're stopped at every turn! Molded from the day we're born into the people men want us to be. Meek and passive. Show some ambition and some aspirations of our own and we're ridiculed and criticized as ball-breakers."

"My family only educated the boys," said another. "'You'll only get married and stay home with the babies, so why waste the money?' is what my Dad said to me."

I told the story of my mother's parents' reaction when she told them her dream of becoming an actress, the loss of that dream.

"I tried to get a loan from the bank," another woman said. "Even though I work and make pretty good money, the manager told me I needed my husband's or my parents' permission. Can you believe it?"

"I wanted to be a stewardess," said another, "because I'd love to see the world. I was told I couldn't be one because I wear glasses, I'm too old and not attractive enough. I'm thirty-two years old! Are stewardesses there as decoration for male passengers?"

So it went, the pain and outrage pouring out.

"All that's going to change," one woman said. "It may take a while, but everything is going to change. Women are rising up at last."

"I believe," said Hadassah, "that women should choose other women as lovers as a political statement. Lesbianism as a choice and as a deliberate political act. Given everything we're saying, why would women whose consciousness has been raised ever want to be with men, or agree to becoming somebody's wife?"

"It's consorting with the enemy!" another added.

"A form of slavery we didn't see," someone said. "How could we have been so blind? Betty Freidan calls it the problem with no name. Women isolated from one another, boxed into our homes, servants to our husbands and children, with no way out and no viable options. Miserable, trapped, and not understanding why, since from birth we're raised with the idea that being a wife and mother is the most blissful thing to aspire to."

The conversations were exhilarating with the promise of change and the power of sisterhood. The power of women's anger.

"What you're all talking about is the most exciting thing that has ever happened in Canada," I said to them. "I had no idea. A hugely powerful social movement that could change the world."

"Where have you been?" Hadassah asked me.

"I've been living in Spain and now Prague. Nothing like this is happening there."

"Time to come home," she said.

The meeting ended. "Anybody want to go to the Quest?" Hadassah suggested. "You bet." "Sure" "Let's do it!" were the responses.

"What's the Quest?" I said.

"A gay bar on Yonge just south of Bloor. Men downstairs, women upstairs, no men allowed up there," she answered, coming over. "Want to go?"

"I guess," I answered.

Upstairs was jumping. Women dancing together, leaning towards one another, talking, lots of laughter. A happy place. Hadassah and I stood at the bar, ordering our drinks.

"Like it?" she asked.

"Wild," I said.

"No guys coming on to you," she continued. "No macho crap going on." We sipped our drinks and watched the action.

"Want to dance?" she asked.

"Me?"

"Yes, you."

She had dark curly hair and dark eyes. She was a good dancer. We danced fast, and then we danced slow. We sat at a table together and talked.

"So what are you doing in Prague?" she asked. I told her.

"Single?"

"Separated. My husband's in England. Haven't seen him in almost a year."

"On your own then?"

"There is someone in Prague."

"Man or woman?"

"Man!"

"I prefer women," she said, tilting her head and smiling at me. "You should consider it."

"There's no gay scene in Prague. It's against the law, and everyone pretends it doesn't exist. No gays in the Czechoslovak Socialist Republic! I had a couple of friends at a pub near where I live." I told her. "David and Gabriel. Nice guys – gay, but had to hide it. During the Nazi era gays were rounded up along with Jews and sent to concentration camps. Under the communists, it isn't much better. One night, David told me Gabriel had committed suicide. He couldn't stand the constant taunting and persecution."

"It's different with women," she said. "It can be a political decision not to support the patriarchal system by consorting with men. To not play by their rules."

"I get that," I said. "I really do get that. Men can be a pain in the ass."

"As they say, a woman needs a man like a fish needs a bicycle." We laughed.

"I love what I read in the *Globe* the other day," I said. "Judy LaMarsh, as mayor of Ottawa, one of the few shining exceptions to the absence of women with any political power, saying, 'For a woman to succeed, she has to be twice as smart and work twice as hard as a man; fortunately, that's not difficult.'" We laughed again. I was delighted we could be so in tune with one another.

When not with my family, I spent my time with my new feminist friends, with Hadassah and other women, attending meetings, listening to their plans, partying. What was I doing, I thought one evening, in that backward country, sitting in pubs drinking with a bunch of men in a society reeking of sexism?

Why was I spending time with a man who was a product of that environment? A man who could say, "She's a pretty good artist – for a girl." That should have declared him my enemy. I was discovering I had sisters and a cause to fight for.

Hadassah wooed me with a powerful persistence, and I was amazed to find myself responding. She was beautiful, funny, irreverent. I loved being in her presence. I'd been curious what it would be like to make love with a woman. As a young girl I'd had a crush, as I thought most girls did, on a couple of my camp counsellors. Why not give it a try? I asked myself. Perhaps we're all bisexual, I thought, but most of us won't discover or acknowledge it. Hadassah and I became lovers. The world turned upside down. My entire notion of who I was and what life could be like shifted. It felt like love – and revolution.

When my three weeks of vacation were up, I promised Hadassah I'd be back, telling myself I'd finish up my commitments in Prague and come back. I wanted to be part of what was going on here. Finally something compelling was happening in Canada that I could care about and dedicate myself to.

———

When I returned to Prague, ugliness was all I saw.

I despised the men in uniform at the airport, who eyed me suspiciously yet condescendingly, because they were men. I resented the men who walked around town like they owned the streets; the men in the pubs, loud and overbearing, taking up too much space. I pitied and was angry at the women who put up with them, who stood in line interminably, shuffled back to their flats to cook, to hand wash laundry, put their children to bed and meekly wait for their men to come home in order to serve them their supper – then be available in case the men felt like a bit of sex. I was furious with the assumption of superiority these men exuded, the way they behaved as though they owned all the public spaces. Why can men sit in a pub alone and no one thinks anything of it, I fumed, while for a woman it takes enormous courage?

Small things that had always upset me in Prague now loomed large. What's the point of beautiful architecture when you have to walk looking down so you don't step in dog shit? I raged silently. And men in Prague were disgusting, coming out of pubs at night and pissing against buildings, as though the city was one big urinal. Everything I saw infuriated me.

I didn't contact Karel. I saw my family, delivered some finished work to Artia, and met with my students. I worked at my desk and went to Malostranská Kavárna for breaks, or walked. I didn't go to U Bonaparta, feeling I would be a traitor to the cause to show up there again. I wrote to Hadassah, "I'll be back. Just as soon as I finish my current work and spend some time with my family here, I'll be back."

One evening I was walking across Charles Bridge when there was Karel walking towards me. He stopped, his face registering shock. "You're back!" he cried.

"I am," I said coolly.

"How long? I kept waiting for you at U Bonaparta. I came by your place a few times, rang your bell but there was no answer. When did you get back?"

"About a week ago."

"What's the matter?" I was silent. "For God's sake, Helen, tell me what's happened!"

What could I say? I just shrugged and turned away.

"Helen, I have waited and waited, yearned for your return every day. And you're here an entire week and don't contact me?"

"You don't own me!" I shouted. He stared at me, stunned.

"Is there someone else?" he finally asked, quietly. "Another man?"

"No," I laughed harshly.

"Helen," he said, taking my arm, "please sit down and talk to me, tell me what's happened." I pulled my arm free but nodded. I owed him at least that. We went to a pub in Kampa. How could I explain? Impossible.

"I'm sorry, Karel. It's that Canada is so different. Being there for that long made it a shock to come back. Everything so difficult, so oppressive, so ... I made friends there, happy friends doing work they love. I envied them that lightness, that ... freedom. Women friends, doing important work. Nothing like here." How could he understand?

"But what about us?" he asked. "I love you. You know that. You are everything to me. You told me so many times, *Karlíčku, mám Tě ráda.* That you loved me. I believed you. Were you lying?"

"I wasn't lying. But everything's changed. There is something else, but not like you think. Not another man." That was as far as I could go. "It's ... the life there. I'm so confused about who I am and where I belong."

"Come," he said when we'd finished our coffee. "Walk with me again." We walked those magic streets of Prague, our footsteps echoing in the dark and quiet night. He walked me home and we stood again outside my street door. He looked at me enquiringly. I shook my head.

"Will you come to U Bonaparta again? Everyone wants to see you." I had in fact brought back gifts, things they had asked for: a pair of jeans, some books unavailable in Prague, a beaver keychain, a Johnny Cash album. I agreed and went. They welcomed me, but surely noticed the estrangement between Karel and me. We were friends now, no longer lovers.

I said to Karel one evening, back in my room, where I'd invited him for a coffee after an evening at the pub, "The thing is, Karel, I don't know any more if I can stay here. If I were to stay, it would only be because of you. And I don't think that's enough." It hurt me to say this but it had to be said. He sat as silent and still as a stone.

I went out to the WC just outside my door, my heart pounding at what I had said. Was it true? Did I mean it? When I came back, Karel had gone. One of my index cards had been rolled into my typewriter. I pulled it out.

"*S TEBOU BYCH ŠEL NA KONEC SVĚTA,*" it read. I would go to the ends of the earth with you. Such a good man and I loved him, I knew I did. It was so hard, holding him at arm's length. What was I to do?

———

"Spolek Pohodlí is organizing a spring ball on March second," Karel said one day, dropping in while I was working. "Would you come with me as my partner? As my friend?" Before the war, February used to be the season for balls in Prague, and this was another one of the group's *akce* – happenings – to protest the misery of communist life. A chance to play and to sparkle.

I went. I actually bought a dress, an ankle-length red dress that I found in a department store on Wenceslas Square, old-fashioned but suitable. I'd never seen Karel in a suit. He looked older, imposing, serious. The ball was at the Royal Summer

Palace on the castle grounds. As we rode the 22 tram, people turned their heads, staring.

Once there, Karel and I stood on the sidelines of the great ballroom, holding our drinks, watching the dancers. What were we doing there? I wondered. I amused myself, bitterly imagining what might happen if I asked a woman to dance. As we stood side by side but apart, our friends watched us, concern in their eyes. Finally Karel turned to me. "Would you be willing to dance with me?" I hesitated, then nodded.

He felt so good in my arms! Warm, solid, real. I lay my head against his shoulder, and his arms tightened around me.

When the ball was over, Karel took my wrap off the back of my chair and without any farewells, we left the palace through the arched entrance and walked in the dark stillness along the paths across the top of the hill. The Royal Gardens rustled all around us and the occasional lamp cast pools of soft yellow light. It was chilly and I took his arm. He pressed it gently against his side. We walked wordlessly across Jelení Příkop, and around the castle walls to Petřín Hill. I wondered if he could hear my heart beating. The sun was a soft pink radiance lighting up the sky in the east. We were approaching Nosticova.

———

At my door, Karel stopped. I took his hand. Inside my room, we looked at one another. The sweetness, the gentleness and the hunger with which we came together, both reaching out at the same time, took my breath away. Feminist principles be damned.

No, I thought. I would be a feminist and still love this man.

———

⁑⁑ Chapter 13

A LETTER ARRIVED FROM MY FATHER INVITING ME TO JOIN him and my mother on a two-week vacation in Austria. A resort called Grüner Baum in Bad Gastein, one of my father's favourite places, not far from Zell am See, where we'd spent that year at the Pension Olga before sailing to Canada.

"Afterwards," his letter continued, "I have invited my entire family. My mother, whom you know as *Babička Na Smíchově* – Grandma from Smíchov; Malý Pavel and his wife Helena, and my brother Otto and his wife are coming from Prague. Rudy and his wife are coming from Canada. We're all meeting in Weimar, East Germany. Much as I dislike the idea of supporting with tourist dollars any Soviet satellite, it is one place where they are allowed to go and where I believe Mother and I can safely visit." And then he added, "I will see my mother, my eldest son and my brother for the first time in thirty years. I have decided it is high time for this reunion." The irony of it stung me. I could live in Prague and know both his family and my mother's, while for him it would be dangerous. He was right. It was high time if this reunion was ever to happen. My father was seventy-six, my mother sixty-eight. Malý Pavel was fifty-two, his wife Helena a year or two younger, and Rudy, two years younger than his brother Malý Pavel, would be fifty. I looked forward to it immensely. There was a postscript from my mother. "Afterwards, I'm planning on joining you in Prague."

I made the trek to Bartolomějská to obtain my exit and re-entry visa, and to the East German embassy for a visa.

Karel saw me off at the station. "Write to me," he begged, "just a postcard now and then. Don't meet any handsome strangers. And please don't come back all changed again. Take pictures, too. I hear Austria is beautiful."

"I promise," I said. Just across the border and he'd never been.

The countryside of southern Bohemia rolled by, dingy industrial sections of larger towns, lovely rolling hills, small villages, dark pine woods. At the border, there was a lengthy stop as policemen walked through the train, checking documents.

As before, I was aware of the transformation in me the instant we crossed the border. An immense relief, a sudden lightness – I could breathe more deeply, move more freely. A wild desire to laugh out loud, to dance, to sing as loud as I wanted.

The train wound through the Alps to Bad Gastein, a spa town perched on a mountainside, a waterfall coursing under its main street. A van from Grüner Baum picked me up. The driver welcomed me with a friendly smile. What a difference from the place I had just left! He chatted all the way, pointing out the places of interest in the town and the names of the mountains on either side. The road was narrow and winding, hugging the mountain. We descended into a deep valley and pulled up in front of the hotel. I ran to my parents, who sat waiting for me out front and hugged them each in turn.

They gave me a gracious two weeks in that magnificent resort. We strolled along a path that wound along the valley floor, the air fragrant with the scent of drying hay. A mountain stream flowed alongside the path, icy cold from the melting glaciers high above. We walked to an outdoor café, the owners a friendly Austrian in traditional lederhosen, and his daughter, who wore the traditional women's *dirndl*. We walked along the Kaiser Wilhelm Strasse into Bad Gastein, a walking trail that skirted mountainsides all the way into town, past the spa hotels where guests came for thermal water cures. We stopped for traditional Austrian *Kaffe und Kuchen*.

The contrast was painful. The beauty, ease and graciousness. Light after darkness. To think that Czechoslovakia could have been – *had* been not so very long ago – this beautiful, prosperous, refined.

We took our meals in that luxurious dining room, its large windows looking out over the pool, at the river full of speckled trout, at the mountains where cows grazed at impossible heights. A sign on our table read *"Familie Notzl."* Evenings we went to the bar in the resort and danced. We took our lunches on the outdoor patio under the chestnut trees. We swam in the indoor thermal pool or the cool outdoor pool.

One evening towards the end of our stay, as my parents and I sat in the bar after dinner, I thanked them from the bottom of my heart for bringing me to this beautiful place.

"This is the life you were used to," my father replied, "the life you could have in Canada." I thought wryly, they sure wouldn't approve of the life I'd found at Christmas with Hadassah.

"I wish we'd come here instead of Canada after we escaped. At least we'd still be Europeans," I said. My father spoke German fluently and was completely at home here.

"I've often wished the same," he said. "Who knew at that time where the borders would be drawn? But Helen, we've done well in Canada. Why can't you be satisfied with that?"

"I don't know," I said, lighting a cigarette. "Are you a Canadian? I know we all have Canadian citizenship. But Dad, do you *feel* you're a Canadian?" This was a conversation we'd never had.

He contemplated me. "I think an immigrant will always be one. Especially one who left unwillingly. We are exiles, making the best of it."

"But where do you feel you *belong*?" I said.

He shook his head impatiently. "We've made a fine home for all of us. That's where we belong. Canada has been generous, has given us a lot."

"Can that make up for everything we lost?"

My father was silent, also lighting a cigarette. "It has to," he finally said. "Yes. It has."

I drank my beer. My mother, who'd been silent through this exchange, spoke up. "Having to leave your home, leaving everyone behind – I don't think you ever recover."

"Nonsense," my father snapped. "Look at all the Czechs in Canada who've made a success of their lives." My mother looked dubious, but said nothing.

"Wherever you sent me – camp, private school, university – though I loved them, I always felt different. An ugly duckling searching for my flock. I thought returning to Prague was the answer. Now I have no idea. I used to think, I'm a Bohemian; what am I doing in Canada? And suddenly I've been thinking, I'm a feminist; what am I doing in Prague?"

"Those women – next you'll be burning your bra!" my mother scoffed. "Don't tell me you're a feminist now."

"Yes," I smiled. "I am."

"All those years, I thought Prague was the answer," my mother said. "Until I saw what they'd done to it. The apartment I remembered so lovingly was a hovel. Nobody promenades in the squares anymore, they scurry like moles through broken streets. Everything I treasured is gone."

"It's not all gone. It's the dissidents who are keeping it alive."

"Hah!" exclaimed my father. "Look what happened to Dubček and Prague Spring."

"I know," I said. "But the people I've come to know are what's left of the intelligentsia: the artists, writers, musicians. They keep life worth living. And our family. They are good people."

"I know they are," my father said.

———

A few days later we were on a plane to Weimar, East Germany. Here the dilapidated state of things was even worse, lacking the former grandeur of Prague. We were the first to arrive at the downtown hotel my father had reserved for the entire party.

"I knew it would be like this," he declared, enraged. The hotel, once fine, was shabby and in bad repair.

The next morning we were waiting in the lobby when Malý Pavel and Helena walked through the front door. I leapt to my feet to greet them, and stopped. My father had risen and stood staring at his first-born son. They stood wordless, looking at one another, the son a mirror image of his father, both struggling to contain emotion. They embraced, pulled back to have another look, my father still holding on to Malý Pavel's arms, then another embrace. Father and son, who had missed out on thirty years of each other's lives, their lives lived two worlds apart. We were all crying.

"*Konečně*," was all my father could say. At last. His son nodded.

The two are like twins, I thought, only the years separate them; perhaps they even share each other's thoughts and feelings, yet they are probably on opposite sides of every issue now.

Malý Pavel shook my mother's hand, then introduced Helena, who beamed and pumped my mother and father's hands. "I'm sorry young Helena couldn't come," her mother said. "She wanted so much to see you again." She'd been left behind as the required hostage.

Otto and his wife arrived soon after, and with them, my father's mother. Despite his usual reserve, my father ran to his mother and enfolded her in his arms, both their cheeks awash with tears. She reached up and put her hand on his cheek. "My son," she said, "my beloved son."

My father had rarely spoken of his mother, yet now I saw how much he loved her. What incredible strength it must have taken to leave. What pain being apart must have caused him all these years. Unlike my mother, he had borne it in silence. I'd only met this grandmother a few times at Otto's, and hadn't warmed to this short, stout stranger with what seemed like a rather sour disposition. I saw her differently now.

The greetings were effusive, joyful, heartbreaking. My father reunited with his brother Otto with hearty slaps on the back, and shortly after, when a taxi deposited Rudy and his wife arriving from Canada, my grandmother reunited with her grandson, and Malý Pavel with his brother. The wives were introduced. The staff at the front desk and other hotel guests passing by slowed to stare at this melee of shouting, tears and laughter taking place in their lobby.

For the next five days everyone talked and talked, doing their best to make up for the lost years. So many stories to tell, so much love to remember and rekindle. We strolled the streets of Weimar, sat in restaurants, in cafés and wine bars, talked and laughed and drank, my father the host, paying for everything, effusive and happy in the role. At dinner, he ordered the best wine, "And keep it flowing!" he'd call to the maître d', and when musicians struck up a song he knew, he burst into song and slapped the table in time with the rhythm. He was happy. A European to the bone, I said to myself.

There seemed to be an unspoken understanding that politics were not to be discussed, that nothing divisive would be tolerated on this occasion. There was only one exception. Sitting over coffee after dinner one evening, my father said to Malý Pavel, "So, have you changed your mind? Are you still a communist?"

Malý Pavel was thoughtful for a moment, then replied, "I don't like a lot of what's been done in the name of communism. But I still believe in its ideals."

My father shrugged and rolled his eyes. "You're stubborn. Like me." They both laughed.

"I always wondered if you joined the Communist party to punish me. Out of anger at my divorcing your mother. You couldn't have found a better way. As a banker, I became your enemy when you joined the party. I've thought about it a great deal. I did abandon you when I remarried, well before we escaped. I have regretted it deeply. I'm very sorry." My father reached out and put his hand on Malý Pavel's arm.

Malý Pavel flushed, and tears sprang to his eyes. He could only nod. Perhaps some healing was taking place.

I watched, fascinated and moved by the intricate family connections and resemblances among us. My father and Uncle Otto, brothers, were opposites in appearance and temperament, my father refined, Otto earthy. That difference between them was echoed in my father's sons, Malý Pavel the spitting image of my father, Rudy resembling his Uncle Otto. And when I thought about my siblings, my older brother Peter had the same look and temperament as his Uncle Otto and Rudy, his half-brother, while I and my younger brother Tom were more like our father and Malý Pavel. How different life would have been, I reflected, watching the coming together of all these personalities, if we'd been surrounded and enriched by this extended family.

When it was time for us to part, we stood again in the lobby, saying our farewells. Tears flowed; promises were made to do it again soon and to write often. Father and son clasped hands hard, then embraced one last time. My father held his mother in his arms, both unwilling to let go.

A taxi took Rudy and his wife to the airport. The Prague contingent drove off in their two cars and my mother, my father and I stood on the sidewalk waving. We spent our last evening together and the following day, my father saw my mother and me off at the train station and made his way alone to the airport and back to Canada.

It was never to happen again. My father's mother died a few years later. My father referred to the reunion often, and considered it one of the finest things he'd ever done.

This time, back in Prague, I lost no time in calling Karel.

It was lovely to see my mother ensconced in her family. She and Růža became great friends and there was a powerful bond between my mother and Uncle Paul. The four of us set out together often, strolling arm in arm, two by two down Wenceslas Square, and sat in cafés over coffee and cake. My mother and I met on our own occasionally. Her being in Prague added another dimension to my experience. Wherever we walked, she had stories to tell about her childhood and mine.

In Old Town Square she turned away in disgust from the huge red banners strung across the facades of the lovely buildings, blaring between images of the hammer and sickle: *SE SOVĚSKÝM SVAZEM NA VĚČNÉ ČASY!* With the Soviet Union Forever!

"What do you think our life would have been like if we'd stayed?" I asked her.

"A nightmare."

I took her to see my room on Nosticova. "It's lovely," she said, and her words warmed my heart. "I'm glad to see you well and happy."

We went for coffee to my favourite local café.

"I want you to meet my friends," I said, sitting back. "One in particular, named Karel. A painter at the Academy of Fine Arts." I knew I was taking a chance – and sure enough, old habits die hard; she threw me that wary look. "You've always been critical and suspicious of every one of my boyfriends. What's with that?" I said.

She hesitated. "I was afraid you were sleeping with every man you met!" she said.

"Really, Mother," I laughed, "not *every* one. This one's very special. We've been together since October. There's a party in a couple of days, a steamboat ride on the river, a boat his group has hired. Why don't you come? We're dressing up in turn of the century costumes. There'll be a band, food and drinks, and dancing."

At first she wouldn't hear of it. I told her about Spolek Pohodlí. "The propaganda they shove down your throat here is absurd – evil, in fact. So you dismiss it, but then what? You create your own values, your own meaning. That's what they do. Come to the party – you'll see what I mean."

She arrived at Malostranské Náměstí on the 22 tram, elegant in slacks and a silk blouse. I was in costume, a long skirt, a brocade jacket and a bonnet tied under my chin. Karel jumped from the tram wearing breeches, stockings with garters and a velvet jacket. My mother's eyes widened when I introduced them. Karel bowed and said to her in Czech, "Now I see where Helen gets her beauty." My mother reddened, pleased.

The whole gang was on the wharf. We piled on and with a blast of the whistle, the steamboat chugged out into the river. The beer flowed, food was plentiful and the band played. Karel introduced my mother to his friends. She particularly liked Milan Udržal, who kissed her hand, his dark eyes sparkling as he invited her to dance. They danced once, then again, and when he escorted her to where Karel and I stood watching, she was flushed, her eyes shining.

During the rest of her stay, she spoke often of that steamboat escapade.

"I'm so glad I came to visit," she said as I was seeing her off at the airport.

"Me too," I said.

"Your Karel is wonderful."

I smiled and waved until she disappeared through the gate.

Karel (left) and his friend Milan Udržal at the roller skating race, 1973

Karel and me at Rubin bar, 1973

Karel's exhibition flyer, front

A triptych of Karel's graphics titled Conversations

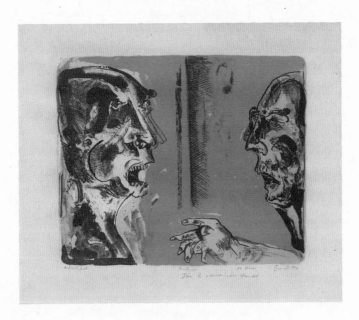

*Čertovka, The Devil›s Channel, just outside the window of my beloved room
on Nosticova in Mala Strana, 1972*

*Spolek Pohodlí and Zlatá Praha on the steamboat. Karel and I are towards the left,
in the middle of the crowd.*

⸆⸆⸆ Chapter 14

KAREL LOOKED ESPECIALLY HAPPY WHEN I CAME TO HIS studio one day to sit for my portrait. He ushered me in, closed the door and told me to sit down.

"I didn't want to tell you before because I wasn't sure it would happen. But it has." He paused. "I've found a place for you to live."

"No!" I leapt out of the chair.

He nodded. Then a cloud darkened his face. "It's not in Malá Strana, though, and not on the river. Nothing like what you've got. And it's small."

"None of that matters," I said. "To not have to be beholden to Mirek anymore!" I threw my arms around him.

"Let's forget about working and go see it," he said. I was already heading out the door.

We took the metro from the Dejvice Station to I.P. Pavlova. "This is where my Uncle Paul and Aunt Růža live," I exclaimed. There on the corner was their building.

"You'd be closer to them now," Karel said. He led me across the tram tracks, through the square and up Bělehradská Street.

"This is it," he said, stopping outside the door of number 61. It had been a fine building once. Statues stood in alcoves between the windows on the upper storeys, but they were chipped and black with soot. Karel unlocked the street door, which opened onto a dark passageway, a courtyard and beyond it a coach house. "That's it," Karel said, sounding worried. "The ground floor is used for storage, and the room is above that."

He unlocked the front door. A set of narrow wooden steps rose up to a small landing and another door that Karel unlocked. It opened onto two small rooms, a kitchen nook and a small bathroom. Three windows overlooked the courtyard.

I walked around, picturing where everything would go; one room would be the living room and kitchen, my table by the window, where I could work looking out over the courtyard. My uncle's oriental rugs would fit throughout and my bed would go into the smaller back room, where Karel and I could be together with no fear of ever being disturbed.

"It's perfect," I cried. "I'll hang curtains and put flower boxes in the windows."

To celebrate we went to Deminka, a pub down the road, both of us radiant.

"I'll only come on your invitation," Karel said. "It's your home now." I had a lovely vision of our future together. A room of my own – in fact an entire little coach house – to share with him as I wanted, with no one else to feel obligated to. I leaned across the table and placed a grateful kiss on his mouth.

I cleaned and painted my two room coach house and moved in over the next week. An unused metal mailbox hung on the door downstairs, which I painted black with white flowers and printed my name in large capital letters: NOTZL – stating my ownership. Copying Mirek's idea, I planted runner beans in window boxes, and standing outside on the overhang, I strung rows of wire to the soffit above. The beans germinated quickly and soon I had a fluttering, lacy curtain of green leaves and pink flowers to look through at my courtyard. I named it *U Fazole*, after the way pubs and hotels were named. At the Beans, my new home.

Karel respected my privacy as he'd promised, but I welcomed him to my piece of the world whenever he was free to come.

———

Several weeks later, I was in Honza's fine studio for my first sitting since my return from Bad Gastein and Weimar. He asked about my trip and I described the reunion with my family.

"I've had a chance to work on this a bit during your absence," he said. "It's coming along."

"Can't wait to see it," I said.

"Not yet," he smiled.

Honza worked silently, adding bits of clay here and there. After some time, his head cocked to one side as he smoothed the clay with a deft hand, he said casually, "I guess you've heard the news by now about Karel joining the Communist party."

I couldn't have heard what I thought I'd heard. My faulty Czech. "Pardon?"

Honza kept working. "Karel. He's joined the Communist party. I thought you'd have heard."

"What?" I said, still thinking I'd misunderstood. "What are you saying?"

He stared at me. "I'm talking about Karel," he repeated, slowly this time. "He's become a member of the Communist party. I guess he hasn't told you."

I felt the blood leave my face. "That can't be true."

"It is," Honza nodded and kept working, a wry smile on his face.

I stared at him in disbelief. "Are you serious?" I croaked out.

He was putting me on. These were dissidents, for Christ's sake. The whole point, the whole meaning of their group and of their *lives* was to protest the system that oppressed them. "This is your idea of a joke," I said.

"Nope."

"Why would he do such a thing? It doesn't make any sense! He wouldn't!"

"Well, he did. The Academy told him he had to if he wanted to keep his job," Honza said. "So he joined."

I was stunned. The ground had fallen out from under me. Honza stood there smirking, and rage towards him came over me.

"You're lying!" I said. "I don't believe you."

He stopped smiling. "I'm sorry to be the one to tell you."

"How could he do that?" I cried.

Honza was silent. He'd stopped working and stood there, his hands by his sides. I cast around, looking at him, at the room surrounding us, at the red clay roofs outside his window, as though looking for clues to this new reality, working hard to grasp what I'd heard. Eventually it hit me that he was telling the truth. Despite everything Karel had said and done, everything he'd told me he stood for, he had caved. And then I began to rail. A flood, a passionate invective burst from deep within me.

"How the hell can anything change in this goddamn country when even the most passionate opponents of this fucking, evil regime end up signing on the dotted line?" On and on I went, venting my shock, my disbelief, my profound disappointment. A diatribe against the system and against Karel, who I never imagined would give in. Honza was silent the whole time.

Finally, exhausted, I ran out of words. He stood, unmoving.

"Let's quit for today," Honza said quietly. He took a cloth, wet it at the sink and covered his work. "Let's go to U Bonaparta. They'll be there by now." I pulled off my hat, grabbed my jacket and headed for the door.

Karel was there, sitting among the group. I couldn't pretend. He noticed it at once. "What is it?" he whispered, taking a seat beside me. I shook my head and took a big slug of the beer that appeared in front of me. Many slugs of beer. I couldn't look at him.

"Let's get out of here. Let's talk." I shook my head. I sat there in the group trying to calm myself, but numb. I couldn't make sense of it. Karel looked as dear and as beautiful as ever, but Honza's news had transformed him in my eyes. I didn't know him. He was a liar. He was a traitor. He was what people derisively called a *karierista*, a careerist, a person who would betray his principles and his friends in order to get ahead. I couldn't talk to him, I sat silent within the group and drank. Finally, when the pub was closing, the group disbanded and Karel and I were out on the sidewalk.

"You have to tell me what the matter is," Karel said. "I knew the moment you walked into the pub. Tell me."

I was afraid to say it. That would make it real. Finally I blurted it out. "Honza told me you joined the party." He stared at me, silent now. "Is it true?"

"I was afraid that was it," he said, his head bent low.

"Is it true?" I asked again. He nodded.

"It is." We stood in the silence and the dark.

"It's against everything I thought you stood for, everything you believed," I said.

"*Helenko*, let me explain. Please try to understand."

The director had come and said he'd been given an order: if Karel wanted to keep his job at the Academy, he had to join the Communist party. Being a professor was a position of influence, they'd said, and they couldn't allow a non-party member to continue to hold such a position.

"It happened while you were away and plunged me into a terrible dilemma. You know how much I love my job. But I'm not a *karierista*," he said urgently, "willing to sell out for the sake of a job. I agonized, weighing my decision day after day. They needed an answer within two weeks. If only I could have talked to you, to confer, to help me see all sides. But you weren't here and I had to make the decision on my own.

"I thought long and hard about it," he went on. "Where could I have the most influence? If I was thrown out of the Academy, how could I have any influence at all on young people? As their teacher, I'm there, I work with them every day. They listen to me. I can tell them what no one else could tell them. The truth."

"But how could you act against your own beliefs like that?"

"Signing that document was meaningless. It's just a piece of paper."

"It's not! It means something much bigger than that."

"Helen, I didn't know what to do."

In the end, though it took me many days, I was able to reconcile myself to what had happened. I realized I'd been harsh and uncompromising, and forgave him. Who was I to sit in judgment? In Canada, I'd grown up with a strong sense of entitlement and of individual freedom that Karel had never experienced. I'd never had to confront the kind of impossible situation he'd been faced with. Over and over, he took pains to explain himself.

"It doesn't change who I am," he said. "I'm still the man you know and have loved. I still believe in everything I've said to you."

Chapter 15

THEN FOLLOWED ONE OF THE HAPPIEST TIMES. IT WAS THE summer of 1974.

"Let's go hitchhiking!" I said to him one day. The Academy was closed for summer holidays and I had weeks before my next deadline.

"Hitchhiking?" His eyebrows shot up. "Nobody hitch-hikes here."

"Maybe we'll start something new."

"Where would we go?"

"Anywhere," I said. "To the countryside. Somewhere beautiful. You decide."

"For how long?"

"A week? Two weeks? We'll come home when we want to."

Hesitant but intrigued, he produced a map, and we pored over it. "I can't believe we're planning this," he said, looking up as we traced several possible routes. "What about southern Bohemia?" His eyes shone at the prospect. "There are wonderful towns and villages I could show you. We'll take a bus to get out of the city."

"Sure. Let's just hit the road and see where it takes us," I said.

"What if no one picks us up?" he wondered.

"It's an adventure! We'll launch ourselves out there and see what happens."

We each prepared a backpack, taking very little. If we needed to, I said, we could come back to Prague and set out again.

One sunny day soon afterwards we boarded a bus heading south. We got off in a small village nestled in a valley with several dozen houses with steep roofs and fenced gardens. The village was surrounded by rolling hills of fields and woods. We walked through the village, packs on our backs, the sun high in the sky. A few women in kerchiefs stood chatting outside a grocery store, shopping baskets over their arms. They went silent and turned to stare at us as we passed. We smiled, nodded, and received a few nods in return. A man in overalls working in his garden stood up and stared as we approached. *"Dobrý den,"* we both greeted him. He nodded in reply, continuing to stare as we walked down the road. We entered the village pub, where again we were the object of curious gazes. Clearly, not many strangers stopped in this village. Hungry, we ordered goulash and dumplings, downed a couple of beers, and set off.

We walked hand in hand at times, sometimes apart, sometimes I'd run on ahead, Karel running to catch up, throwing his arms around me; then we strolled on. Past dark stands of forest, past fields of wheat, corn, and hay, uphill and down. We walked from village to village, stopping in pubs to refresh ourselves. Often villages were only two or three kilometres apart. Everywhere villagers stared at us, some silently, some with a greeting or a wave, old women kneeling in their gardens, men in overalls, digging. There weren't many cars. The occasional truck toiled past. We let them go by. That first day, we were happy to be out and walked for miles, from one village to another, past fields harvested and plowed or high with corn-stalks or waving fields of wheat.

Towards evening, we were between towns when we heard a truck behind us. I turned, held out my thumb. The surprised driver screeched to a halt.

"*Kam jdete?*" he called out. Where are you going?

"*Do příští vesnice,*" Karel answered. To the next village. We'd agreed he should do the talking. I didn't want to frighten anyone with my foreignness. The driver indicated with his head – hop in. We scrambled in. The truck was an old one. Karel thanked him for stopping. "It's getting late and we want to make it to the next village. Do you know if there's a *pension* there?"

"You from Prague?" The driver's head shot around, wariness in his pale blue eyes.

Karel nodded, said something I didn't catch, and the driver relaxed and warmed to him. He was surprised to see hitchhik-ers, he said. "You hardly see any these days."

"No," Karel agreed. "No one I know does it."

"And what about you, Miss?" the driver leaned over and asked. "You from Prague too?"

"I'm from Canada," I ventured, "but I was born here, so I'm living in Prague now."

The driver's eyes widened as he turned to stare at me, his face transformed by a wide grin. "I have a brother in Canada!" he exclaimed. "Escaped in '68. He's happy there and doing well. He's in Vancouver. Do you know Vancouver?" he asked eagerly.

"I do," I told him. "I'm from Toronto."

"Oh yes, he wrote me about Toronto. A friend of his lives there, so he's visited. But he loves Vancouver, he's a skier so he loves the mountains. You can be skiing, he tells me, and you can see the ocean! It must be wonderful." He was silent for a moment. "Stupid me. Why didn't I run when I could?" We nodded. "I was afraid. And how could I leave my parents? They were old, it would have killed them." He sighed. "My brother is happy. But I'll probably never see him again. He was due to do his military service when he left. He'd be arrested as a deserter if he came back. Lucky you," he said, glancing at me, his watery eyes brimming.

He dropped us off at a pension in the next village and we waved to each other as he drove off.

The landlady led us up to a small room on the second floor where, after eating, we spent our first night making love under the eaves, the window open wide to the warm, dark night.

We set off again the next day after buying some provisions. "We don't want to eat in pubs and sleep in pensions the whole time," I said to Karel. That day we walked, got a couple of rides and ate our lunch sitting in the sun at the edge of a field of sweet-smelling cut hay. Towards evening we were walking along the road and came to a cornfield.

"Let's pick some and have them for dinner," I said.

"Corn is for animals!" Karel exclaimed. "You don't eat it, do you?"

"Of course!" I ran into the cornfield and tore off four cobs and added them to my backpack.

That evening, we found woods and a stream far from any village or habitation. I built a small fire, and after soaking the cobs in the stream, I put them still in their husks into the coals, just as we'd done at our family cottage in Haliburton. I felt Karel's eyes watching me with surprise and concern and was keenly aware of the gulf between us – my taking for granted that it was all right to do all this, to steal corn, to enter these woods, to light a fire, to bake corn and consider it acceptable for human consumption. When the husks were blackened, I pulled the cobs from the fire and when they'd cooled a bit, showed Karel how to remove the husks and bite into the corn. "Too bad we don't have butter and salt," I said, "they're even better that way." Warily he stripped the husk and took a tentative bite. *"Ale to je požitek. Bašta!"* he exclaimed. Why, it's delicious. A treat!

"Let's stay here for the night," I said. We brushed our teeth by the stream, put on our sweaters, lay our jackets on the mossy ground and used our backpacks for pillows. We kissed goodnight and were soon fast asleep under our leafy canopy, lulled by the stream trickling over the pebbles.

For ten glorious days we continued, sojourning through the beautiful countryside of southern Bohemia. We visited churches, strolled through parks and cemeteries, visited galleries, sat in town squares. Karel told me stories, relating historical events that happened in the places we visited, told me about the art and architecture we saw, describing the grandeur of what had been. Everywhere we were witness to the devastation that had happened to this once magnificent country.

One evening as dark was approaching, it began to rain. No car or truck had come along in some time, and there was no village in sight. We had food with us, but what would we do for shelter? We quickened our pace, making for woods we could see ahead, telling ourselves at least we'd find a bit of shelter under the trees. Entering the woods, we could see some sort of structure deeper in the forest and moved closer to explore it. It was a deer feeding station, a wooden manger piled high with hay and covered by a peaked roof.

"It's perfect!" I cried. That's where we spent that night. Dry and sheltered, we lay together, the dark woods rustling all around us, the rain drumming on the roof above. Breathing in the sweet smell of hay, we lay with our arms and legs entangled in that small, cozy nest.

"I will remember this forever," I said to Karel as I was drifting off to sleep.

Another night we were walking through a village when once again it started to rain. We were already close to the outskirts and had found no pension, hotel or pub.

"This town feels creepy," I said to Karel. We had noticed there were three men walking behind us.

We realized we were being followed and walked faster. So did the three men. We broke into a run. We rounded a corner at the edge of town, and there in front of us was a barn, its door open a crack. We pried it open, darted inside, and closed it behind us. No animals, just storage. A wooden ladder led to a loft. Quickly we climbed it and hid in the hayloft. The three men, like a posse, rounded the corner and stood below us, staring down the darkened road. We could see their outlines through the cracks between the barn boards. "They're gone," one of them said. They turned back and disappeared into the night. We slept for a while and well before daybreak, we crept down, squeezed out of the door, and running as quietly as we could, left that village, relieved to be out on the open road again.

Oh, we were adventurers, Karel and I, moving through the world, open to every experience. Again and again Karel would say he couldn't believe what we were doing, that it was something no one he knew had ever done. It was about freedom, adventure, danger, laughter and love, being together day after day, in such joy. It was about being young and unafraid, undaunted, courageous in spite of the oppression, distrust and fear all around us. It was about wanting to live life wide open, experiencing it to the utmost. Karel had given me so much. This adventure was something I could give him.

After ten days on the road, a car approached us as we made our way out of the woods and we stuck out our thumbs. The car stopped. Too late we realized it was a police car. Two officers strode over and demanded our papers. We produced them. Karel was anxious. No big deal, I thought; we weren't harming anyone.

"What are you doing out on the road like this?" one of them asked.

"We're hitchhiking," Karel said. "It isn't against the law, is it?"

The policeman flashed Karel a threatening glance, then, looking at my passport, said, "This may be done where you come from, Miss, but it's not done here."

They ordered us to quit and get back to Prague immediately. They didn't offer us a ride.

We crossed the road and began to walk back. The police car took off, its wheels squealing. Half an hour later a truck stopped and took us to the next village where we caught a bus back to Prague. Although it had been cut short by a few days it had been the adventure of a lifetime. Karel and I returned to Prague triumphant.

———

My thirtieth birthday was coming up: August 26, 1974. I'd been in Prague for close to two years and had known Karel since October of the year before. I'd recorded our meeting in my journal: *October 19, 1973. Met Karel Z. today at Rubín.* Our time together felt much longer, as though we'd lived a good part of a lifetime already.

The first year after I'd arrived in Prague had been hard. Lonely, missing John; the fight for a residence permit. And then Mirek. I was ashamed of having been dependent on him, hated having allowed myself to be close to such a man.

Life had altered dramatically since those early days. My residence permit was secure, I had ongoing work, I'd developed warm relationships with my family, and most of all, Karel had come into my life, as had the friends I'd made through him.

Hadassah still wrote to me, counting on my promise to come back. Since the ball at the Royal Summer Palace, that intention had faded, and when I thought about my pledge to her, I regretted having made it.

Since childhood, my birthday had been a time of melancholy for me; summer drawing to a close, the end of fun and freedom, back to school and responsibility. The long dreary winter lay ahead relieved only by the joy of Christmas, which ended too soon. And then there were harsh January and February to endure.

But this year I wanted to celebrate and one evening, sitting together over coffee at U Fazole, I consulted Karel about how I might do that.

"Host a party," he suggested. "Here it's the celebrant who hosts the party and pays. Invite everybody!"

"Where? How?"

"You could rent Mánes," he said. Mánes was a spacious art gallery in Old Town directly on the river. Karel and his friends knew the owner, even though they were not allowed to exhibit there. "I'll help you make the arrangements."

He designed the invitations and had them printed. I handed them out to our friends at U Bonaparta and U Tygra. The word went out, and on the evening of my birthday, the crowd gathered. An open bar. Lots of hors d'oeuvres I'd had catered – small open-faced sandwiches, smoked meats, cheeses, sausages, bite-sized schnitzels, and plenty of sweets. A band played in one corner, friends of Karel's.

People brought me gifts, mostly art offerings. Pepa Steklý brought me a drawing he'd created in the shape of a church, the doors opening to reveal an interior with an exquisite stained glass window. Milan Kohout brought me several of his graphics, as did Jana. Another friend gave me a lithograph titled "Where the light is so gentle, it removes silk stockings." Another brought a large rolled-up lithograph, a great warm orange sun on the horizon, and a line of figures waiting to climb a ladder, each walking away holding a shining piece of the sun. These were treasures I would keep forever.

The party was raucous; we talked, laughed, and drank copious amounts.

Midway through the evening, Karel was talking with a group of friends and I had a chance to sit at the bar by myself. How amazing it was, given the dream of returning to Prague I'd had for so long, that here I was, hosting this crowd of Czech artists and writers, some of them former and possibly future celebrities. Tonight I wasn't just a tag-along with Karel, but the evening's host. Catching sight of my lover among his friends, I felt immense gratitude towards him for opening up this world to me. At thirty, I had achieved my dream. Yet where did I stand on that dream now? What about the life and work I'd been so excited about in Canada?

So much of my life in Prague depended on others. I lived in rooms others had made available to me. An aspect of that made me feel like a kept woman, which I hated. I thought of Blanche in *A Streetcar Named Desire*, relying on the kindness of strangers. And then, looking out at the crowd, I knew I was only a part of this as Karel's girl. These were men's groups. As far as I knew, all the women in Spolek Pohodlí and Zlatá Praha were there as girlfriends of a member. I would never belong in my own right.

In Canada, I could achieve something and attain some degree of personal power. But perhaps that wasn't important. It if was, why hadn't I stayed in Canada to rise within the ranks of the National Film Board? It could have been a wonderful career. Achieving personal power hadn't been important to me; all that had mattered was getting to Europe and eventually to Prague. Maybe staying in Prague, loving Karel and creating a life was more important. Perhaps I could find a cause and make it my own.

What was it about this place called Prague that wouldn't let me go? The deep, mysterious joy I found walking through its gas lit streets at night. It was the only place where that restless need, that agonized yearning, was stilled, the one place on earth that reflected back to me who I was and what I aspired to. It was rowdy, irreverent, intense, passionate, creative. Yet it was also macabre, absurd, and dangerous. Maybe what I loved was that living in this environment made a person stronger, requiring one to be creative in forging a meaningful life. The choice here was to rise up as these dissidents did and create an alternative, or to be cowed and destroyed.

Karel came back, put his arm around me and we danced. We held one another, we sang, we celebrated with our friends until early morning.

At the end of the evening, I was presented with the bill. Between my income from Artia and my students, and my black market exchanging of dollars to crowns, it was an amount I could easily afford.

But – could I really live in such an oppressive environment, once the adventure wore off? What a dilemma! Karel and this ragtag bunch of boozing Bohemians, this heavy life in communist Prague on the one side; and on the other, Canada, Hadassah and the women's movement, women embarked on vital work I could be a part of, that spoke to issues deeply important to me.

⚡ Chapter 16

THE DECISION WAS TAKEN OUT OF MY HANDS.

September came and it was time to get back to work. Karel returned to his teaching, and having finished *The Big Book of Ghost and Monster Stories*, I was given two new stories. My weekly English lessons with the three engineers began again. The fluttering green curtain of leaves outside my window at U Fazole was heavy with bean pods. It was a cozy place to come home to and a quiet workspace. Karel stayed often but also respected my privacy and need for space.

I visited my aunt and uncle regularly; they were just down the street now, across Tylovo Náměstí. I could see Růža's face waiting for me at her window and I'd wave as I approached. They invited me to their cottage in Černošice occasionally; we took the train and climbed the hill lugging bags of groceries. They had turned the wooden henhouse, all that had been left to my family when the property was confiscated, into a cozy cottage. Through the trees, surrounded by a chain-link fence, was the villa that had once belonged to our family. On the other side was what had been our orchard, now a housing development, twenty or so houses side by side with little plots of land surrounding each, their occupants probably unaware they were living on stolen land.

I invited my aunt and uncle to come and visit me in my new home. Until then, I hadn't been willing to share with them my uncertain living arrangements, temporary and contingent as they were. Now I felt secure. They looked dubious as they crossed the courtyard and climbed the narrow stairs, but smiled with approval once inside, and we chatted happily over coffee and cake one afternoon, sitting around my kitchen table.

I told them about Karel. They were impressed by his credentials, a docent at the Academy of Fine Arts. They appreciated art and had a fine collection of Czech painters' works hanging on their walls. "I want you to meet him one day," I said. "I'm sure you'll like him."

I visited Malý Pavel and his family regularly as well, and he was generous with his time, helping me whenever I needed.

———

One evening in mid-October, I was working at my desk when there was a familiar knock on my door. Happily, I ran to open the door. Karel stood there, a worried look on his face. He strode past me, drew a card from his jacket pocket. "Look at this," he said. "I don't know what to think."

I recognized the card. I'd seen many like it during my early days in Prague.

"It's from the police," he said.

"I know."

"Read it," he said. It was an order summoning him to appear at the police station on Bartolomějská at two o'clock on October sixteenth. Two days from now.

"What could it be about?" I asked.

"I have no idea," he said.

"Something about your work? Has anything happened?"

"Not that I know of," he said. "I don't think I've done anything to attract their attention."

"Something to do with ..." I hesitated. "With your joining the Party?"

He shook his head. "There's nothing going on there. It's done. No need to summon me."

"Just checking in with you?"

"I don't see why."

We sat at the table, staring at each other and at that piece of paper with a growing sense of foreboding.

"Maybe they're about to try with you what they did to me when I was applying for a residence permit. Maybe now that they have you, the demands for more will start," I said. "Turn you into an informer."

His eyes blazed. "No way!"

"I know," I said, "but they could try."

"They can try all they want. They'll get nothing."

I made coffee and we continued to speculate on what his summons might mean until we'd exhausted all the possibilities we could think of, then out we went into the dark streets of Vinohrady, telling each other it was probably a formality of some kind and meant nothing.

The next afternoon, I lifted the hinged top of the pretty black and white mailbox with the name NOTZL declaring my presence. Inside lay a card addressed to me. A similar card to Karel's with a similar message. I was to appear at the police station on Bartolomějská two days after Karel, October eighteenth. Was it because Karel was a member of the Communist party now? Were they about to start hounding me again? Or could Karel's card, too, be about me?

A shiver went through me. Now I was frightened. What could they be interrogating us both about? My mind cast back, searching for anything that might have brought us to their attention. Hitchhiking? Surely not. I could come up with nothing plausible. But perhaps they didn't need anything plausible. Perhaps my father had been right all along. Were we in danger?

It was a Wednesday and we were meeting at U Bonaparta. It was Karel's turn to see the fear in my face. He got up and led me outside the instant he saw me.

"I got one too," I blurted as we stood facing one another on the sidewalk. "A card like yours. Two days later. I have to appear at the police station on the eighteenth."

"*Ježíš Maria*," he swore.

———

We met at one o'clock on the sixteenth at the tram stop at Národní Třída and walked holding hands down the street towards Bartolomějská, each trying to reassure the other. I felt pale and my hands were cold.

"We've done nothing," he said to me, squeezing my hand. "I'm sure it's just some administrative thing. Wait for me here." We were outside a pub, U Medvídků, At the Little Bear, where we'd often sat together. I watched after him as he continued down the street and turned left at Bartolomějská. I took a seat at one of the wooden tables, ordered a beer and waited. I tried reading the book I'd brought with me, but was unable to focus. I sat and stared, unseeing, at the posters on the walls and the few people coming and going. It seemed like forever before the front door swung open and Karel walked in. Or stumbled in, hurrying to my table, breathing hard.

"What in God's name have you been up to?" he whispered hoarsely as he slid onto the bench across from me.

I stared at him, my hands that had reached for him, turning into fists. "What do you mean?"

He was speechless, as though his mind, still whirling, was unable to form words.

"What do you mean, what have I been up to? You know everything about me!" I was shocked at an accusation coming from him.

"They think you're a spy!" he burst out. "It was an interrogation about you!" His hands shook as he lit a cigarette. "The things they said!"

"But Karel, you *know* me! How can you believe anything they said?"

"Oh, don't worry, I defended you. I argued with everything they accused you of."

"What? What did they accuse me of?"

"Terrible things! That you're a spy. An enemy of the state. An evil influence, come to infiltrate and corrupt people – like me – towards decadent Western thinking. A parasite – imagine! – a *parasite*, living off other people. I defended you. I told them you worked, earned more money at times than I did. Paid your way, paid rent, paid all your bills on your own. They couldn't care less. I couldn't budge them. They claimed they had proof. When I challenged them, asked where they were getting this stuff, they said it was none of my business. They warned me about you and that was it."

I sat still, horrified. Where was this coming from?

"There was more. That you'd pretended to be non-political, but in fact were violently anti-communist, considered it oppressive and evil. Calling the regime nothing but criminals who'd robbed you of your country – a regime that had welcomed you and allowed you to live here. That everything you'd said to them had been nothing but lies. Told me the interview was over and threw me out."

The words were indeed an echo of some of the things I might have said, words that every one of Karel's friends had expressed at one time or another at the pub and elsewhere. How did the police get to hear these words from me?

"Karel, I've done nothing you don't know about and I don't know why this is happening. I'm going the day after tomorrow. I'll find out what's going on. I'll convince them. I'll bring along documents, pay cheque stubs, whatever I can find. Who doesn't rail at the government sometimes? We do it in Canada as well, I'll tell them. I'll convince them they're wrong."

We lived in dread for the next two days. Then it was my turn, and this time it was Karel waiting for me at U Medvídků. I entered that too familiar building once again, and waited in that long corridor, facing that row of closed doors, my feet wearing down the tired linoleum in front of my chair. Kafka came to mind yet again, the Czech writer of the absurd and sinister. A door opened. I sat on the chair facing the desk. Two uniformed men, one standing, one sitting at the desk, a file in front of him. I couldn't remember if I'd seen these men before.

"*Pas,*" barked the man at the desk. I handed over my passport. He opened it to an empty page and smoothed it flat against the desk with his fat fingers. He picked up a large stamp, pressed it against an inkpad, and without a word or a glance towards me, banged it on a page in my passport. He picked up a pen and bending over my passport, scribbled a few notes between the lines of the stamp. Then he pushed it back across the desk toward me and sat back in his chair. I looked from him to the man standing by the window. The man at the desk leaned forward and crossed his arms on the desk.

"You are hereby charged with anti-State activities. This is a very serious crime. You have until midnight tonight to get out of the country. If you are here beyond midnight, you will be arrested." I froze and my mind whirled, unable to take in what he was saying. He continued, "Your residence permit is void, and what is in your passport now is the charge against you and the requirement to be out of the country by midnight." He sat back. Again I stared at him, and from one to the other. And then the enormity of what he was saying hit me like a rock.

"But why?" I said, realizing I urgently needed to find my voice. "What do you think I have done?" He simply repeated the charge and the imperative that I leave the country.

"But what are the charges?"

"I have already told you. You are charged with anti-State activities."

"On what grounds? What is the charge based on?"

"We are under no obligation to explain the charges to you."

"But I need to know! I am innocent. The charges are false, whatever they are! Tell me what they are and I will answer them!"

He shook his head impatiently. "Be out of the country by midnight or you will be arrested."

My desperation made me indignant. "Surely the accused have the right to know what they're being charged with, so they can defend themselves and explain! That must be protocol, if not law, in every country in the world! I have the right to know!"

"Not at all," he said acidly. "We are under no such requirement."

"But tell me what you think I have done, please! I haven't done anything wrong, truly, and I don't know why you think I have!" The man at the desk simply shook his head. The other stood leaning against the wall, his arms folded. I tried again and again. They refused to tell me anything. They said nothing to me of the things they had said to Karel two days before. I was unable to answer any charges because they gave me none.

"I have been working. I pay my own way." I told them of my translation work, told them the editors at Artia were happy with my contribution. "I swear I'm innocent of whatever charges someone has brought against me!"

They were immovable. Until now they had looked bored; now they looked impatient. "There is nothing you can do or say. I've warned you several times already – if you're here after midnight, we will come and arrest you." The realization that I was powerless, that the situation was hopeless, gradually dawned on me. I sat paralyzed. The man started to get up from his chair.

"I can't leave before midnight!" I cried. "There's only one flight to Toronto daily and it's before noon." I looked at my watch. "It's almost noon now!"

"That's your problem. We don't care where you go. Take the train, take a bus, anywhere beyond the border. Just as long as you get out."

I was reduced to pleading. "I have family to say goodbye to! Work unfinished! My things to pack! Please – give me more time!" The two men exchanged glances. The one standing shrugged one shoulder, then nodded. "Very well," said the man at the desk. "Give me your passport."

My hands shaking, I pushed it back to him. He opened it to where he'd stamped it and scribbled something. He passed it back to me and stood up. "You have until noon tomorrow." He opened the door. I stumbled out in a daze.

The afternoon passed in a flurry of frantic activity. I was a mixture of numbness and panic. I packed. I ran to the post office and called my father asking him to book me a seat on the next morning's flight. I called Artia. I couldn't call my aunt and uncle, couldn't knock on their door to tell them this news. I didn't call Malý Pavel. Might his phone be tapped? I asked Karel to contact them both for me. I sorted through my things. What to take, what to leave? I had to leave a lot. Karel agreed to take care of my things once I was gone. To keep what he wanted. To take my rugs back to Uncle Paul; they would finally meet one another, but under these terrible circumstances. To take my unfinished translations to Artia. We were wild with grief and despair. Karel went to ask a friend to drive us to the airport in the morning.

We lay together, awake all night. Crying, holding one another. Making love. Whispering plans to see each other again, somehow. This couldn't be the end.

"I'll write to you every day," he said.

"I'll write to you too," I said.

"We'll meet somewhere outside this country," he said. "I'll get out somehow. I'll get an exit visa to attend some important exhibition. I'll make my father arrange it." I nodded. "If only you weren't married," he moaned. "If we were married, I could leave with you!"

"I'll apply for a divorce the moment I get to Canada!"

"Would you marry me?"

"Yes! Oh, yes," and we cried again. He stroked my face, my hair. "*Lásko má*," he whispered. My love.

Morning came. Karel's friend arrived. I walked from one room to the other, touching my beloved things, my table and chair where I had spent so many hours working, the tiny kitchen, the Czech patterned dishes, Uncle Paul's rugs, the posters on my walls, the bed with the pink and black Indian cotton bedspread, the black coffee table I'd made. The curled leaves of my runner beans rustling outside my window. With lipstick, I wrote on my bathroom mirror, *Čekej na mně*. Wait for me. I said goodbye to U Fazole, Karel by my side. Shaking, I made my way down those steps and out into the small courtyard, looking back one last time at my windows, the mailbox with my name boldly painted on it. We crossed the courtyard and climbed into the waiting car.

We were silent on the way to the airport. We needed days, no, years, to say everything we wished we could say to one another, and we had said all that could be said for now. We sat in the back. Karel held my ice-cold hand.

In the departure hall, I held on to Karel tight, tears coursing down my face. He pulled me away. They were announcing my flight. Boarding had begun. "You have to go," he said.

"I can't!"

"You have to!"

I tried. I took my suitcases and walked toward the exit to the gates. I couldn't do it. I dropped my suitcases and ran back to him. He had to pry my fingers off his arms. He was crying too.

"*Helenko, musíš*. You have to. We'll see each other again. We will."

I forced my feet to walk towards the gate. I looked back once to take him in one last time, then turned and walked through the door. Like an automaton, I produced my passport, checked my bags, hardly knowing what I was doing. Numbly I sat at the gate, waiting, then following the other passengers blindly, I walked onto the plane and let the stewardess point me to my seat. I had three seats to myself at the very back of the plane, and I wept all the way back to Canada.

PART THREE

Chapter 17

I COULDN'T HAVE ANTICIPATED HOW BROKEN I WOULD BE. Hadn't I considered coming back to Canada and taking part in all the marvellous things happening with the women's movement? Hadn't I less than a year ago promised Hadassah and my other women friends I would be back to work with them? Those friends were small comfort now, and Hadassah was devastated at my indifference. I had no feelings for her, or for anyone or anything. We met only once. "I'm sorry," I said. "I just can't." I was hardly able to function, stunned at how much losing Karel mattered.

My parents were relieved to have me back in Canada. I lived at their home in Don Mills until I could somehow get myself established. I sat with my friends, listening to them talk, unable to care. I looked for work. Nothing interested me. I slept in, spent an hour or two reading the classifieds, made a few calls. My parents hovered, anxious, wanting to help but having no idea what to do. Despair flavoured my days.

A couple of women friends invited me to come share the house they rented on Laurier Avenue in Cabbagetown, and I accepted with gratitude. I needed friends around me. Sylvia Spring, my filmmaker friend and Eve Zaremba, a writer, were both passionately involved in the women's movement. I hoped some of their zeal would inspire me, reigniting what I'd felt earlier – cold ashes now.

True to his word, Karel sent me a postcard every single day, full of news and longing. Every card ended with the word "Čekám." I'm waiting. I'd consulted a lawyer and was stricken to discover that because I'd lived abroad for four years, the law required me to wait a full year before I could apply for a divorce. I wrote to Karel, telling him the bad news. We were waiting for that year to pass. As well as his daily postcards, he sent photos of Spolek Pohodlí sitting around our table at U Bonaparta, Jana's beautifully crafted invitations to *akce* they'd organized, happenings taking place without me. One day I received a beautiful photo of Karel sitting in front of my finished portrait, at which I burst into tears all over again. At the end of December, New Year's greetings came from him and other artists in the group. A flyer announcing an exhibit of his paintings in a small gallery in Tábor. His letters were full of news, loneliness, love – and hope.

I wrote back, though not as often. Nothing felt real, and I moved in a fog, feeling dead inside, with little to say and nothing to give. Despite my aching heart, Karel seemed like another world, inaccessible. I was locked out. Every postcard only reminded me of what I had lost, yet again. Too much loss. I couldn't bear to think of it.

I found a job as an enumerator for Might's Directories, going door to door throughout the city, collecting data on residents and business owners to be listed in the directory. The job gave me an income, enough to pay my living expenses, and nobody owned my time.

But exciting things were going on around me. The Secretary of State had allocated funds for women's projects to be made available the following year, 1975, which had been designated International Women's Year by the United Nations. One evening, I sat with my women friends in our living room on Laurier, listening to their plans.

"Let's create a women's coffee house," Alexa, a poet, said. "A café run by women, for women. Readings by women writers. Women's paintings and photography on the walls, women musicians on weekends. A meeting place, exclusively for women."

An idea was forming in my mind. "I think you're aiming too small," I interjected. "We need something bigger, something that will make a real difference."

What flashed through my mind were Spolek Pohodlí and Zlatá Praha, those artists and writers prevented from exhibiting or publishing, but by supporting one another, creating ways to get their works seen and read nevertheless. What we really needed, I thought, was a place that presented the work of women to the general public and gave women the exposure they weren't getting in the established venues and galleries.

I spoke up again at a later meeting. "What I think we should do is found an arts centre with a theatre for performances and concerts, an art gallery, a library, some workshop space and a café, all showcasing the work of women to the public," I said, feeling involved for the first time in many weeks. "We want women's work to gain exposure and be taken seriously. A place where our work can be seen and celebrated. Not some little café as a hangout for women only."

"That'll never happen," someone replied. "Pie in the sky."

"Sounds amazing, but let's aim for something achievable," said another.

I broke off from the others and pursued my vision. I applied for grants and talked to artists and prominent women to enlist their support and involvement. The response was positive. Soon I had an impressive list of potential board members and an advisory council: the well-known writers and artists Margaret Laurence, Helen Lucas, Maryon Kantaroff, Joyce Wieland, and Member of Parliament Flora MacDonald. Next, I began scouting around for a location.

I had found something in which to invest myself, and despite my numb heart, I could focus on it relentlessly. The loss of Prague and Karel were still a profound anguish, but I put my head down and did my work.

I found support everywhere. Harbourfront donated office space. Marcella Lustig of Redlight Theatre joined me and agreed to become the resident theatre company. Joanne Ruderfer, owner and director of a successful downtown dinner theatre, agreed to be my theatre director. A high-powered board grew. Grant funds were promised. Continuing my search for a building, I sought and received the support of Toronto's mayor, David Crombie, and councillor Art Eggleton, who offered me several vacant city buildings. In the end, we reached an agreement to lease the former City Morgue, a beautiful red brick and stone Georgian building on Lombard Street in downtown Toronto, for a dollar a year. In exchange we committed to raising funds to renovate the building and install the facilities we needed. Grants came from the Secretary of State, Wintario, the Ontario Heritage Foundation, and the Toronto Arts Council.

Now that we had funds, I hired Marie DunSeith, a professional fundraiser. Bud McMorran, a vice-president of the TD bank, agreed to chair the capital campaign. Originally calling ourselves the Women's Cultural Centre, we changed the name at a board meeting in order to make it clear that the audience we were aiming for was the general public. The Lieutenant Governor of Ontario at the time, the Honourable Pauline McGibbon, graciously agreed to lend her name to our Centre, and we became the Pauline McGibbon Cultural Centre.

But all these things took time. In those early years, I put heart and soul into the project that gave my life in Canada some meaning, while still enumerating door to door daily to earn a living. Letters and postcards kept coming from Prague, a stab in the heart each time, and helplessness and despair were my response. I wrote to Karel. My letters were short: Thank you for all your cards, for your photos. I miss Prague, I miss you terribly, this first year is taking forever. I can't bear it.

My mother applied for a visa to visit Uncle Paul and Růža and was refused this time, a result of the anti-state activity charge against me. Karel couldn't get out, and I couldn't go back.

————

One evening at a board meeting in our offices at Harbourfront, we were planning our strategy. It was an excellent board of men and women, among them Ron Thom, architect, Pamela Cluff, architect, Tom Lewis, accountant and treasurer, Diane Pugen, artist, and Miles O'Reilly, lawyer. The need for a fundraising chairman was discussed.

"Grant funds are coming in," I reported, "But to reach the corporate sector, our fundraising consultant tells me we need someone with some clout on Bay Street to work with Bud McMorran, who's lending his name to the campaign."

"I think I know someone," volunteered Tom Lewis. "A fellow named Walter Keyser, president of Heitman Associates Canada. I'm his accountant. He knows everyone on Bay Street, has a terrific reputation for integrity – and he's interested in the arts. A great guy." The board asked Tom to approach him.

Walter appeared at the next meeting to determine if there was a fit. He was maybe forty, and very good looking. Dressed in a well-cut dark suit, he was of medium build with dark hair, hazel eyes, a straight aquiline nose and a strong jaw. A wonderful smile. He was well-spoken and interested in what the Centre was all about. The questions we put to him, he answered with sincerity and clarity.

"I'd be happy to take on the job of fundraising chairman if you think I can help you and your group," he said with a smile. "I'm intrigued at the prospect of helping to make something like this happen. The first of its kind, I believe. And long overdue." When he withdrew from the meeting, the board voted him in unanimously.

There was a great deal to do. With a jigsaw, a sheet of plywood, a string of white Christmas lights and a can of green paint, I built a five-foot hinged dollar sign with small round holes numbered from zero to $400,000, our campaign target. Light bulbs would be screwed through the holes into the string of lights from the bottom up as our campaign progressed. At the next meeting of the fundraising committee, of which I was an ex officio member, Walter suggested the boardroom in his offices at the Toronto-Dominion Centre would be a better location for future meetings. "It's a lot easier for committee members coming by public transit," he pointed out. "And a bit more impressive, perhaps, if we want to invite potential donors to meetings." My wooden dollar sign was moved and stood in the corner of his boardroom for the duration of the campaign.

We met regularly as the campaign progressed. Meetings were enjoyable; we were excited, optimistic, fully engaged. The group worked well together. Walter steered the committee adroitly, never heavy-handed, yet expecting members to take responsibility for the tasks they committed to. We all felt we were embarked on important work with people we enjoyed working with. Often we'd go for drinks after meetings in nearby bars.

———————

I realized Karel's letters and postcards were no longer coming every day. Days went by when there was no mail from him. When at last something did come, I still felt that stab of grief and a deep longing. Our life together seemed far away, yet the pain would return, bitter and raw. I felt helpless and in limbo.

Then one day a card from Karel appeared in my mailbox. I snatched it up eagerly. It was his familiar handwriting. But it no longer said "*Čekám*" at the bottom. Before I could read the contents, I noticed the stamp. A French stamp. I felt myself grow cold as I scanned his short message. "My darling, I have looked for you and waited for you everywhere I wrote you I would be. You didn't come. Tomorrow I go back to Prague. Karel." It was postmarked Paris, ten days before.

I sank down on my sofa, staring at the card. He'd been in Paris and I hadn't known. He had succeeded in doing what we'd planned to do as we lay together that last night at U Fazole. He'd got out of the country on some pretext, an exhibition, perhaps, and made his way to Paris, so we could meet and he could come back to Canada with me.

I jumped up, pacing back and forth. How could I not have known? Karel had been in Paris looking for me. My mind cast around furiously. Could I have missed his letter informing me of his plans? Not seen it, mislaid it among a pile of bills? *Forgotten* it?

Or could it have been intercepted? I knew mail was censored. Sometimes my mother received letters that had phrases and whole sentences blacked out. Could they have intercepted and stopped letters between Karel and me? Yet I'd been receiving his all along, so maybe that wasn't it.

There must be something I could do! I stalked from room to room, racking my brains. My mother had been turned down; I would be too. Could I write and ask him to try again? They wouldn't let him out twice. He must have fought long and hard to get an exit visa.

It was too late. Only eight months after I'd been forced out of Prague, Karel had come looking for me. And now he was back in that prison of a country. The enormity of my loss overwhelmed me, and I cried and cried. We will try again, I vowed, once I get my divorce. I'd never be allowed back. But if he got out once, he could try again. Maybe next year.

Days later I found the will to write to him, telling him how devastated I was that we'd missed our chance and letting him know I hadn't received his letter about meeting in Paris. Otherwise I would have been there. He didn't answer. For many weeks, there was nothing from him.

———————

My father became very ill. He developed a blood clot in his left calf and despite blood thinners and surgery to clear the blockage, gangrene set in and he had to endure the nightmare of having his leg amputated. A prosthesis was made and he learned to walk again. His ordeal horrified me, but I ached with love and admiration for him. A year later, another clot formed in his right leg; it too developed gangrene and it too was amputated. Diabetes was diagnosed. He was seventy-eight years old. Again, that courageous and valiant man learned to walk, now on two prostheses. He walked with canes, but he walked, and returned to work, going to his office every day, president of the three companies he had founded.

By a tragic coincidence, my husband John was back in Toronto. His older brother, Herbert, had died, choking on food as he sat at dinner with his family. John came back from England for the funeral and stayed. He called to let me know. We met, and though it was clear our marriage was over, I turned to him for comfort. When I told him about what my father was going through, John comforted me, "He'll pull through," he said "He's a tough old bastard." I was desperate enough to try to lure John into my bed. He turned me down, pulling his arms free of me as I tried to coax him into my house on Laurier. Loneliness and such profound loss made me starved and reckless. I had a few affairs with unavailable men, either married or from out of town, and experimented with relationships with my lesbian friends. I considered this progress. My heart was numb, but I was hungry for the comfort of a warm body.

———————

One day my father complained of pain in his abdomen; his doctor diagnosed gall stones and scheduled surgery. They discovered he was riddled with cancer, the cause of everything he had endured. He never came out of the hospital. He drifted in and out of consciousness, sometimes aware of us, sometimes in another world, in his past, speaking Czech or sometimes German, the languages of his childhood, when Bohemia was part of the Austro-Hungarian Empire and his father an official in the Emperor's court.

I sat by his bedside holding his hand. I told him about my love of Prague, how much I missed it. I told him how proud I was of everything he had accomplished in his life, everything he had given and made possible for me. I told him about the Centre, and how it was progressing. I didn't know how much of what I said he heard, but when we were alone, I told him everything that weighed on my heart.

One day, close to the end, my mother came to visit him while I sat by his bedside. Her reserve and the pain his betrayal had caused her so many years before kept her at a distance that had become a habit. How was she to bridge it now? She greeted me and went to stand by the window, her face registering the deepest grief. My father, restless, was muttering unintelligible words in German. "Why don't you come and sit here and hold his hand?" I said to her, getting up from the chair by his bedside. She sat down, tentatively took his hand, and burst into sobs, bowing her head, her tears falling on their hands, now entwined.

Early one evening, I was at home when my sister Irene called to say my father was asking for me. I flew to him. He was having one of his lucid moments. We were all there. I held his hand. He turned to us and said, "I had to get sick to learn that you loved me."

I cried, "We have always loved you! You had to get sick before you allowed us to love you!" His eyes crinkled and his lips formed a ghost of a smile. He died in the dark hours of that morning.

———

I opened my mailbox one day and finally, there it was, that familiar pale blue airmail envelope with a bright Czech stamp on it. I held it to my heart, the joy and relief washing over me. I turned it over. Yes, there on the back was the name Zavadil. But something made me uneasy. Something was wrong. The handwriting on the return address.

I tore it open. Black ink. Only two short sentences. No words of endearment. My eyes flew to the signature. Not Karel's.

"Dear Miss Notzl," it read. "I wish to inform you that Karel is now married. We would appreciate it if you would conduct yourself accordingly." It was signed Karel Zavadil, Sr. Again I stood at my mailbox, reeling from what I'd read. My world caved in again.

I told myself it couldn't be true. His father was lying to me to get me to give Karel up. But if it *was* true – how could he have married another woman? Over and over he had written words of love and yearning, begging to hear from me. I had written to him every few weeks, as it was difficult for me. We were waiting for the year to elapse. Could our love have died over something as insignificant as my not writing as often as he'd hoped?

This time there was something I could do. An acquaintance of my mother's was going to Prague and agreed to take a letter to him. I poured all my bewilderment, grief and loss into a long letter which I wrote and rewrote, wanting to get the Czech right, asking if what his father had written was true.

It wasn't long before I received Karel's reply, which had been mailed by a friend who was going to Yugoslavia. His bewilderment was as great as my own. He hadn't heard from me since I'd left. I didn't understand – I'd been writing, though not as often. He must be exaggerating. But he'd come to the conclusion, he wrote, that I didn't love or want him anymore, that I had forgotten him and found someone else. Eventually he'd met another woman and she'd become pregnant. "I couldn't bear the thought of a child of mine," his letter read, "growing under her heart being destroyed or growing up without me. So yes, it's true. I married her." He had no idea that it would cause me such pain. He thought I had abandoned him.

Days of numbness followed. I went about my life, working, meeting friends, seeing my family, but part of me was simply not there.

Weeks later, finally, everything changed. I was downtown after a meeting with a potential donor. I was walking along Adelaide Street when suddenly I stopped and looked around. Something was different. I stared intently at the people strolling or hurrying past me. They were vivid. I could see their faces and their bodies in motion clearly, their clothes, the way they walked. I stopped, startled, and looked up. The sky was a deep and brilliant blue. The clouds that drifted slowly along were a bright white and had a depth that amazed me. Most astonishing was how sharply the tall buildings were outlined against the sky, like knife edges, solid, real and clear. A simple thought leapt into my mind: I am here.

I continued walking slowly, my heart light, inhaling the air around me in slow, deep breaths. Karel was lost to me. Maybe the siren call of Prague was over at last. Maybe I can be free to live this life. Maybe this could be enough. Not just enough, but good.

Chapter 18

SEVERAL MEMBERS SUGGESTED WE INVITE WALTER KEYSER to join our board, convinced he'd be an important asset. I called him at his office and asked him to meet me. We met at the wine cellar at Graf Bobby on Front Street. I put my question to him.

"I'd be honoured to join your board," he said, smiling broadly. "Thank you for inviting me."

We sipped our wine.

"So how did you come to head up this project?" he asked. "Tell me about yourself."

I told him about Prague, growing up in Canada, Spain, about John from whom I was separated, about living in Prague the last two years, about the group of dissidents I was lucky to have spent time with there. "I figured women artists and writers could use the same kind of support, making their work more accessible."

He nodded thoughtfully. "And your husband? What happened to him?"

"He's here in Toronto now, but it's over between us." I told him about having to wait for a year before being able to divorce. "There was someone in Prague ... but that had to end." He didn't inquire further. "Now tell me about yourself."

He told me he grew up an only child in London, Ontario, his father's background German, his mother's family British. He moved around as a child, as his father, an employee of the Bell Telephone Company, was transferred often. Difficult, he said, having to make new friends every few years. Money was scarce and he'd joined the army to put himself through university. Got his degree in business administration at the Ivey School of Business at Western. Was recruited to the Bank of Canada in Ottawa by Jim Coyne right after university, getting him out of four years' compulsory army service in Germany, which would have been in exchange for his university education.

He looked down at his wine, then up at me. "Then I made the biggest mistake of my life. I got married. Way too young. I was twenty-one. A father at twenty-two. And again two years later."

"Mistake?" I said.

"Tied down way too young. I had no adventures like you're describing." He was silent. "It's not a happy marriage. I spend a lot of my time away on business. On purpose. Happy to be away."

I nodded in sympathy, surprised at his telling me all this, my heart going out to him.

"How old are your children?"

"Two daughters, twenty and eighteen. The older one lives with an abusive boyfriend. One day I had to go and threaten to have his knees shot out from under him if he ever touched her again. The younger one took off to Vancouver with a boyfriend. I think he may be a drug dealer. I have no way of reaching her."

I stared at him. That he who was so sophisticated, so refined, could have such a family. And then I couldn't help it, I started laughing. Soon we were both laughing until tears rolled down our cheeks. At his story and mine, and the absurdity of life, at the gulf between us that was being bridged as we talked.

"I'd better be going," I said when we'd caught our breath.

"Can I take you out to dinner sometime?" he said.

I stopped. "What about your wife?"

"She's at our cottage in Grand Bend for the summer. I go the odd weekend."

It was time to leave. He walked me to my car and we agreed to have dinner together the following Saturday.

"Can I pick you up?" he asked. I lived in a basement apartment with my black dog Laurie, a gift from my two brothers at Christmas to help me heal from the loss of Lawrence in Spain. I loved my apartment on Parkside Drive, directly across from High Park and lush with plants lit by plant lights in the high windows. But it was a basement and my bed was a foam slab on the floor. I wasn't about to let him see it. I knew he lived in Forest Hill, one of the wealthiest residential areas of Toronto. The contrast was too great.

"No, I'll be downtown already. Where shall I meet you?"

"How about Hazelton Lanes?" he asked. He walked me to the mustard-coloured MG Midget convertible I'd found in a used-car lot. We shook hands and I took off for home.

———

I agonized over what to wear to our dinner, tearing through my closet for just the right thing. I didn't wear dresses much. Suits, yes, I needed those for important meetings, but not for a dinner date. I tried one thing, then another, the rejects piling up on the floor of my bedroom. Laurie sat up on my bed watching intently. I finally chose black slacks, a white silk shirt and a tweed jacket, raced to Hazelton Avenue, and strolled to our meeting place. When Walter caught sight of me, his face broke into a wide grin. He took my arm as we walked to the restaurant.

He was confident and self-assured as he spoke to the maître d', at home in fine restaurants, like my father had been; the life I'd been raised with. Dinners at the King Edward hotel, the maître d' bowing, "Good to see you again, Mr. Notzl, your usual table is ready." The waiters greeting every request with a bow and a "Certainly, Mr. Notzl, right away." The irony struck me, sitting once again in a fine restaurant with a man who knew his way around. This was familiar territory. Yet new. This time it was my life.

Over dinner we told each other more of our stories. He was an avid listener, his face full of interest, warmth, generosity. I told him about my life in Spain, my life in Prague. About the shock of being thrown out of the country. I told him about my father's death.

"I'm so sorry. I knew about that, actually," he said. "I called to speak to you one day and you were at your father's funeral."

"I regret you won't get to meet him," I said. "You're very like him."

"I guess I'm a younger version," he laughed. "I'm only 40!"

"I'm 32," I told him. "And here I am starting all over again."

"And doing an amazing job of it."

"Thanks. What do you do other than work?"

"I collect ancient maps," he said. "My specialty is maps of the exploration of the Pacific northwest. I've been collecting them for some years. I travel to New York quite often, where some of the best map dealers are, so I have an extensive collection."

"I love travelling," I said. "More than anything. Do you travel a lot?"

He nodded. "On business. Too much."

"Really? You don't like it?"

"I don't like travelling alone. Eating dinner alone, staying in hotel rooms alone. No, I don't like it."

"I love travelling alone. I love the feeling of moving through the world, finding my way, exploring and discovering. You experience everything more directly, I find, when you're alone."

There was a pause as we contemplated one another.

"So what made you decide to get involved in the Centre?" I asked.

"I'm interested in the arts, as a supporter, that is. I'm on the board of the School of Fine Arts here in Toronto, along with Tom Lewis. He's been my accountant and good friend, and when he told me what your group is doing, I was intrigued. I like spending time with people interested in the arts. I'd be too much of a workaholic otherwise."

A picture of Karel and his group sitting around their table at U Bonaparta flashed through my mind, those Bohemians with their beer and cigarettes, their rage, their wild humour, their outrageous happenings, Jarda's soup-destroyed flat – and wondered how Walter would enjoy spending time with that group of people "interested in the arts." For a moment I missed Karel and that life terribly.

"And to tell you the absolute truth, it was because of you. You fascinated me. I wanted to get to know you." He grinned. "The fact that you started this organization and built it to where it is today – such determination. I admire that immensely." He paused. "Not to mention you being smart, savvy – and beautiful. How could I not want to get involved when there's such a woman heading it up?"

His words washed over me. I felt my face flush.

Later, when we were getting ready to leave, he leaned forward and asked, "Would you come back to my place for a nightcap?"

"What about your wife?"

"She's still at the cottage. Please? I don't want this evening to end."

I deliberated only briefly, then nodded.

I followed his black Cadillac up Avenue Road and west to Russell Hill Road. He pulled into the driveway of a large brick and stone house and led me into an elegant living room.

———

We sat in the rich leather armchairs. I examined the paintings on the walls. "You have a beautiful home," I said.

"Thanks," he said. "But unhappy. We have not been happy together for a long time. Yes, it is a nice house."

His sorrow was palpable. I was captivated and admired him tremendously. I would let him lead the way, let him take me as far as he was willing to go. A summer fling, perhaps, with his wife away. Snatching what happiness we could find to ease the pain of broken relationships.

We ended up kneeling on the carpet, poring over the maps I'd invited him to show me, large maps he'd had to spread out on the floor so we could examine the details he described. Suddenly we stopped talking, turned to one another and kissed, like two starving people. He took my hand and led me upstairs.

Very early the next morning I kissed him goodbye, ran down his front steps, jumped into my MG Midget, and headed home down the wide, leafy street just as dawn was breaking, full of joy.

We embarked on a summer affair. We spent an ecstatic two months together, keeping it a secret from our colleagues, dining out together almost every evening, and spending a glorious weekend in New York, where we stayed at one of the finest hotels, danced at Regine's and drank cocktails at the Sherry Netherland.

When his wife came back from the cottage in September, Walter disappeared. He stopped calling me and would not take my calls. I was shocked, and discovered that it mattered very much. I realized I'd been hoping it would be much more than a summer affair. We saw each other on Centre business, attended meetings together but parted when they were over. He treated me politely but was cool towards me. When I looked at him directly, he avoided my gaze.

Marie DunSeith, our fundraising consultant, invited us both to her New Year's Eve party. Walter was there with his wife. I came with a man I'd begun to date, a forensic photographer. Walter's wife seemed a sour, unpleasant woman, critical and demanding, issuing orders. Walter deferred to her. I hated her, hated his putting up with it.

Months later, he called one evening and asked if I would meet him at Graf Bobby again. This time I was there first. When he came down the steps, I watched him walk toward me, regret in his expression, and sorrow. What I felt was anger. We waited in silence for our wine to arrive.

"I'm sorry, Helen," he said. "I couldn't leave her just like that. I had to see if we could make it work. I owed her one last try."

"And?" I said.

"I've discovered ours was much more than a summer affair for me." I was silent. "I've decided I'm going to leave my wife, but I want to do it right. I need more time. I want to ask if you'll wait for me."

I sipped my wine. I wanted very much to believe him.

"Please," he went on. "Would you wait for me?"

"Do it and find out," I snapped. And then I softened. "I would, if you're sure."

"I'm more sure than I've been about anything in my entire life."

As I was getting into my car, he reached out and touched my arm. "I'm very sorry to have hurt you. Nobody said it would be easy."

It took him another month, but he left. He left her for me. Many times over the coming years he told me I had saved his life. His daughter Lynda and I went out for lunch one day after Walter and I had been together several months. I worried that she blamed me for breaking up her family. Instead she thanked me. "I've never seen my father so happy," she said. "He's been so tense the last few years that he's been carrying around a bottle of Maalox, gulping it down straight from the bottle to try and cope with the stress."

I introduced him to my family, inviting him up to Chinook. They raised their eyebrows at my bringing home such a man. My mother was enthralled with him, envied me, flirted with him a little.

For a while Walter and I lived together in my basement apartment, his Cadillac parked out front. Laurie resented him at first, nipping his toes as we lay together on my foam-slab bed. They came to love one another. His first dog.

One day during that first summer together, we were driving home from Chinook, where we now spent most weekends. Looking out at the houses we passed, their windows glowing in the dark, I said, "How I envy those lucky people who live in the country and don't have to drive back to the city at the end of a weekend."

"I have an employee who's relocated to Edmonton, and his house in Caledon, just northwest of Toronto, is for sale," Walter said. "Would you like to go and look at it one day?"

We went a few days later. It was a fine house on ten acres of wooded, rolling land.

"Like it?" Walter asked.

I was too overwhelmed to answer. Could this be my life? From a Bohemian living in borrowed rooms in Prague to a chatelaine in the Canadian countryside?

We discovered a charming restaurant nearby called the Teddy Bear's Picnic where we went for dinner. "Before we head home, let's go look at the house again," I said.

We stood in the darkness side by side under a maple tree behind the house, the lawn sloping gently toward a pine wood. Wordlessly I took Walter's hand, marvelling at the life opening up before me, and wept.

"Yes," I managed to say. "Yes."

We rented the house, moved in, and a year later, we bought it.

———

The Pauline McGibbon Cultural Centre opened in September of 1979 to great fanfare, a weekend of celebration. The Honourable Pauline McGibbon cut the ribbon on Friday morning. Saturday evening we celebrated the opening of the DuMaurier Theatre on the second floor, thanks to a $50,000 donation, the opening concert attended by Pauline McGibbon, Ontario Premier Bill Davis, Toronto Mayor David Crombie, and other dignitaries. My mother sat in the front row, her eyes shining with pride. Walter sat beside her.

The art gallery, the library and the restaurant, called *Polly's*, all had separate and well-attended openings that weekend. The culmination of four years of hard work by a dedicated group of women and men – staff, volunteers and supporters.

———————

Walter asked his wife for a divorce; she refused. I did nothing about my divorce. I didn't care about marrying. I kept my apartment in Toronto, and called it keeping my back door open, just in case.

Walter came to love travelling, and so we travelled. That first winter in our Caledon house, we went to Martinique, a French island in the Caribbean where neither of us had been before. We fell in love with it. One night I woke up in our bungalow on the beach at Diamant Les Bains, a sultry, fragrant wind blowing off the ocean through the window at the head of our bed. Suddenly feeling a tremendous sense of urgency, I shook Walter awake and told him I wanted to have a baby. I, who had thought marriage and motherhood were not for me. But now I loved this man and I wanted a child.

On April 6, 1981, when I was thirty-six, our son was born. We named him Adam, a name I had loved for years. The first man. A miraculous, beautiful baby who only moments after his birth looked at me with alert and knowing eyes, and we greeted one another. He had my father's deep brown eyes. My life opened up like a flower, rich and heady.

Walter's wife saw the birth notice and sued for divorce, using the notice as her grounds. I contacted John, and got a divorce as well. Simple, amicable. On October 30, 1982, Walter and I were married at the Belfountain Church near our home. His older daughter was one of my bridesmaids, as was my dear friend Joanne Ruderfer. I wore a dove grey flowing organdy dress and a hairpiece I'd had made, with pink and white flowers and a small dove grey veil. My mother looked beautiful in her silk shantung suit and orchid corsage. Adam, a year and a half old, sat on his nanny's knee in the front row, and as my friend Ruth Morawetz at the organ played The Wedding March, and I began to walk down the aisle, Adam saw me and joyfully cried out "Mommy!" We celebrated with family and friends back at our home.

———

It was 1986, twelve years since I'd been thrown out of Prague. Walter and I had been married four years. Adam was five.

"Let's go to Europe this year," I said.

"I'd love that," said Walter.

"And just on the off-chance, I'll apply for a visa to Czechoslovakia," I said. My mother had tried several times and been refused.

"We'll do a grand tour," Walter said. "Fly to Paris, rent a car, drive south to Provence, across into Italy, up into Austria ..."

"And to Prague, if we can," I added.

I applied, and to my joy a visa was granted for the three of us. Perhaps I was no longer a threat, now that I was married.

Chapter 19

THE GRAND TOUR OF EUROPE WAS MARVELLOUS, THE THREE of us on our great adventure, where I could share the world I loved with Walter and Adam, who at five, was a joy to travel with. We became boulevardiers sitting at sidewalk cafés on the Left Bank; we were parents enjoying a Sunday in the Jardins du Luxembourg, pushing our son on a swing. We drove the winding lanes through the vineyards of Burgundy and tasted the best French wines. We ate bouillabaisse in Marseille, went to outdoor concerts in Salzburg, and I took them to my father's beloved Grüner Baum in Bad Gastein, where we spent a few days wandering in the high Alps.

It was all wonderful – but I was frantic to get to Prague. Finally, I was travelling again on that road through Austria towards the Czech border as I had all those years ago, this time in a luxurious red Citroën instead of on a second-hand scooter. I was fearful of Walter's reaction. Would I be ashamed of my country?

I was. Leaving the elegance and graciousness of Vienna and Salzburg, we arrived at the same chilling barbed-wire barrier I'd sat in front of twelve years before. "Oh my God," Walter said. Adam stared wide-eyed at the grim, heavily armed soldiers who approached us, demanded our papers and ordered us out of the car. Walter held Adam in his arms as the soldiers searched our car inside and out.

Released, we drove through the countryside, with me at the wheel. This was my return. Walter and Adam stared out at the sad fields, the unloved villages.

"Wait until you see Prague," I said. "It's been allowed to deteriorate, but it's magnificent all the same." I described the castle, the river, the gas lit lanes of the Little Quarter, and my heart beat faster.

Once in Prague I found my way to Wenceslas Square and pulled our Citroën up to the Ambassador Hotel. How wondrous strange to be back, driving a big car, about to stay in what had once been a grand hotel. During my two years there, I'd never entered it.

There were few other cars. Two doormen appeared and with a great deal of bowing and scraping, removed our luggage and whisked it inside. A crowd gathered to stare at us and our car, walking around to view it from all angles. The doormen returned, shooed the bystanders away and assured us we could leave the car there, they'd see no one touched it.

The hotel had a tired elegance, with red carpets that were once plush, faded brocade drapes and velvet upholstery. We were given a suite on one of the upper floors, with a balcony overlooking the great square. We stood surveying the scene below, the broad avenue that curved upward toward the museum, fronted by St. Wenceslas on his horse.

"I want you to meet Uncle Paul and Růža and my brother Malý Pavel and his family," I said. "I'll call them tomorrow. Let's just be us today."

I couldn't wait to get outside. I led them to the top of the square, where Adam gazed in wonder at the massive horse and rider, and then we walked all the way back down. Hungrily I drank in the sound of the Czech language all around me, wanting to shout, "It's me! I'm back!" We walked through the winding streets to Old Town Square, where on the hour we watched the ancient astronomical clock with its disciples appearing, the cock crowing as they disappeared. We walked across Charles Bridge, looking at the swans on the river, the castle above, and then to Malá Strana, and Kampa. I was like a wild thing, needing to hurry, anxious to revisit every familiar place.

I realized I was looking for Karel. He haunted me. I searched the faces of men who passed us on the streets. What would I do if I saw him? Would I even recognize him after twelve years? Would he recognize me? Everywhere we went, I was flooded with memories. On Charles Bridge, I remembered the roller skating race. Looking out over the river, I recalled the steamboat party. On Kampa Island, I pointed across the Čertovka to the two windows that had been my room on Nosticova, and saw Karel standing dripping wet at my window. He was everywhere.

Walter knew about Karel, of course. I'd told him about having had a relationship with a dissident artist, being invited into his group, and how the relationship had ended when I was thrown out of the country.

"I'd love to see Karel and my other friends from back then," I'd said, hoping he didn't sense my urgency.

I took us up Nerudova Street, that steep street that climbed toward the castle, and once again, like on that Wednesday so many years ago, I stood outside U Bonaparta pub trying to work up the courage to enter. I so much wanted to see him, but I was afraid. He had married another woman. Would it be painful to see one another, or excruciatingly awkward? Most of all, I was worried about how I would behave, not wanting to hurt my husband. Would I discover I still loved Karel, and have to bear the pain that I couldn't have him? Or what if I found I *could* have him? I didn't know which I feared more.

"I'll be back," I said to Walter and Adam, and pushed open the door. A burst of noise, of voices and laughter. It looked just the same, dark wooden tables, a vaulted ceiling. The pub was full, every table occupied. A quick sweep of the crowd didn't turn up any familiar faces. I walked up and down among the tables, searching, being stared at by strangers. Longing to be recognized, to hear that familiar voice call out *"Helenko!"* I went last, my knees unsteady, to the front and looked around the partition to what had been the Spolek Pohodlí table. It was occupied by a German-speaking group. I left, both relieved and bitterly disappointed, and rejoined Walter and Adam. We continued into the castle gardens.

Walter adored the city and was awed by the beauty of the architecture, the wide, tree-lined avenues of Old Town, the charming lanes of Malá Strana. He was shocked by the rudeness of people, of clerks in stores, of waiters in pubs and restaurants, even in the hotel dining room where we had breakfast every day. The terrible service, their delight in saying no, their ignoring our signals when we needed service.

The next morning, I called Uncle Paul to announce our arrival.

"Helen is finally in Prague!" I heard him call to Růža. "Come to dinner! Tonight!" he urged me.

The reunion was joyful, tearful. My uncle opened the door, reached for my hand and held it tight, skewering me once again with that chilling look, then drew me in, his thin arms holding me hard. He drew a handkerchief from his pocket and wiped his eyes. Růža, crying too, hugged each of us in turn, Walter a little tentatively, but when she felt her embrace returned, laughed through her tears and hugged him harder. Adam she hugged and kissed on both cheeks, and when he laughed shyly, she did it a second time. They ushered us through that dark hall and into the anteroom where I'd spent so many evenings long ago. Uncle Paul, looking frailer, sank into the faded red armchair by the coal stove where my grandfather used to sit. His back was stooped and his face, hollow now, was a mixture of grief and joy.

They loved Walter and doted on Adam. Adam was afraid of Uncle Paul, his shock of white hair, those pale, staring eyes, his gnarled hands. Růža, flustered, couldn't do enough. She sat beside me, stroking my hand. She offered cookies and candies to Adam, who took one of everything she offered. She ruffled his hair, offered more. She took him by the hand, opened a door that led to the next room, a large salon, and showed him the huge tiger skin rug on the floor. Adam, frightened at first of the fierce head, the mouth wide open revealing sharp fangs, overcame his fear and lay on the skin, his head on its head, his arms outstretched on top of its front legs.

My uncle raised an arm to get my attention. "Your friend Mr. Zavadil called after you left. To return our rugs," he said.

"Yes," I said. "I asked him to do that for me that last day."

"We had to learn what happened from a stranger," my uncle continued. "You didn't come to say goodbye."

"It happened so fast," I cried. "Imagine everything I had to do to end two years of living here. I'm sorry. I was a mess."

"We were interrogated at the police station as well. They told us nothing. If only you had come and told us yourself."

I crouched by his chair, taking his hand. "They refused to tell me what I was charged with. Only that I had to be gone by noon. I still don't know." We were both crying.

But now I had a fine, handsome husband and a beautiful young son and we were together at last: a reunion, a new family. Once the grief and loss had been spoken, joy broke through and we celebrated.

The next day I phoned Malý Pavel. Our reunion took place at the sidewalk café in Old Town Square, in front of the astronomical clock. Again I was struck by how much he resembled my father; it was as though my father had been returned to me. We leaned towards one another, talking, as the years melted away. Walter and Adam joined us later, having given us this time to catch up. I'd always regretted that my father had never met Walter and never known of Adam. Here was an opportunity for Walter to get a sense of what my father had been like. They liked one another instantly. Thanks to Malý Pavel speaking some English, they could carry on a basic conversation.

Malý Pavel invited us to their cottage in Lázně Libverda in the mountains of northern Bohemia, close to the Polish border. Helena, Malý Pavel's wife, showered us with hospitality and love. Their daughter, young Helena and I hit it off as never before. We were more like contemporaries now, she in her thirties and I forty-two. Her daughter Markéta was seven, a lovely, free-spirited girl who immediately adopted Adam as her cousin and best friend. Free and uninhibited, she ran about the cottage yard without a stitch of clothing on. They collected snails and swung in the hammock, the snails leaving shiny trails on their arms, their faces.

"Let's invite them all to visit us in Canada," I said to Walter during the weekend.

"Would they be allowed?" he said.

"Worth a try, no?"

"Definitely."

When I proposed it, Malý Pavel looked dubious.

"We'll issue a formal invitation guaranteeing to pay all expenses. You'd stay with us, of course."

"I suppose we could try," Malý Pavel said

"Imagine us seeing Canada!" Helena Sr. said, her eyes brimming.

We saw Malý Pavel and his family several more times, dining at their home on Letná and hosting them at dinner. Uncle Paul and Růža too invited us to their home for several more dinners and allowed us to take them out.

"Thank you, my darling," Walter said as we drove back to the hotel after an evening with them. "Suddenly I am blessed with a wonderful Prague family."

———

It took me close to the end of our stay before I found the courage to make the call I was longing to make. Walter and Adam were down at the hotel's sidewalk café. I called Karel's parents' number. My hand shook as I dialled the number. A man's voice answered.

"*Prosím?*"

"*Dobrý den,*" I began. Good day. "May I speak to Karel please?"

"Who is speaking?"

"It's Helen. From Canada."

"No, you may not. He's not here. He doesn't live here anymore."

"Would you please give me his new number? I am here on holiday with my husband and son and would like to speak to him." There was a long pause. I could hear a woman's voice in the background.

"*Moment.*" He put his hand to the receiver and spoke to the woman. A few seconds later she came on.

"*Dobrý den, paní.* Karel is not in Prague. He's on holidays with his family. What is more, we don't want you bothering him and causing trouble. You know he is married now and has a family. My husband wrote you to tell you that. Please leave him alone."

"Mrs. Zavadilová, I am married now too, happily, and I have a family as well. We are here together. I don't intend to cause trouble. Perhaps I could just say hello."

"No. I don't think that's a good idea."

"Please! It's just as a friend now. Everything is different.'"

"I tell you, he's at his mother-in-law's cottage with her and his family. It wouldn't be right."

I thought fast. "I understand. Then please, could you just tell me the name of the village, at least I can send him a post-card greeting."

She hesitated. "Kytlice," she finally said.

———

The next day the three of us piled into our car and headed north. I'd found the village on the map, in the mountains of northern Bohemia. Two hours later, we pulled into a small village and found the central square. I located the post office and asked the woman behind the counter if she knew where the Zavadil cottage was. She gave me directions.

I drove down a country lane beside a hillside that rose steeply to our left. Several hundred metres down the laneway, a small flat area was carved into the hillside and a footpath led up through the trees. I could see the corner of a low wooden cottage at the top. I pulled the car over and turned off the engine. "This must be it," I said, the blood pounding in my temples. We got out of the car.

What was I doing? Would Karel be angry and see my arrival as a violation? And what about Walter? Despite having agreed to this adventure, what must he be feeling? It didn't matter. I had to do it.

We started up the hill. After we'd climbed a few metres, a man came into view sitting on a bench at the top, looking out over the hillside. He saw us at the same time and sat, silently watching us. It was him.

"It's Karel," I said to Walter.

"*Ahoj!*" I called out. The universal greeting.

He stood up so suddenly that a small dog he'd been holding on his lap tumbled to the ground. He said nothing for a moment, staring at us. And then he called out, in that long familiar voice, "*Helenko! Je to možné? Jseš to Ty?*" Is it possible? Is that you?

I couldn't speak.

He stood still, silent as a statue, watching us as we climbed the rest of the way. I could hardly stand my own excitement. Please God, I prayed, don't let my feelings show.

We got to the top. He looked just as I remembered him. Older, yes, more mature. Just as handsome. Just as solid. Those same penetrating brown eyes, soft hair, ginger moustache and short beard.

We shook hands. Electric. We drank in the sight of one another. I introduced Walter and Adam and they shook hands. An older woman emerged from the cottage and Karel introduced his mother-in-law. She was flustered, but cordial. "Welcome" she said in accented English, "do sit down," indicating the rustic outdoor chairs. "Míša is at the swimming pool with the children. They will be home soon." We sat. "I will bring some refreshments," and she disappeared.

"It's nice that she speaks English," Walter commented. "It'll give me someone to talk to."

"How did you find us?" Karel asked, in Czech. I told him about the call to his parents. "They'll be angry that we came," I said. He shrugged.

Karel's mother-in-law reappeared with drinks and snacks. She held out a plate of cookies for Adam, who thanked her politely and took one.

Karel and I couldn't take our eyes off one another. Twelve years! We'd been young then, I thirty, Karel twenty-nine. Now I was forty-two and a mother, Karel a father, forty-one, with two boys I was about to meet. It felt like a lifetime since we'd parted, yet it was all still alive between us. I wanted to touch him, to make him real to me again. I was shocked at how fast my heart beat, how eagerly I watched him, listened to him. Was it the same for him?

There was so much I wanted to know. Was he happy? How could he have married? Why hadn't he waited for me, as he said he would. Čekám – he'd written it at the end of every post card, every letter. Did he love her? Was he feeling anything like what I was feeling? If he was, what were we to do about it? And was he painting? Was he successful? Had I the right to ask? How could I find out any of what I most wanted to know? It was excruciating sitting and making polite conversation, pretending it was enough.

Voices sounded from down below. "Míša and the boys are back," Karel's mother-in-law announced.

Would she be stunning? Would she despise me? I was frightened, wondering what she knew about me, if anything. Up they came. His wife circled, hiding behind some tall shrubs. I heard her whisper to Karel, "*To je ona?*" Is that her? Karel looked at me and nodded. She darted into the cottage with a quick apology – in Czech – "I'll just clean up a little, we'll be right back" – and herded the boys into the cottage. She reappeared soon, shook hands with all of us. She was a plain, humble sort of woman, tall, with straight brown hair and a gentle manner.

"We knew company had come," she said, sitting down at the table. "Everyone was talking about the strangers that drove into the village in a big, red foreign car and asked directions to our cottage. I wondered if it was you," she smiled at me bravely. Then, timidly, she asked if her boys could go down and have a look at our car.

"Yes, of course," I said. I looked at the two boys, Karel and Martin, ten and eight years old. They were handsome, but not beautiful, the way Adam was, I decided. This older boy, Karel junior, I thought, is the reason Karel and I aren't together. It was his conception that made Karel marry this woman. I'd come prepared to hate him, but how could I blame a child?

"Adam, why don't you take the boys and show them the car?" I said. Adam jumped up and led them down the hill. We could hear them calling to one another in Czech and English, managing to understand one another the way only children can do.

The tension was becoming unbearable. Karel stood up abruptly. "Let's go to the pub," he snapped. Míša was silent. Her mother looked at Karel and at me. "I'll stay here with the boys," she said, calling them back up. We shook hands, thanked her for her hospitality, and followed by Karel and Míša, made our way down the hill. We collected Adam and drove into the village, Karel directing us to the pub.

Karel took the seat at the end of the table and I sat kitty-corner to him. Míša spoke a little English, not as well as her mother, but well enough that she, Walter and Adam could carry on a conversation. Finally Karel and I had a chance to talk to one another. Our beers arrived – and the intervening years vanished. It was just as it had been twelve years before. Elbows on the table, drinking, unable to take our eyes of one another, we plunged into conversation.

"Helen, what happened?" Karel asked urgently. "Why didn't you write to me? I poured my heart out to you every single day, sending photos and long letters, telling you everything that was happening here. Telling you I was waiting. I got nothing back from you. Nothing! And finally, after I'd given up, that letter from you, out of nowhere, that stunned me. Your pain at learning I was married. That you still loved me! After almost a year of silence."

"Karel, I *did* write to you," I said, shocked. "I got your post-cards and letters, and I wrote back. I did!"

"I'm telling you, I didn't get a single thing from you in all that time. Not a thing from the day you left!"

"What are you saying? That's impossible."

273

"I thought you'd left me, forgotten me. I lived in hell, waiting, disappointed, every single day. You can't imagine how that was."

"I never forgot you," I protested. "Nothing else mattered. We were waiting. And then your letters stopped. Until that terrible day I got the letter from your father."

"That's right, my father wrote you," he said. "You told me in the letter that finally reached me. Imagine – him having the gall to contact you."

"Informing me that you were married! Telling me to leave you alone." Impatiently I brushed away the tears that were rolling down my cheeks. I darted a look at Walter, beside me. Karel and I were speaking Czech, of course, so he couldn't understand us. But I wondered how he was doing. He was working hard at carrying on a conversation with Míša, on his left, his arm around Adam, who sat between them.

"I couldn't believe it was true," I continued. "How could you have married someone else? How *could* you have? I thought he'd lied, sent the letter hoping to break us up. That maybe he was afraid you would escape and come after me. I wanted you to tell me it wasn't true. But it was. You were married. It took me a long time to get over that."

"Why didn't you come to Paris? Why didn't you answer me?"

"I didn't know you were going! I received no letter telling me so. All I got was your postcard from Paris telling me you'd looked for me everywhere and were heading back. Too late to do anything by then."

We sat looking at one another, taking in the enormity of what we were saying.

"If I wasn't writing to you," I said slowly, "why did your father send me that letter, telling me to leave you alone?"

Karel's eyes darkened. "And how did he know your address in Canada?"

I watched the light dawn in his eyes, just as I too was figuring out what this must mean. "From the return address on your letters!" he said. "So he saw them and I didn't. He intercepted them. It was my father who caused all of it." His face was white, his mouth a thin, angry line.

"I managed to get to France, just as we'd planned that last day. My father actually helped me. I doubt I'd have been given an exit visa without his intervention. But then you didn't come." He burst out, "He knew you wouldn't come! He made sure you didn't know."

"But how?" I said. "He wasn't mailing your letters for you, was he?"

"Of course not, I always mailed them at the post office. You were getting my letters up until then. But not the most important one."

"Could he have made sure it was intercepted somehow?" I asked. "We know the mail is censored even now."

Karel nodded and pulled on his cigarette. "That must be what he did. Maybe they read them all, and let the others go through. Or maybe you didn't get all of mine either."

We were silent a moment as the realization sank in.

"To think you were writing to me all that time and I didn't know it. That my father, the bastard, kept your letters from me. Watched me suffer. He saw how upset I was," Karel said. "It would have been easy for him to intercept your letters, just by him or my mother getting to our mailbox first. Or maybe they never reached my mailbox. A word from him at the post office would have done it. And all that time, I thought ..." His words faded and he looked at me, deep sorrow in his eyes.

"Now we know," I said.

I took a sip of my beer, reached for a cigarette, appalled by the lengths to which the regime would go to prevent something so simple, so human as two people in love being together. How many clerks spent countless hours steaming open envelopes to read the personal messages they held? The longings, the grief, the truth trying to be spoken, met with black felt pens or wastepaper baskets. The absurdity of it, and the cruelty, destroying lives and breaking hearts.

"Tell me what happened after I left," I said. "Did you ever learn why I was thrown out?"

"Our friend Honza, the sculptor, turned out to be an informer, for Christ's sake. The whole thing was a setup right from the beginning. Asking you to pose for him. It was an assignment from the police, to keep an eye on you and report to them. When he told you about my being forced to join the Communist party before I had a chance to tell you, that was a setup too, to get your reaction. Well, he sure got it. He repeated everything you said to the police. I suspect he taped it."

"Honza!" I exclaimed. "Oh my god." I recalled all those hours in his studio, chatting amiably. The outrage with which I'd reacted to his news, unsuspecting, assuming Honza was one of us. Karel snorted. "He was informing on all of us. We threw him out when we found out. He was paid two thousand crowns for every piece of information."

"They probably had their eye on me the whole time," I said, thinking of the stranger in the café sending me that poem he'd scribbled on a scrap of paper.

"It wasn't just Honza – your old friend Mirek was an informer too," Karel said. "After you'd gone, a friend of mine told me he'd been sitting in a pub with a group of friends,

Mirek among them, shortly after you'd moved out of his room on Nosticova. He was talking about you and my friend overheard him say, 'Helen's not going to be here much longer.'"

Mirek, paying me back for not wanting to have anything more to do with him. So that's where the charge of being a parasite, living off others had come from. Mirek's revenge. I suddenly wondered what he'd had to do to get that room I had loved so much. Could requesting that room have been what turned him into an informer? Or maybe he'd been an informer already, the reason he befriended me in the first place. I reeled as the ground under everything trembled and realigned itself.

Every now and again, I turned to check in on Walter and the others. "You okay?" I asked him. He nodded, shrugged. He was doing a valiant job keeping things going with Míša. Adam was happily drinking apple juice and telling Walter about his new friends, Karel and Martin.

I marvelled at Walter, and was perplexed by him. How could he have been so accommodating to my wanting to find Karel and coming all this way to find him? Did he have any idea? Here I was, my heart pounding, the years vanishing as Karel and I sat talking as though there was no one and nothing else in the world but the two of us. Walter was a man of great kindness and generosity. But was this willful blindness? Or was it unconditional love and trust and incredible generosity on his part?

"It's been hideous here since you left," Karel went on. "One terrible thing after another." Shortly after I'd left, he told me, he'd been attacked by a couple of thugs, who'd beaten him up and left him unconscious in the street. He suspected they were connected to the police. "But now you are here, and we're sitting in a pub together again. I never thought I'd see you again. Enough of my bad news. Tell me about you."

How could anything I said breach our two worlds? I told him I lived in the country outside Toronto. I tried telling him about the cultural centre I'd founded and run. How could he make any sense of my life in Canada? Maybe all he too wanted to know was, Was I happy? Did I still love him? Did I love Walter? What did I feel when I thought back on that year we'd spent together so long ago? I couldn't tell him any of that.

Míša's voice broke through. "It isn't very polite of you two to be talking so much and ignoring the rest of us," she said, in Czech. Karel dismissed her with a look and took a long drink of his beer.

"Míša, we have so much to catch up on. I've been anxious to know what happened!" I said. But I sat back, knowing she was right and that I was neglecting Walter. I didn't want to hurt him. No matter what happened, I didn't want to hurt him.

And then it was time to go. We had the drive back to Prague ahead of us, and Karel and Míša were due back for dinner. Quickly, Karel pulled a notebook out of his pocket, wrote down his address and phone number, tore out the sheet and handed it to me. He pushed the notebook towards me, and I wrote down mine.

We stood on the sidewalk, awkward, saying all those things people say when parting. Shaking hands. Smiling. I tried to memorize Karel's face, tried hard not to cry, to swallow the lump in my throat. I couldn't help it – I had to touch him. Very quickly, like it was nothing, when he extended his hand, I put my arms around him and held him. Oh my god, he felt good. But just for a second.

And then I stepped back and walked to the car. Walter and Adam got in, and as I drove off, I caught glimpses of Karel and his wife in my rear-view mirror. Standing apart, they watched us until we rounded the corner.

₰₰₰ Chapter 20

IT WAS 1989 AND EUROPE WAS ABLAZE WITH CHANGE AND hope. The revolution that many behind the Iron Curtain despaired would never come finally happened. Lech Walensa in Poland, Mikhail Gorbachev in the Soviet Union and Václav Havel in Czechoslovakia. I sat glued to the television day after day as events unfolded. Havel, the dishevelled dissident playwright who had spent years in prison, now led the movement in Czechoslovakia. I watched news footage of the streets of Prague jammed with students, and then thousands upon thousands of people lining the streets, filling Wenceslas Square. The crowds stayed despite violent confrontations. The future hung in the balance. And then it was over. Václav Havel, with whom I had sat drinking beer at U Tygra with Karel and Zlatá Praha, who had spent years in jail as a dissident, led the movement that finally toppled the communist regime and became president of the newly liberated country.

There was wild rejoicing throughout the Czech community in Canada. I was sad for my father, who hadn't lived to see this day. Forty years of terror and oppression were lifted and a nation released. And a poet and playwright in charge. Glorious!

Excited as I was about the events unfolding in Europe, Walter and I were busy with our lives in Canada. I'd left my role as president of the Pauline McGibbon Cultural Centre shortly after Adam was born in 1981. I wanted to go back to university, so I earned a post-graduate clinical Master of Social Work degree, worked as a therapist at a number of agencies and developed a private practice. We renovated the small barn on our property, hired a young woman with an Early Childhood Education degree and established a day care centre, a marvellous solution for an only child living in the country. We called it *Goslings*. I loved the Canada geese that soared overhead twice a year, heading south or returning, their wild, haunting cries moving me to tears. The first time it happened, I was shocked at my reaction. I stood stock still and watched them, silently crying, Wait! Wait for me! Despite my busy life, the old longing lurked just below the surface.

Our centre launched human goslings into the world. Starting with just one other neighbour's child, we ended up with four more staff and twenty children over the next five years. Their parents became our friends, an added bonus.

Later we realized we'd missed an enormous opportunity not paying closer attention to what was happening in Czechoslovakia. Suddenly, real estate was available in Prague. I found it curious – and infuriating, when I learned of it – that where there had been such a shortage of flats that families were forcibly moved in with strangers and space allocated by the metre, now there was an abundance of property available. A mystery! Entire apartment buildings came on the market at extraordinary prices. We could have bought a five-story Renaissance building on the river for $100,000. Busy as we were, it only occurred to us when the opportunity was past.

Uncle Paul had died in 1985. My mother succeeded in getting a visa to attend his funeral. For him, the revolution came too late.

For Helena Sr. too. Malý Pavel had finally accepted our invitation for him and his family to visit us in Canada. He, his daughter Helena and young Markéta came and spent three weeks with us the summer of '88, but without Helena Sr., who died suddenly of a heart attack earlier that year. Adam and Markéta, now seven and ten, became great friends, playing together in our pond; Helena and I went off to Toronto and hung out at the Bamboo Pub on Queen Street, and Malý Pavel spent most days working in our pine woods, sawing and clipping their lower branches, critical of the neglect Canadians tolerated in their forests. We were thankful later to have them cleared, and dubbed them Malý Pavel's woods.

Cirque du Soleil was in town, their first appearance in Ontario, and we took our Czech family. I was enthralled. During the intermission, I couldn't wait to hear Malý Pavel's reaction. "They're not bad," he scoffed. "But the Moscow Circus – now *that's* a circus!" Throughout his stay, he was unwilling to acknowledge the value of anything he experienced.

Their visit integrated them into our Canadian family. Adam and Markéta became lifelong friends, as did Helena and I.

———

I thought about Malý Pavel, Helena and Markéta now, and about Růža, wondering how the revolution was affecting them, what new opportunities had opened up for them and how they were relishing the new freedom. And of course I thought of Karel. I pictured Spolek Pohodlí sitting together in the pub, raising their glasses, celebrating night after night, their cause finally vindicated.

———————

One night, when Walter and I were fast asleep, our phone rang. Groggy, I looked at the clock at my bedside. Four o'clock. I staggered to the phone in the next room. A phone call in the middle of the night is always disorienting and frightening.

"*Ahoj, Helenko*. It's Karel." I was speechless. "How are you?"

Walter called from the next room, "Is everything all right?" Then he was standing at the door in his pyjamas, yawning. "Who is it?" I made a helpless gesture and mouthed Karel! and returned the receiver to my ear. Walter went back to bed.

It had been so long since I'd spoken Czech that words simply wouldn't come. Karel and I'd had no contact since our visit three years earlier.

He began to talk. As he did, I realized he was drunk. "I'm at my new place of employment," he laughed. "You won't believe what heights I've risen to in my career. Want to guess? I am a stoker in the boiler room of the central Prague post office. Every day six in the morning to one in the afternoon, earning an honest wage. No end of opportunity in the former workers' paradise."

"Jesus," I said. "What's happened?"

"The revolution happened. So guess what? I was fired. I'm not allowed to teach anymore – might corrupt the youth in this new regime. Why? For having been a card-carrying member of the Communist party. What do you think of that?" He laughed again.

"My God!"

"But no, this job has its benefits. It's warm, it's dry, and I can use the phone here, since there's nobody here but me, which is how I can afford to call you. We have the generous post office to thank."

"You've been thrown out of the Academy," I said, finding my Czech voice, stunned by the terrible irony. "Here I thought the revolution was what you all wanted. I imagined you celebrating."

"Turns out you were right all along. I should never have signed. It took fifteen years, but I ended up thrown out of the job after all. Every one of us, even though they knew we'd been forced to sign. As if we'd had any choice. So be it. Here I am, stoking a boiler." His voice softened. "And here we are talking on the phone! I want to hear your voice. How are you?"

I struggled to tell him. It was like talking to someone on a different planet. I tried. Working, seeing clients, Adam going to a private school, playing baseball, Walter and I volunteer coaches.

What I left out was the ache, this hole in the middle of it all that never went away; that still welled up when I listened to Hana Hegerová and the other CD's I'd brought back from Prague. The Vejvanovsky CD Karel had played as I sat for my portrait, and the 45s of *Řeka Lásky* and *Nedělní Ráno* he'd sent me after I left, those songs that were everywhere when we'd been together – our songs. That was long ago and life had moved on. Life was Walter and Adam and our home in Caledon, our work, my clients, our friends. I'd also taken up writing, taking courses, organizing writers' groups and emceeing readings at the Idler Pub.

The gulf between our lives was so wide, there seemed to be no way of bridging it. Yet to be hearing from Karel, so unexpectedly, shook the foundations of my life. Neither of us asked about our marriages.

"*Tak kdy prijedeš do Prahy?*" he asked. "*Teď už je to jedno-duchý.*" He was asking me when was I coming to Prague; it was easy now. And my heart leapt. Yes, I should come. I hadn't thought about it lately. But yes, I must go to Prague again and see the transformation.

"*Nevím,*" I said. "*Ale ano. Přijdu.*" I don't know. But yes. I'll come.

We said goodbye.

The old ache flared up.

I didn't call him, but over the next few months Karel called me several times, always late at night, usually drunk. Sometimes he was barely articulate. Angry, I'd hang up on him. Other times I let the phone ring and ring until my answering machine took the message. "Helen, it's me," he would plead. "Answer the phone!" I'd wait in silence with clenched fists until he hung up.

Chapter 21

IT WASN'T UNTIL TWO YEARS LATER THAT I FINALLY managed to get back. Five years since we'd driven to Kytlice to find Karel. Seventeen years since that morning at the airport.

Walter couldn't get away, but I had a ten day window between clients. It was summer, and as the plane began its descent, I stared, my face pressed against the window, at the villages dotting the countryside around Prague, the green patchwork of fields, scarcely able to contain my excitement.

The plane landed and we were released into the terminal. No more police checking visas. Smart new uniforms on the customs agents, who actually greeted me: *Dobrý den!* The terminal was the same; a few new shops had opened, a café, but otherwise it was just as I remembered it. Setting my suitcase down, I stood where I had clung to Karel, where the gates had rolled shut behind me seventeen years before. I ordered a coffee and sat, remembering.

I'd called Helena to let her know I was coming and she arrived to meet me. We threw our arms around each other and she led me out into the sunshine and to her car. A sign of growing affluence – quite a few late model cars in the parking lot. As we drove into town, not much had changed. I welcomed the familiar sights. The same red and yellow trams, the same sooty buildings, only now many of them were covered with graffiti.

"It was against the law under communism," Helena said wryly. "Labelled hooliganism and punished severely. People react to freedom in odd ways." Another sign of changing times was the many casinos and gaming bars that had opened all over town, often several per block. "Another scourge," she added.

"I must tell you, Helena, I expected great things," I said. "Celebrations in the streets. A fresh coat of paint on every building."

Helena laughed. "It's only been two years. Recovering from four decades of what we went through will take a long time."

We drove through the familiar streets. It was thrilling to be back.

Helena had arranged for me to stay at Malý Pavel's flat. "He moved there when my mother died. It's a bit of a hole in the wall – I hope you'll be okay there." She sighed. "He's been terribly disillusioned since the revolution. Right now he's holed up at the cottage."

She was right. It turned out to be a one-room flat crowded with dark furniture, bookcases towering against every wall, a narrow cot huddled in one corner. Helena threw me a questioning look as she threw open the windows.

"I'll be fine. I'm grateful to have it." We made plans to meet for dinner the next day. I was anxious to hit the streets.

I wandered everywhere, in a daze, visiting all my beloved places. First to Malá Strana, and I walked again down Nosticova, where so many of my memories lay, my footsteps echoing down the narrow, cobblestone street, to number 2. It looked just the same. I tried the street door, hoping I could catch a glimpse of the courtyard – but of course it was locked.

Crossing the bridge to Kampa Island, I leaned on the fence and through the trees caught sight of the windows of my old room across the narrow Čertovka River. There was the tamarack I'd planted, reaching up to the second storey now. Up the steps to Charles Bridge, around the square, past U Glaubiců, checked the door to Rubín – closed until evening – and climbed up Nerudova. I stood outside U Bonaparta. I didn't go in. Not yet.

I wandered through the city – crossing Charles Bridge, gazing up at the castle, and in the distance, the Summer Palace, and Petřín Park. Through Old Town, along its winding streets to Wenceslas Square, the Museum, the saint on his horse. I was exhilarated and suddenly felt profoundly at home, the first time in many years. The language of my childhood that still gripped and held me whenever I heard it resonated all around me. I didn't know whether to laugh or cry, to race around so I could revisit everything, or sit and contemplate the magnificence I saw at every turn; so I laughed and I cried, raced everywhere, then sat and just stared, feeling foolish but not caring.

Of course I'd been ridiculously optimistic about the changes I'd expected to find. Helena was right – it would take many, many years to repair the neglect and ugliness visited upon this city. I was grateful not much had changed; my beloved places were just the same, my memories intact.

I had important calls to make, so I returned to the flat, picking up some groceries on the way. Uncle Paul was gone now, but Růža was still alive. She'd had a phone installed, and I called her, receiving a joyful welcome and an insistence that I come to lunch the next day.

All that time, I'd been wondering whether I should call Karel. Did I really want to reopen that door? So often when he'd phoned me, he'd been drunk. Is that what I'd find? I couldn't bear it. We were both married, had families. What was I thinking, bursting in on his life again? Yet our meeting in Kytlice five years before had been so intense. How could I leave it at that? He'd been begging me to come every time he'd called. No, I had to call. How could I be in Prague and not try to see him?

With a sudden sense of urgency, I took a deep breath and dialed his number. He answered. That still familiar voice.

"*Ano?*"

"*Ahoj, Karle.*" I could hardly speak. "It's Helen. I'm in Prague."

"Come. Today."

"Where?"

"U Švejku. A pub in Dejvice. On the same street where my studio was, in my parents' flat. I'm just heading out. Come this afternoon."

"Yes."

He gave me directions. Dejvice, where he'd first invited me to see his paintings. Where I'd sat blissfully day after day in his sun-drenched studio. I was shocked by the excitement I felt – and suddenly, the fear.

As I put my groceries away, I noticed my hands were shaking. I took my time unpacking my suitcase. Was I jeopardizing everything – my life in Canada, my wonderful husband, my beloved son? What if I fell in love with Karel all over again?

———

At four o'clock that afternoon, I climbed up out of the Dejvice metro station and looked around. There was the park and the path he'd described. "Look for a blue-tiled building," he'd said. "Head for that." I did, and found the street. Nikola Tesly. Further down I saw the sign. U Švejku. A cellar pub. Through the sidewalk-level windows I could see a section of the interior.

I stood outside the door for a moment, just standing, quieting my pounding heart, then pushed it open. I was on a landing, three steps up from the floor of the pub. Tables of mostly men. I scanned the room. Close to the tap, a man who'd been sitting with four others stood up. It was Karel. We stared at one another. I couldn't help it, I broke into a joyful smile and crossed the cement floor.

He took my hand, pulled me towards him and kissed me on both cheeks. "What are you looking at?" he snapped at his friends, who were staring. "This, if you must know, is Helena. From Canada." I nodded to them and sat down. He flagged the barman, who brought me a beer and added a pencil stoke to the chit in front of Karel, a chit which had many strokes on it already. We sat looking at one another without a word. Where to start?

He did. "So you've finally come back."

"Seventeen years."

"A lifetime ago." He took a drink. "How long are you here for?"

"Ten days."

"Alone?"

"Yes."

He lit a cigarette. I looked around the room. I didn't like this pub. Dissolute old guys guzzling beer. I didn't like his friends, either. They didn't look like artists or dissidents. They looked like boozing buddies.

"So what finally brings you here?" he said.

"To see the changes, reunite with my family. And I wondered how you were doing after all this time."

He took a swallow of beer. I noticed his hand was shaking. "I've already told you that – like shit – when you troubled to answer the phone."

"I'm sorry." I couldn't explain how disoriented I was at the sudden collision of those two worlds whenever he called. And angry, helplessly so, at his being drunk.

"You're looking good," he said. "Life in Canada treating you well?" There was a sudden hard edge to his voice.

"Yes," I said. "It is." We couldn't take our eyes off one another. "When did you start coming here? Do you still go to U Bonaparta?"

He waved the hand holding his cigarette. "That's all finished. I don't go downtown anymore. This here is my local."

"What about Spolek Pohodlí, Zlatá Praha? I was hoping to see them again."

"Gone. That's all finished." He took another drink, then looked at me. "God, it's good to see you."

Suddenly all I knew was that I was here at last, Karel was sitting with me and I was fantastically happy.

"It's fabulous what's going on here," I said. "I watched those incredible images on television. I couldn't believe my eyes. Finally! Finally all that cruelty and evil is over. And imagine – no armed guards at the airport, no visa required, no more treks to the police station. Amazing!"

He looked at me with those deep brown eyes of his. "You don't know a damn thing about it."

"Tell me then."

"It's changed, all right, but not for the better. It's been a disaster."

"What do you mean?"

"I'm telling you, a nightmare. First the revolution itself. My sons were out there, day after day. Míša too. People streaming into the streets, first the students, thousands of them, then others, hundreds of thousands."

"Yes, that's what I saw on television. I was ecstatic!" I said.

He drank. "Police were hauling students off the streets. Some were killed, some just disappeared, their families never found them again. I was terrified for our boys, holding my breath every night until they came through the door. When it finally succeeded, Míša was over the moon. In the end, I couldn't help it, I hated her for it."

"Karel, I don't get it," I said. "You were a dissident, hung out with Havel, one of the leaders of the revolution. The communists were finally defeated! I thought that's what you stood for."

"What I stood for?" he snarled. "I was an artist, and a teacher. Art was what I cared about. That revolution stole everything from me. I told you – it got me thrown out of the Academy. They labelled me a communist and threw me out. All of us – as if we'd had any choice back then. Now you show up spouting this crap about how great it is. I guess it is for you, you can blow in and out now whenever to please, while I'm stuck in a boiler room shoveling shit for a living."

I was overwhelmed. "But ... but Karel, you're free now," I stammered. "You can do whatever you want – paint, teach, whatever." He didn't answer. "Are you painting?"

"For Christ's sake, aren't you listening to me? I'm telling you – I'm broken. Everything has gone to ratshit. I don't do anything because nothing's worth doing. I've lost everything! I sweat it out in the boiler room, sit here with these drunken assholes all afternoon, go home to pass out, then drag myself back to the boiler room. Every day. That's my life now, thanks to the revolution."

I stared at him, lost for words. "Do you still have a studio?" I finally said.

He snorted. "I go there, but not to paint. I live there for days at a time – when I can't stand being at home. When I can't stand myself. I stay there until I feel human again."

"Start painting again, Karel. You have to. You were so good."

He exploded with rage. "Goddamn it, can't you hear me? Go to hell with that idiot talk. You can't create out of nothing! I'm nothing!"

He was slurring now, weaving in his seat. He lit another cigarette, ignoring the one burning in the ashtray, and signalled the waiter for another beer.

"Karel, you're wasting your life," I said, unwilling to give up. "You're moping around, feeling sorry for yourself. You have to paint again!"

He downed half his beer, wiped his mouth on his sleeve and set his stein down hard, sloshing the beer on the table. "And you are nothing but a boring, naive, stupid North American."

He might as well have hauled off and hit me. I drew back, reeling, then grabbed my jacket and stood up. "Karel, I wanted to find you, as though it was the most important thing in my life." He shook his head, which was hovering close to the table. "I was actually afraid – but I needn't have worried." I turned to leave.

He turned bleary eyes on me. "Helen, I'm sorry. Please, come again. Tomorrow. I'll be better, I promise. Give me another chance." He crossed his arms on the drenched table and cradled his head on his arms.

Anger fought against heartache. The latter won. "All right," I said, "I'll come." Outside I burst into tears.

I slept fitfully that night and had terrible dreams of disorientation and loss. In one I was at home trying to make tea and couldn't figure out how to do it. Adam was there, watching my mad and desperate attempts with growing horror. My best friend Sylvia appeared, announced that Walter was leaving me, put her arm protectively around Adam and led him away. I had lost everything.

Suddenly I was glad of my anger and fierce disappointment; they would protect me and help me keep my distance. I wouldn't go back that evening.

I set out for Aunt Růža's. She opened the door and I enfolded her in my arms. She had shrunk – she was thin and wiry now, her face gaunt. Uncle Paul's red chair by the coal stove was empty, and there were other changes. Pale rectangles dotted the walls where paintings had hung. Through the partly open door I glimpsed the beautiful old drawing room, which was almost bare. The piano was gone, as were the Persian rugs that had once been heaped on top. The tiger skin Adam had played on no longer stretched across the floor.

"It's not all good, what's happening," Růža said as we sat once again over coffee at that familiar table. "You've noticed I've had to sell things off. Prices have gone up terribly and pensions have been lowered. For older people it's a disaster. What good is freedom if you don't have enough money to live on? Of course we're happy to be liberated – but some people, especially the older ones, preferred things the way they were. They promised we'd be taken care of from cradle to grave – one of their slogans. We came to expect it." She shook her head. "Nobody's taking care of us now."

Růža's nephew was the one selling things off for her. What would she do, I wondered, when everything was gone? I also knew my mother, seemingly oblivious to Růža's plight, expected to reclaim the paintings and other possessions she'd left behind and entrusted to Uncle Paul.

Over the next years, I left Růža with money every time I came to Prague. Later, I wished I'd done more – wished I'd transferred money regularly from my bank in Canada. Why do these thoughts, so obvious in retrospect, come too late?

After lunch at Růža's that afternoon, Helena picked me up and we drove out to Černošice to see the villa that had belonged to my family.

Properties confiscated by the communists were being restituted – a new word created to describe the process – to their former owners. My mother had written to Malý Pavel asking him to apply on her behalf to have our villa and acreage returned. He was not a lawyer and couldn't afford to hire one, and so was acting alone. It was a delicate situation. As my father's wife, my mother assumed the property would be hers. Yet according to Czech law, all of my father's children would also be entitled to a share of it, which I didn't think my mother realized or acknowledged.

I was anxious to see the villa again. Imagine owning it and possibly living here one day, I thought. Perhaps there was something I could do. Perhaps adding my voice to the application would strengthen our claim; Malý Pavel certainly wouldn't have the means to restore it.

Helena parked by the side of the road and we stood outside the high chain-link fence. Tall trees hid both the henhouse and the villa. We ventured up the curved laneway to a gate. As it was the weekend, and the villa was now a school, no one was about. Beside the gate, I was able to climb the fence and get high enough to see the villa and take photos. It was worth fighting for, I decided. I would discuss it with Malý Pavel.

All day, thoughts of Karel weighed heavily on me. Finally, telling myself it was because I'd promised, I set out for U Švejku.

When I got there, he was fumbling to pay and leave, and was very drunk.

"Let's forget it for now," I said, turning to go.

"No, stay!" he urged. "Stay and have a beer with me. We need to talk." He took my arm and pulled me back to his table. The same friends were there. They avoided looking at us.

We sat down and a beer was deposited in front of each of us.

"Karel, I don't want to see you when you're drunk," I began.

"Then we'll have to meet mornings," he said.

I laughed. He was serious.

"I mean you've got to stop drinking."

"What the hell! You're not my wife!"

I caught my breath. "No. I'm your friend. You've got to stop drinking – you're killing yourself."

"*Do prdele!* What business is that of yours?"

"Damn it, Karel, you were so fine. You're throwing it all away."

"Fuck off with that bullshit!"

Leaping from my chair, I yelled, "I won't let you speak to me like that!" and I walked out. I flashed a glance back when I got to the door. He was taking another swig of his beer, with no intention of coming after me.

And so it ends, I thought as I stumbled back to the metro station. I won't go back, and he doesn't have the will to pursue me.

———

I dragged through the days for the rest of my stay, spending time with Helena, visiting Růža and taking her out.

I was desperately lonely and no longer knew what I was doing there, disillusioned by everything I saw. Finally I'm seeing things as they are, I told myself. Ugly people in the streets, terrible restaurants staffed with rude waiters, crap in the shops. My visit suddenly felt meaningless. I was nothing but an outsider visiting relatives and old haunts. I felt detached and cold, and was critical of everything. The people around me were strange, intrusive, disgusting, the men sexist pigs.

I couldn't seem to find the pain I felt over Karel; I knew it must exist but I couldn't touch it. What I felt was anger, withdrawal and a self-protective coldness that reminded me of my mother. Surely there is loss and grief, I told myself. But how odd that I couldn't feel it. Was it that I finally knew where I belonged – back in Caledon where my real life was? Is that why this pilgrimage suddenly felt meaningless? Was I free at last? But I was also full of tension, unable to sleep, my nights full of bad dreams when I did drift off, and my body ached. I didn't feel free.

As the days wore on, I realized I was waiting for Karel. I was praying he would come for me. Each time I came back to Malý Pavel's flat, I expected he'd be waiting for me. I hoped for a note taped to the door. When I was in, I kept expecting a knock on the door, a tap on the window. He's not going to come, I kept telling myself; an alcoholic loves nothing but his booze. Yet I was waiting.

———

I missed Walter terribly, wished he was with me, and felt great love and yearning towards him. And yet I seemed utterly unable to express it. Writing a postcard, I couldn't bring myself to write "I love you," even though I wanted to very much.

I phoned him and was in tears when I heard his voice. He sounded so warm, so kind, so loving. He said he was sorry my time in Prague wasn't turning out the way I'd hoped, and he comforted me, describing the wonderful holiday we'd have when we were together again. I have to find a way to get through this impasse, I told myself. I have to.

Malý Pavel returned to Prague, I moved in with Helena, and the three of us met over lunch. Malý Pavel was subdued, and when I mentioned the revolution, he waved his hand dismissively, shook his head and refused to discuss it. I brought up the subject of Černošice, wondering if I could help in any way. Again he shook his head, told me he didn't hold out much hope of succeeding but the request had been made and he would handle it.

I packed that last evening after dinner at Růža's with great relief to be going home at last.

Karel did not come after me.

Walter was waiting for me at the airport, his beautiful, kind face beaming when he caught sight of me coming through the gate, and I was full of joy and gratitude when I saw him in the crowd. Our life resumed as it had been. Busy with work, lots of writing as I tried to sort myself out, pages of densely written journals, a yearning for life, for connection, for something – where do I belong? why am I so often sad? – going in a hundred directions at once, wanting everything, passionate, searching.

"Help me," I wrote to the universe in my journal, "I am lost."

My mother was diagnosed with lung cancer in 1992. She was eighty-six. She'd never smoked but my father and all her children had at some point.

One day, about a year and a half into her illness, my mother and I were having lunch at Chez Marcel, a little French bistro on Yonge Street where I often took her – taking her to lunch was the way I was most comfortable being with her. My heart was aching with sadness and fear. I rested my head against the wall beside me and spoke my anguish. "I don't know how I'll be able to bear your dying. I have never known and can't imagine the world without you in it."

"But Helen," she said, "I'm sick and I'm old. It's my time."

Such simple words – nothing, really, of great significance. Yet it felt like the kindest, most honest thing she'd ever said to me. She was comforting me by helping me face the truth.

After my father died, she'd sold their home and bought a small bungalow in Leaside and with my brother Peter's help, had it renovated, turning it into a lovely two-storey home, where she lived alone. Even well after her diagnosis, she continued to host family dinners and sat at the table, the proud matriarch, happy to have brought us together, enjoying our conversations and banter.

Peter, who affectionately called her *Tiger*, was her mainstay, having taught her skills like writing cheques, which she'd never learned while my father was alive. I visited her as often as I could, opening the front door to find her reading the newspaper at her kitchen table. She would look up, radiant with welcome and cry, *"Jé! Helenka!"*

As the disease progressed, she would come and spend weekends with us in Caledon, her oxygen tank in the spare bedroom, the thin plastic tube trailing after her as she'd come into the sunroom to read or to chat. My siblings and I took turns inviting her. I'd take her into shops, and from her wheelchair, she'd reach out hungrily to touch and savour things – the cool smoothness of a silk scarf, the softness of a cashmere sweater, the heady scent of roses. She was avid for life.

"If only I could see spring flowers just one more time," she'd cry.

There were several crises, her lungs filling with fluid, her panic at feeling she was drowning, rushing her to the hospital to have her lungs drained. But she weathered every one, outlasting doctors' prognoses by two years.

In early 1994, her doctors gave her no more than two months to live. So – April or May. I tried to imagine what life would be like in June, and the summer, and all the time after that. I needed to do something to help fill the enormous chasm her death would create.

I thought of Georgian Bay, the untamed wilderness that had brought me solace and comfort as a child. A place to grieve and to heal. Walter and I rented a cottage in Georgian Bay for the month of August. "For two years now, I have carried the burden of knowing she would die soon," I wrote in my journal. "I need to put it down now."

My mother saw her spring flowers, and against all odds was still active as the summer progressed.

How could I go away and leave my mother? Peter saved the day by inviting her to his cottage on Manitoulin Island for the month.

By October it was clear she needed more care than we and the visiting nurses could give her. We registered her in the palliative care unit at Baycrest.

Irene and I met at our mother's house, made tea and took three mugs up to my mother's bedroom. We laid her suitcase on the bed and held up items from her extensive wardrobe for her to choose. Thin and frail now, my mother sat in the small chair by the window.

"So this is the end. I am going there to die," she said.

"No!" we insisted. "You can come home any time and still spend weekends visiting us."

Once there, though, if was as if she no longer had to fight. I would wheel her down to the coffee shop or the flower shop on the ground floor, but in a matter of days even that was too much. She became bedridden and spent most of her days sleeping.

One evening towards the end, I was alone with her. On a visit to our home, she had found Robert Munsch's children's book, *Love You Forever*, among Adam's things, and was so moved that she bought copies for everyone in the family. I sat by her bedside and read it aloud over and over, not knowing whether she could still hear me. Then in my own words, I let her go. "Don't suffer anymore," I said to her quietly. "When you are ready, you can go. We'll miss you terribly – but we'll be all right." I thanked her for my life and told her I loved her.

―――――

She died two days later, around four o'clock on a dark December morning. When I arrived at the nursing home, my siblings, exhausted, had gone to the cafeteria. No one else in the room, the curtain closed around her bed. Her face white and slack in death. I couldn't touch her. A hard expression on her face, the lower jaw jutting forward, belligerent, like a bulldog. Was that the feeling with which she left the world? My brain fought and struggled to take this in – this was my mother now and forever. What she had given me or said to me was all she would ever give or say to me.

I wanted to reach forward, open an eye, see if she was still in there. Force her, beg her, to see me. To take her frail, thin shoulders in my two hands and shake her until her eyes flew open and she stopped this cold behaviour, until she softened, and smiled.

And when the urge to shake her passed, another urge, to hold her, rest her halo of white hair against my broad shoulder, wrap my aching arms around her. But no, I thought. She would be stiff and hard. I might have to break her bones to make her body accept my embrace. All I could do was wait until the terror passed and then stand by her bed – so large now, her body so tiny, empty – to stand and look upon her and bid her farewell.

"Thank you, my beloved, for my life."

———

What astonished me at her funeral was realizing I didn't know the woman described in my family's eulogies, the loving woman who devoted her life to her family. Their words transmuted her thwarted hopes, dreams and ambitions, her possessiveness, her isolation from others into devotion to her family. But eulogies are like that; they're not the time for baring our bruised and yearning souls.

When it was my turn to speak, I told the story of the courageous, valiant woman who had led Peter and me across that barbed-wire border to safety.

Of the two conflicting messages I'd received from my mother – resignation to my lot as a woman, and the exhortation to be different, to have a life vastly different from hers – it was the second that informed my life, and I realized this was her gift to me. And so I was able to acknowledge the legacies from my mother: her courage and ambition, her love of family, of music, her passionate thirst for life. And her fervent wish for my happiness and success.

I left the lectern and walked to where her coffin lay, surrounded by flowers, and spoke the words of a song that had always moved me, *The Last Farewell*.

"For I have loved you dearly,
More dearly than the spoken word can tell."

But no, not only dearly, I thought; desperately, secretly, angrily, heartbrokenly. And now, gratefully.

———

Spending the month at the cottage had rekindled my love of Georgian Bay, so the next year, Walter and I bought a two-acre island in the Sans Souci area of the Bay, a portion of the cost paid for by my inheritance from my mother. The three of us camped on the island for the first few years, cooking our meals over a fire, sleeping in a tent under the pine trees, or in the small cuddy in our boat. Roughing it like this was new to Walter, but he came to love it. Eventually we had a post and beam cottage built overlooking the wide, sparkling bay.

Walter seemed determined to make my every dream come true.

Weekends we skied at the Caledon Ski Club, close to our home. We began holidaying in Puerto Vallarta in Mexico, and bought two weeks of timeshare vacations, enabling Walter, Adam and me to spend Christmas and New Years at the Sierra Beach Hotel each year.

Adam was happy at Country Day School, an academically demanding private school in King City. He was on the rugby team and played the saxophone in the school band.

I continued my work as a therapist and group leader at Family Transition Place in Orangeville, as well as running a private practice out of our renovated barn.

I'd begun the habit of writing three pages in my journal every morning. Karel didn't appear in those pages at all. Most of what filled them was grief over the loss of my mother and profound regret at not having had a true relationship with her.

There were times I saw my mother in my behaviour towards Walter. I'd find myself looking at him with the same critical eye she had turned on my father and me. I held back from loving him as openly and unreservedly as I longed to. I loved him, I knew, and was immensely grateful for his steadfast love, his kindness and generosity. But I withheld myself from him. I spent pages trying to figure it out and trying to change. Was it the result of that terrible wrenching from all I knew and loved when I was four? Was it fear of loss, having learned that happiness is fragile and could be ripped out from under me at any time? Or was it having learned, watching my mother's anguish, that happiness lay elsewhere and out of reach, and so I longed for what was distant? Scorning the blessings I had and yearning for the unattainable.

I was raised by a woman damaged and thwarted by exile – and sexism. She was bitter but hadn't the strength, the resolve or the tools to fight. I became a fighter, and perhaps she resented that. Perhaps I'd made her look weak and afraid. She once told a friend of mine that she was afraid of me. She saw me as an alien creature; we'd been alien creatures to one another. I didn't want to be like her, didn't want her life with its limitations and bitter resignation. I'd rejected and fought against her – against what she represented – yet secretly yearned for her love and acceptance. A difficult paradox to live with – for both of us.

We never got past the awkwardness and distance between us. I couldn't reach her with the things I said, and she would inevitably say something that hurt or offended me. She was critical of me, her body language and facial expressions told me so – yet I didn't know how or wasn't willing to be who she wanted me to be, and nothing I did was enough.

As a child, I'd often felt the terrible pain of unrequited love with my mother and wondered if Walter ever felt that with me. I hated to think so. He never complained or called me on it. He continued to shower me with his love and delight at our being together.

———

Five years later, Walter turned sixty and we decided the three of us would spend an entire month in Europe to celebrate. We exchanged our timeshare weeks for two weeks of mountain-wandering in Switzerland and a few days at Grüner Baum in Bad Gastein.

And then – Prague.

Adam, Walter and me in Martinique, 1982

Walter, Adam and me visiting my long-lost brother, Malý Pavel, his wife Helena and their granddaughter Markéta at their cottage in Libverda, 1985. Photo by Walter

Helen Notzl

The Velvet Revolution, February, 1989.
Four photographs from *Portfolio Československý Listopad, 1989*, Agentura RADOST

November 17 // Albertov, Prague. The sign says FREEDOM.
Photo by Tomki Němec

November 20 // Wenceslas Square. The sign says TRUTH WILL PREVAIL.
Photo by Radovan Boček.

Alexander Dubček, (left) Václav Havel // after the government's resignation.
Photo by Herbert Slavík

Opening the Czechoslovak-Austrian Border.
Photo by Karel Cudlín

Spolek Pohodlí at U Bonaparta with members of Zlatá Praha discussing the 1989 revolution. Lithograph by Milan Kohout, 1992

Karel's portrait of Markéta (left) and Helena

Chapter 22

THE TRAIN SPED ALONG THE TRACK FROM SALZBURG AS WE lounged in our own luxurious first-class compartment on velvet upholstered seats, our feet propped up on the seats opposite. We dined in the elegant dining car; the menu was presented in German, English and Czech, and the staff, it turned out, were Czech. I thrilled once again to hear my language spoken.

My visit five years before had been a bitter disappointment. A few late-night drunken phone calls from Karel had followed, attempts at apologies; I'd ignored them and they'd dropped off. And yet Prague without Karel? I couldn't imagine it. I hadn't decided what I'd do, but felt nervousness along with my usual excitement at returning.

Helena was waiting outside the train station, which still bore its pre-revolution squalor. No change there. Our greetings were joyful, Helena effusive, her rosy face glowing as she hugged us each in turn. She, of course, spoke no English, so I translated everything.

"Walter looks just as gorgeous as he did ten years ago!" she said. "Tell him I said so." And turning to Adam, "What a handsome young man you've grown to be! I bet the girls fight over you!" Adam, now fifteen, flushed, pleased.

"Let's go to Malá Strana, have some drinks in an outdoor patio and catch up. Then I'll take you to the flat."

As we drove through the downtown core, construction was going on everywhere. Large sections of Wenceslas Square were dug up, new cobblestones being laid. Scaffolding covered many buildings, and this time there were construction workers applying stucco, retiling roofs, replacing windows. There were still many dilapidated buildings, but progress was being made. There was a hum to the city now. Prague was coming alive.

The people in the streets seemed to walk with a bounce to their step, or strolled in a more contented way than I'd seen before. Malá Strana, my old haunt across the river, was also undergoing drastic renovation. Several of the lovely buildings around my old local square, Malostranské Náměstí, and at the foot of Nerudova, shone with fresh stucco and paint, their facades and statues restored.

We sat at a café on the square and caught up.

She told us about the flat she'd bought, where she'd invited us to stay. It was a future gift for her daughter Markéta, for when she grew up and needed her own place, and in the meantime, after our stay there, it could be an income property. Helena had been married – her husband, whom I'd never met, was also a dentist – but the two had divorced some years ago. Markéta lived with her.

"Once the revolution came, I could finally take my certification exam as a dental surgeon. I've opened my own clinic, and it's thriving." She swore us to secrecy – the flat was to be a surprise for Markéta when the time came.

"It's tiny, though, and in a *panelák*, one of those prefab cement high-rises the communists threw up in the outskirts. I've fixed it up and hope you'll be comfortable there. And it's a half-hour bus ride from the centre. I hope that's okay. That, believe it or not, is where the majority of ordinary Praguers live. You, having lived in Malá Strana and Vinohrady," she said to me, smiling, "were extremely lucky."

"Don't I know it," I said. "Tell me, how's Malý Pavel?"

Helena's face darkened. "He's been diagnosed with lung cancer and had a lung removed. The prognosis isn't good. He's out of the hospital now. He refused to let anyone visit him there, not even me. I bring groceries and cook meals for him. He's getting stronger and goes out for short walks now."

"I hope he'll see me. Please ask him." She agreed to try.

"I wish I'd known him better," I said. "Even back when I lived here and he helped me so much with my translating – I didn't know how to get close to him."

"Neither did I, and I've had a lifetime of trying," Helena said. "His was a very hard life." She told me more than I had known. His – our – father divorced his first wife, Malý Pavel's mother, when he was ten years old. He took it hard. Became withdrawn, sensitive, an intellectual, an esthete. Rudy, his younger brother, who escaped to Canada with us, was his opposite; loud, jovial, overblown, with a strong sense of entitlement, and his mother's favourite. Their mother was cold and distant. He was a dutiful son, but the relationship brought him little comfort or nurturing. Instead she pined for Rudy, whom she was never to see again."

"He married well, didn't he?" I said. "Helena was so warm and loving."

"He couldn't really take it in," Helena said.

I'd seen that during my visits years before, Helena Sr. showering Malý Pavel with her bountiful love, only to have it awkwardly deflected. I was a little like him, I realized; Walter was the more generous, demonstrative one.

"Then, when you all fled the country, he was in his early twenties, and that was another abandonment, by both his father and brother. And what's more, he was punished for it. Thrown out of his job as editor of *Rudé Právo* and sent to work in the mines." My idealist brother I'd not known existed for so many years.

Helena was to become a dear and close friend, and the source of much of the family history I was anxious to learn.

———

It took a good half-hour to drive out to Řepy, the suburb where we were to stay. The lovely buildings of old Prague and the renewal taking place were replaced by street after street of cheaply constructed towers with tiny windows, stained stucco and rusted balconies. Older women lugged shopping bags, men in undershirts stood smoking on corners, while exhausted-looking young women pushed strollers. Life was hard here.

We found ourselves in a graffiti-covered elevator that groaned its way up to the sixth floor. The hallway smelled of stale food and sweat. Helena threw me an apologetic glance. But when she opened a door at the end of the hallway, a tiny, perfect apartment was revealed, white walls, crisp linen curtains, everything in shades of cream and white, ferns and flowers adding splashes of colour. Helena had created an oasis, a generous gift for Markéta. We made a date for later in the week, and Helena left us to settle in.

We were curious about the neighbourhood and set out to explore it before heading downtown. I was appalled. It was a

Prague I'd never known. A desolate cluster of buildings with peeling stucco, crumbling concrete, balconies stuffed with the overflow from overcrowded apartments. I'd noticed a few tables with umbrellas across the road and we set out to explore – perhaps a bright spot in this dreariness. "Maybe a place to eat?" I said. "Let's check it out." What had looked like a warehouse turned out to be a shopping centre with a grocery store, a pub and a restaurant. The outdoor seating outside the restaurant was rickety and broken, so we went inside. Prefab concrete, stark, echoing, noisy. A blue ceiling fan pushed the smoky air around. We were hungry. "Let's try the scrambled eggs," I suggested. "Can't do much to those."

The cheapest, ugliest tin forks came with our eggs, distressing me so deeply, I wanted to cry. I sat there, furious. Here were the results of that glorious experiment Zdeněk the police interrogator had described to me so eloquently over champagne at the Palace Hotel, while beautiful buildings – gothic, renaissance, art nouveau – had been left to crumble. Ugliness had ruled, aesthetics and beauty the enemy. Ordinary people, the workers, as the communists called them, lived in surroundings like these while the communists erected for themselves places like the Hotel Praha. Heavy, Soviet, oppressive – but lavish. The real meaning behind this ugliness was in that formula. Give the people concrete slabs so the party elite can have their marble.

We got on the bus and then the tram, heading towards the centre. There was graffiti everywhere, the glass broken on bus shelters, tram windows so scratched they were opaque. What a relief to see sudden small bursts of grace when scarlet geraniums bloomed in window boxes. Look for the good, I told myself. Seeing the dirt and neglect is easy.

A young, dark-skinned boy climbed into the tram, a harmonica hanging from his neck, yelling at a still younger boy, perhaps eight years old, who was crying. They sat down, the older boy getting ready to play, when they saw the ticket controller making his way down the tram. They leapt up and dashed out just as the tram doors were closing.

Billboards everywhere. Advertising had come to Prague. *Zlatá horečka* – gold fever; an image of a screaming woman – a Coca Cola ad; Lucky Strike – *A máte Ameriku v kapce*: And you have America in your pocket; McCain Golden Fries; Sony; Peugeot; Toyota; street cars, instead of their familiar, iconic red and yellow, a striking powder blue advertising British Midland Airways, a Boeing 747 splayed across their sides.

We spent the rest of the day downtown, picking our way through the construction going on everywhere in the centre. We stood on Charles Bridge, watching the swans gliding on the river. We sat in an outdoor café in Old Town Square, marvelling at the renewal going on all around us.

How could it be, I thought silently, grimly, that I still, despite everything, saw Karel everywhere I went? When would this damn obsession *stop*?

———

Anxious to see Růža, I called her several times the next morning, but there was no answer. We headed into town, bought a bouquet of flowers at a street kiosk on Wenceslas Square and walked up to her street. Her building had not been touched but the intersection was completely torn up. Narrow boards were laid over deep excavations, and yellow tape closed off sections of the road, pedestrians having to detour far out of their way.

I rang Růža's bell. Waited, rang again and again. Eventually the intercom buzzed.

"Růža, it's me, Helen."

"*Prosím?*" a tiny voice said. Pardon?

"Helen. From Canada."

"*Promiňte, neslyším.*" Forgive me, I can't hear.

"Helen!" I hollered.

There was silence, but the intercom buzzed again, and I pushed open the street door. I took those stairs two at a time, Walter and Adam followed. I was shocked when she finally opened the door. She was skeletal. She peered at us, and when she finally realized who we were, the hand holding her handkerchief flew to her mouth and she started to cry. I stepped in and took her in my arms. She felt like a small bird, hollow-boned, weightless.

"Oh," she cried, reaching up to hug Walter, then Adam. "And here is your fine husband –and your beautiful Adam. It's a miracle! God has answered my prayers."

We followed her slow progress down that dark hall into the sitting room I knew so well. She walked with two canes now, and when she touched the doorframe, I realized behind her thick glasses she was almost blind. She insisted on serving us coffee and biscuits, and brought juice for Adam.

She had shrunk terribly, her skin thin and translucent, the bones of her skull and jaw prominent. She was completely alone, she told us. Her nephew and son and their families were on vacation, as was the nurse who came to her daily. A student nurse came occasionally to do her shopping and help with daily chores.

"I live my life in this room now," she said. "I eat, watch TV, look out the window here. I sleep on that daybed so if something happens to me in the night, I can bang on my neighbour's wall. She's a widow like me, and alone." The last of the family that had been moved into the other half of the apartment.

Růža's apartment was almost empty now, no paintings left on the yellowed walls. The bathroom was horrible, the tub and sink brown with rust, the cement floor grimy underfoot.

I thought of the construction at the intersection, how Růža must long to go out into the sunshine, to sit in the square across the street, and the impossibility of her navigating those broken sidewalks, those yawning pits, she with her two canes and her near blindness.

"Růža, let's go out!"

"I couldn't!" she said, her eyes wide.

"We'll take it slow. I'll help you."

We walked together, her hand gripping my arm, Walter holding her other arm. She was agog at the bustle and pace of life around us. We guided her around the corner and down one block to the newly restored Deminka and took a window table.

"Imagine me," Růža said, sitting up straight, a wide smile on her face and tears in her eyes, "*me* sitting at Deminka, where I haven't been for many years, surrounded by my beloved Canadian family." When we took her home, we promised we'd come often and take her out whenever she wished.

———

We visited Růža numerous times, and each time we took her for an outing. We cried when we parted. "*Drž se, Růžo,*" I begged, hugging her frail body. "*Vrátím se brzo.*" Hold on, Růža,

I'll be back soon. She assured me she'd be fine, her nephew and son would return from holidays, as would her regular nurse.

"Budu se držet, Helenko," she vowed, clinging to me, her thin arms surprisingly strong. I will hold on, so we can see each other again. But she didn't. She died that summer. I received notice of it from her nephew, too late to come to her funeral.

———

On my own one afternoon, I took the tram to Malostranské Náměstí and walked to Kampa to see from across the Čertovka the room where I lived all those years ago. Twenty-five years. Renovated, it was beautiful. I'd forgotten just how steep those narrow steps were leading down to the river, which was high and fast. The building was painted a pale green with fresh white trim. I could see my two windows, now overlooking a lovely garden. Ivy climbed the wall around my window. A white globe light illuminated the restored patio at the edge of the river and a flagstone path ambled its way through the garden. I went around to Nosticova, to see the front. The walled park with its footbridge over the Čertovka was just the same, as were the cobblestones on my street. Number 2 was now Pension Dientzenhofer. I could actually stay there again, I thought. But of course it would be unrecognizable.

The high wall that had been next door was gone, and a park revealed. The building at the corner was being gutted and completely redone, covered with scaffolding. I looked into the glassless window openings and felt the cold, cave-like air wafting out. Everything would be restored, I thought, returned to its original, glorious state.

I mourned, I raged and I exulted at what had happened and what was happening to my city.

I found myself speaking my thoughts to my mother. I'm back, trying to find your Prague, the Prague you could have opened up for me, if only you were still here. Where you and I spent the first four years of my life together. Where my grand-parents lived, the ones you taught me to view as angels, and this paradise lost. I'm back, trying to find that lost kingdom. How do I crack its shell so it reveals its heart and soul to me? Still I come back, searching for home.

What did you do when you lost your mother, I asked her silently, when you left her behind forever? Where did you go for consolation? I have spent my life searching for the solace of home and still it evades me.

Everywhere I went in Malá Strana, I saw Karel. But he doesn't come here anymore, I reminded myself, there's no way I'll run into him. I considered calling him. But would it be unfair to Walter and Adam, and another huge disappointment for me? I held off.

———

Helena arranged for us to see Malý Pavel. We met at a small outdoor café, Pavel arriving with Helena. He was pale, emaci-ated and stooped. When I hugged him, he felt fragile, brittle.

I told him how happy I was to see him. He simply shook his head. He hardly spoke. He drank a coffee, exchanged a few words, then sat silent, letting our conversation flow around him. I tried to engage him. How thrilled I was that Prague was coming alive.

"Helenko, forgive me. I am an old, sick, and broken man," he said. He rose, apologized for leaving so soon, and explained he was tired and needed to go home to rest. Helena offered to accompany him; he refused. When she stood to insist, he snapped at her. He walked slowly down the street and disappeared into the metro station.

"He has eluded me, just as my father did," I cried to Helena.

"He has eluded everyone," Helena said.

My half-brother whom I had admired so, yearned to know better; the bright, solitary, left-wing intellectual, now disillusioned, broken. I will not see him again, I thought. My premonition was correct: his words to me that day were the last I ever heard him speak. Malý Pavel died later that year.

———

We were in Prague five days before I could no longer resist the need to find Karel. I'd lost his address and phone number. All I had to go on was U Švejku. Would he still be going there, five long years later?

Dejvice metro station, the building with the blue mosaic tiles, and I was on my way by myself, Walter and Adam having decided to take a boat tour along the river. Some of the buildings had been restored on Nikola Tesly. Ahead I saw a fine-looking café with outdoor tables. The pub is gone! I thought. But no, passing the café, there it was, another block further on. U Švejku written on the window and Lada's graphic of the good soldier painted on the window. Just the same.

I was afraid to enter. But neither could I leave. I pushed open the door and stood at the top of the steps, exactly as I had five years before. I couldn't believe my eyes. There he was, sitting in the same chair, at the same table.

I stood looking at him for several seconds, just taking him in, quieting the pounding of my heart. He saw me and sat, staring at me. I crossed the room towards him.

He jumped to his feet. "I must be dreaming," he said. He reached out and took my arm. "I have to touch you to make sure you're real."

"I'm real," I said.

I sat down. He's still drinking, I thought, prepared to be disappointed.

"Look what I'm drinking," he said.

"Water?" I said, hope rising, noting the small clear glass instead of the usual stein.

"Wine, with soda. We had a celebration last night and I'm recovering." Hope quashed.

The barman came around, put a beer in front of me, put it on my own tab.

"I want to apologize for the last time we met," Karel said, leaning towards me. "You caught me at a terrible time. I was a mess, everything going wrong, the seven plagues of Egypt. I was drinking like a maniac and was horribly rude to you and I'm very sorry." He spoke the words humbly and sincerely. "I've felt bad ever since. You wouldn't answer my calls. I thought of writing to you, but didn't think you'd want to hear from me after that. I hit bottom."

It was as if five years hadn't gone by.

"Tell me," I said.

"I couldn't believe how hard it hit me when I lost my job at the Academy," he said. "It was my whole life until then. I'd been there eighteen years." I nodded. "I had that job stoking coal in the post office boiler room and at first my friends hung out there and we made a joke of it. But they drifted off and I lost touch with them. Then the post office switched from coal to gas and I was fired. I got a job as a doorman at a television station owned by Americans and Canadians. Then that fell through.

"My father died, I hated my wife and couldn't stand being home – though I know she was an angel putting up with me. I lived mostly in my studio, but then when the building was restituted to a former owner, he raised the rent to something I couldn't possibly afford. I was at my wits' end."

I shook my head, my heart going out to him.

"And then – oh thank God, or luck, finally something went right – I met someone who was opening a private school offering degrees in advertising and marketing. They offered me a job teaching graphics, and that's what I've been doing for two years now."

Tears filled my eyes. "That's wonderful."

He tapped his teeth – the Czech version of knocking on wood – and said, "It's going well so far."

His mother was in a retirement home now, he told me, and he was living in her apartment. His boys, now twenty and eighteen, were both in school, Karel Jr. attending the school where he taught, Martin in art school, aspiring to being a painter and teacher like his father.

"I can't believe how good it is to see you," he said, and reached out and gently stroked my cheek with his knuckles the way he used to do. "I still have the belt you gave me" – he stood up and pulled his sweater up to show me – "I wear it all the time. And I still have the mirror you left behind at U Fazole, where you'd written in lipstick, *Čekej na mně*." Wait for me.

I was dazed, happy and immensely relieved. And the way my heart was reacting, I was frightened again.

"Are you seeing your friends – our friends – these days?"

He was. "I discovered Zlatá Praha still meets at U Tygra Tuesdays and I've started joining them again. Poor Pepa Steklý, that gentle soul," he continued. "Died a year ago. He was gay, you know. Got beaten up, both legs broken. He died in the hospital." Pepa, who'd given me the drawing of a church whose doors opened to reveal an exquisite interior.

"And your old friend Mirek, who turned out to have informed on you, died," Karel went on. "Friends of mine told me he'd fallen asleep in Klárov Square, drunk, and froze to death." The square close to where I'd lived in my little room, the photographer's studio, with Mirek's runner beans fluttering at the back of the courtyard.

Life deals harshly here with sensitive souls, I thought. Mirek had reached for me like a drowning man. He would have taken me down with him. Karel had reached for me in the same way.

"After I hit bottom, it took me a long time to realize it was up to me to dig myself out."

It seemed he'd done it. He looked good. Ruddy, bearded, crinkly eyes, smiling. The desperation and rage were gone from his eyes.

"I have to go now," I said.

"Will you come again?" Karel asked.

"I'm here with Walter and Adam. We're only here for another three days."

"Try."

He reached out and touched my cheek again. I turned and walked out the door.

————

The next morning I woke up with the strains of *Nedělní Ráno* running through my head, sensing they'd been playing all night. The Czech version of Bob Dylan's *Sunday Morning Coming Down* that had been one of our songs way back. I debated whether to go back to U Švejku. It's a bit much, I thought, to come the very next day. Besides, we've caught up on all the news. What else is there to say?

The main thing is, I told myself, I'm happy he's back on his feet. What I don't want is to have his ruined life on my conscience.

Chapter 23

WHAT FOLLOWED WAS A PERIOD WHEN I WAS BUSY WITH MY private therapy practice, giving lectures around town. I also joined a writers' group, and wrote a series of Island Stories about life at our cottage in the summer. One of my stories was accepted by the CBC and I was invited to read it on air. Yet unsatisfied with all of it, I filled notebooks struggling to find meaning in my life. A therapist I saw said, "I think you're a wild woman." I gave a jolt of recognition. The book *Women Who Run With the Wolves* landed in my life and I read it like a starving person, finding some sustenance at last. But what kind of a sustained and productive life can a wild woman live? How much of me had I set aside to be this middleclass wife and mother? I wrote myriad questions and attempts at answers – illuminated now and again with bursts of joy and gratitude for my life, acknowledging the gifts I'd been given.

I dreamed of Karel one night and woke up feeling bereft, my longing for him reawakened. My reaction was dismay; how long would I go on yearning for the impossible? When I looked at the photos of himself Karel had sent me, I saw a balding, fat-bellied middle-aged man with a red nose, and thought, What am I thinking? I had every chance for love and intimacy right next to me, day after day.

Unhappy with practising traditional therapy, I moved to alternate forms, first solution-focused (rather than problem-focused), then narrative therapy, which is based on the premise that we live our lives according to a story that we've been told or have created, often destructive. My job as therapist was to unearth evidence from clients' lives to craft a new story, digging for evidence they had forgotten or discounted.

Then I discovered coaching: through skilful questioning, searching for what a client most valued and wanted, setting concrete goals, then creating the path to achieving them. I took a two-year course and became a life coach, then studied further to qualify as an executive coach, working with managers and leaders to further develop their leadership skills. I became an associate with the Niagara Institute, the leadership development arm of the Conference Board of Canada.

Waiting for a client's call one day, a lightning flash of inspiration hit me. Thanks to technology such as Skype, coaching was portable. Most sessions took place over the phone. Coaching could be my way of returning to Prague! I would fly there several times a year, build up a clientele, and after initial meetings, coach them by phone from Canada.

The border was open. Multinational companies were flooding in, investing, taking advantage of the new markets and low wages. Over the past forty years – two entire generations – the country had lost its middle class, its professionals, its intelligentsia, its executives. The work ethic had been eroded on every level. A common saying during those years captured the prevailing attitude about the state as the sole employer: "If you're not stealing from the state, you're cheating your family." It would take a long time for the country to catch up and become ethical and productive again. The need for coaching that developed basic managerial and business behaviour would be enormous.

The siren call was suddenly impossible to resist. I had to make it happen. Walter agreed it was a great idea and voiced no objections.

I did my homework. I created coaching information kits, met with the Czech Chamber of Commerce in Toronto, researched businesses that had offices in Prague and lined up meetings. I enrolled in a Czech class at the University of Toronto Slavic Languages department, taught by a wonderful professor, Veronika Ambros, another Czech who had fled and made her home in Canada.

It was November of 2003. As I had so many years earlier, I stared out the airplane window, full of excitement as we circled the airport. Seven years since I'd last been there. The doors opened and we streamed into a renovated airport, airy and bright, all chrome and glass. I stepped into the crisp sunshine and breathed the air deep into my lungs. The sky above was a bright blue, life was vibrant all around me. Rows of taxis, passengers being greeted, the sweet magic sound of Czech, and many other languages as well. Across the parking lot was a brand new hotel, a large, modern drug store. Everything clean, up-to-date, efficient.

From my taxi I stared at the familiar landmarks as we zipped along. Construction everywhere, scaffolding covering buildings, construction workers hammering, plastering. The newly restored buildings were freshly stuccoed and painted in their original delicious pastel colours; pale grey with light blue trim, lemon yellow with eggshell trim, pink with grey, leaf green, ochre, sand. I caught a glimpse of the house on U Lužického Semináře where I had lived in the photographer's tiny studio. My room was a souvenir shop now, opening out onto the street. We passed the walled Valdstein Gardens and through the open gates I caught sight of a blaze of fall colours, clipped hedges and raked gravel pathways.

The taxi deposited me at the Blue Key, a small, charming new hotel I'd found over the internet, just one curve away on Letenská from Malostranské Náměstí. The staff greeted me warmly and for the same low price, without my asking, gave me a suite, beautifully decorated in blue and white. The Blue Key was to become my home away from home for the next few years.

I was alone and could wander through the streets of Prague to my heart's content. I'm back, I whispered to the statues on Charles Bridge, to the river, to every familiar place I walked. There again across the Čertovka River were my two windows. My tamarack tree was gone, no doubt outgrown its space. Malostranská Kavárna, where the police informer had sent me his poem on a scrap of paper, was a Starbucks now. I climbed up Nerudova and found U Bonaparta. It was unrecognizable, a tourist menu in English hanging outside the door. I went in. All signs of Bonaparte memorabilia gone, and no sign of anyone I might have known.

I continued walking up the steep street and stood at the low wall overlooking the city, the city at my feet. That beloved scene, the waves of red clay tiles, the church spires, the river. I was bursting with excitement, with profound gratitude to be back – and still, that old deep sorrow.

———

Helena and I had a wonderful reunion over dinner the next evening. She lived now in a spacious apartment in Vinohrady she'd inherited from her aunt. We promised we'd meet often during my stay. I told her about my new work and my plans to build a coaching business in Prague.

"That's great news," she said, "I'll get to see you often." And after a pause, asked, "What about Karel?"

"It's been seven years. He was pretty good the last time I saw him. I never know what to expect. He still phones occasionally, sometimes sober, often drunk. It's a way of life with these guys. Do I want to get tangled up in all that again?"

The next few days were a flurry of meetings: the various chambers of commerce, the Canadian Embassy, Radio Free Europe. Canadians working in the Prague offices of their companies. Each person suggested other names to connect with, and I spent hours in my hotel lining up meetings. A whole new way of being in Prague was opening up for me.

But Karel was everywhere. I still searched the faces of passersby but recognized no one. It was ridiculous, I told myself; as if time had stood still – as if I'd even recognize him or his friends. Finally I couldn't help myself. I called him. Nervous, excited, I sat in my room after breakfast and dialed his number. It was as simple as that. He answered. That familiar, beloved voice.

"*Ano?*"

"*Ahoj, Karle.* I'm here in Prague."

"*Ježíš!* When can I see you? How long are you here for?"

"Two weeks. Tomorrow?"

"Today? This afternoon?"

"I could."

"Come to U Švejku anytime after four." Oh no, I thought, hesitating. "Don't worry," he said. "Things are good."

"All right. I'll come this afternoon."

Filled with both excitement and apprehension, I emerged from the metro, got my bearings, crossed the park and stood outside the pub. Take three, I thought and pulled open the door. He was waiting, and jumped to his feet as I came toward him. We kissed on both cheeks – like old friends. I nodded to his companions and sat down. A beer arrived, which I welcomed, and I drank half of it before putting the stein down.

Karel looked good.

"It's good to see you," he said.

"You too." I was shocked at what I felt. My heart was pounding like a teenager's. Anything I said would be inadequate. Suddenly nothing mattered but that I was here, Karel was beside me, and I was blissfully happy.

"So what brings you to Prague this time?" he said.

I told him about being a coach. "If I succeed I'd be coming several times a year."

He looked at me, a long, serious look. He was so dear, his dark eyes sincere, searching. I had to turn away.

"What about you?" I asked, pulling myself together. "Are you still at that graphics school?"

"I am," he said. "It's working out well."

"Doing any of your own painting?"

"Not yet. But I've been thinking about it lately."

"I'm glad." I remembered seeing his paintings for the first time, overwhelmed by their power, their passion. "I have the graphics you gave me hanging on my walls in Canada," I said.

He looked away. "I don't have many left. Sold a few, but there wasn't much call for paintings like mine back then. When I was at my lowest I was giving them away to buy cigarettes and booze." He paused, then continued, "I still have your portrait, though. I couldn't part with that."

My heart leapt. Oh Karel.

Suddenly he stood up, signalled the barman, threw money on the table and grabbed his jacket. "Let's get out of here." With a nod to his friends, he strode towards the door. I followed.

"Sorry," he said out on the sidewalk. "I had to move. Sometimes I don't know what to do with myself. Let's walk."

We walked side by side in silence through the darkening streets.

"Listen, Helenko," he broke the silence. "You should have your portrait. Take it home with you."

"Surely it's too big," I said.

"It could be done," he said. "Have it wrapped really well – don't take it out of its frame or the oil paint will crack – and take it on the plane. I'll arrange it. I'd like you to have it."

We walked through the quiet streets of Dejvice, its broad avenues, frequent squares and small shops. What was I to do about this beautiful, sad man whom I had loved so much and lost? I didn't know whether to jump for joy at being with him again or weep bitterly at the loss of him and at what the years had done to him. And ... how could I still feel like this? When, I silently raged, would this pain and longing end? When would I be free to live my life as it was, grateful and content? Not now. Not yet.

We both stopped at the same time and turned towards one another. How desperately I longed to throw my arms around him and hold him to me. To feel that joy again. We stood, our arms at our sides, taking in one another, our faces serious. He was the one who turned away first and started walking again. I couldn't help myself – I reached out and took his arm. I felt his body tense.

"We're just walking, that's all," I said. His arm softened. We continued walking, my hand lightly in the crook of his arm. Now and again he gave it a tiny squeeze against his side, as though assuring himself I was really there.

It was getting late. "I'd better go," I said. "I have an early appointment."

"When can I see you again?" Karel asked.

"I can't tomorrow. The day after?"

"All right. Let's meet outside the café in Malostranské Náměstí. Where we used to meet. Four o'clock?"

I agreed. Karel walked with me to the Dejvice metro station. When he bent to kiss me on both cheeks, I had to stop myself from grabbing and holding him. But I ran down the escalator like I was dancing.

I was there by 3:45 and walked round the square, remembering. U Glaubiců, my first local, was still there, unchanged. Rubín, the steep stairs into the wine cellar where I'd first laid eyes on Karel. Lost in memories. And then I saw Karel, leaning against the café window sill, smoking. His eyes lit up and he came towards me.

We walked up Nerudova Street, through that narrow passageway, down the steep steps. Karel had been my guide to Prague, my entree to the city and its people. He had brought the city to life for me and helped make it my home. And now, so many years later, he was doing it again.

He led me under a low arch – I could never have found such a place on my own – to a tiny wine cellar with just three tables. "They have exquisite Moravian wine here," he said as we sat down. Over several glasses of wine, we talked. How could we still have so much to say to one another? Me with my imperfect Czech. It didn't matter. I struggled, but he understood everything I said. We talked, we laughed, a few times I cried, as we tried to make up for all the lost years.

When we left the wine cellar, night had fallen. We climbed up the silent street and entered Petřín, a lovely park stretching across the entire hillside. The lights of Prague glittered below us. I remembered the ball at the Summer Palace, so many years before, Karel and I crossing the park just as dawn was breaking, heading back to my room on Nosticova, coming together again after months of estrangement.

I stopped. "*Karle,*" I said. "*Karlíčku.*" My old pet name for him. We stood looking at each other. Suddenly he threw his arms around me, drew me to him and held me tight. We stood clinging to one another. All my pain and sadness melted away. "*Lásko má,*" he murmured. My love.

To hell with worrying about everyone else, to hell with his being married. This was *my* life, *my* love. "Come back to my hotel with me," I whispered. His arms tightened around me for an instant – and then fell to his sides and he drew back. He turned from me and walked away.

"*Karle!*" I cried, running after him. He whirled and faced me.

"Would you leave your husband and son?" he demanded. "No, you won't. You'd leave me over and over again and then what should I do? Jump off a bridge?"

Tears coursed down my face. I couldn't answer him; I understood he loved me still. But he was right, I would not leave Walter and Adam.

"What about you?" I cried. "It's you who married first, you who stopped waiting for me."

He made a dismissive gesture. "It's you who would keep leaving. I couldn't bear to go through that again."

I was crying. He was in tears himself. Wordlessly we walked down the path to the street below. We passed a pair of lovers sitting on a bench in the dark, murmuring to each other, their arms entwined. If only, I thought.

He walked me to my hotel. At the front door, he looked at me, then without a word, gave me a quick hug and walked away. I stood watching him as he disappeared under the arches to the tram stop. I knew he still loved me; I was desolate that he'd turned me down, though I knew he was right to. But more than anything, I was afraid he wouldn't want to see me again after what had happened between us.

The next day, while I was out, he left a message at the reception desk. "Call me when you have time. I'd like to bring you your portrait to take home."

———

I'd committed myself to a whirlwind of meetings over the next few days, but felt completely disoriented. Who was I, anyway? An entrepreneur focused on establishing a business? An exile still trying to come home? Or the romantic heroine of a long-ago love story as poignant as Casablanca, meeting my long-lost lover almost thirty years later, still obsessed by him and this beloved, accursed city?

I made the rounds, meeting people through the Canadian Embassy and the Canadian Chamber of Commerce, the British and American Chambers of Commerce, handing out business cards everywhere. The HR director at Radio Free Europe, IWAP, the International Women's Association of Prague. The interest was there. Each of them invited me to speak at one of their regular meetings.

One day, needing a break from it all, I went to the café in the magnificent art nouveau Municipal House. The chandeliers sparkled, an elegant silver trolley of pastries trundled by, and as the small orchestra in the corner began to play *Summertime*, all the longing I carried inside overwhelmed me – for my parents, for the past, for everything that was gone. My parents had met in this café. I imagined my mother, young and beautiful, sitting with her parents, waiting for a man named Otto, whom she had recently met. Her parents had wanted to meet him. Otto was delayed, and his much handsomer older brother, the director of the bank across the street, appeared – tall, dignified, a little arrogant, coming to apologize on his foolish brother's behalf and suddenly smitten by this ravishing blue-eyed beauty with a milk and blood complexion, as they say in Czech.

Helena, Markéta and I got together many times; concerts, galleries, a festive lunch of roast duck, sauerkraut and dumplings at Helena's apartment; a gypsy music club with Helena, her friend Kamil, Markéta and her partner, Zbyněk, an evening of dancing, drinking, love and laughter.

Karel was in my thoughts virtually every moment. Finally, I had some free time and I called him. I'd done a lot of thinking. He was right. We would not be lovers again. He had saved me from that danger. But perhaps I could have him as a beloved friend. Would he be willing? And could I be satisfied with that? He invited me to join him at a different pub, near the river, U Rudolfina. I was there first, went in and walked through the pub. A smoky dive. A motley group sat in the back room. I went outside and waited. Karel arrived. My heart leapt as it always did when I saw him; this time with simple relief and pleasure at seeing him. We kissed on both cheeks – I was grateful for that – and he led the way in. Sure enough, we joined the characters in the back room, Karel's friends.

"That fellow there is the best painter in Prague," Karel told me, indicating an old guy with bad teeth.

The man nodded at us and called out, "Are you Karel's wife?"

"No," I laughed, the irony stinging.

"Yes," Karel said, also laughing.

Every now and then the man called out to me down the long table. "You are a beauty! A true beauty!" Another man across the table pulled out a harmonica and began to play Czech folk songs, the group singing along. It was that kind of scene and there I was – among Karel's Bohemian friends again.

At the end of the evening he walked me back to my hotel. We stood looking at one another on the sidewalk outside my hotel, silent, though a flood of thoughts were exchanged – love, regret, desire, renunciation. And then, as he had done so many times in the past, he brushed my cheek with his hand, turned and walked away.

A few days before I was due to leave, Karel arrived at my hotel in a friend's car and delivered my portrait. He gave me a letter he'd written, testifying the portrait was a gift, to prevent any problems at the border.

"Let me know how it turns out, getting it to Canada," he said, and got back in the car and they drove off.

The caretaker at the hotel wrapped it for me, covering it with layers of bubble wrap, then paper, and another layer of plastic, firmly taped. "Take it to the airport by taxi and then to the oversize luggage window – should be no problem," he said when he delivered it to my room.

All those days of sitting for Karel as he painted this enigmatic portrait – I was taking the result home now, a trophy, a prayer.

Karel in front of his portrait of me

Chapter 24

I BECAME A FREQUENT VISITOR TO PRAGUE OVER THE NEXT few years. The staff at the Blue Key came to know me well and gave me the same suite every time. I joined IWAP, a group of three hundred women, either spouses of, or more rarely, themselves employees of multinational companies doing business in Prague. They offered newcomers' luncheons, outings, balls, theatre and dinner evenings – all opportunities to make friends with English-speaking women from all over the world. I was invited to be keynote speaker at one of their monthly meetings. My topic, using the principles of coaching, was taking an active role in creating the life you want. It was well received and led to other engagements, including one at the American embassy, a talk I called "Becoming the CEO of Your Life."

I met the president of the Canadian Chamber of Commerce, Peter Formánek, a Czech who'd escaped to Canada in 1968 and come back with his Canadian wife, Suzanne. They were to become great friends. Through them, I met ambassadors from many countries, politicians, business people and other members of the international community. It was like no other lifestyle I'd ever encountered, people open and accessible to one another up to the highest levels.

All the chambers of commerce held monthly meetings, as well as social events such as weekly pub nights. They were always on the lookout for speakers, and I was invited to speak at the Canadian, American and British chambers. Coaching was a new concept at the time and members were intrigued. The social events were used for active networking, and gave me an opportunity to meet further prospective clients. I expanded my talk to a two-day workshop I gave at the CEELI Institute called, "Creating Your Future: How to Create the Life You Want." With a new friend and colleague, Eva Gordon Smith, a Czech who'd grown up in England and now worked in Prague as a consultant, we gave a workshop called "Leadership and International Communication in Business." I met Dana Stein, a Czech woman well known for her ground-breaking work in memory training. Together we presented a five-day workshop for seniors entitled "Empowering Seniors for Independent Living," my two days dealing with attitudinal and lifestyle aspects, Dana doing three days of memory training.

I offered complementary sessions with each talk or workshop and often a dozen or so people signed up. Sure enough, I enlisted coaching clients from all this activity. We'd have our initial meetings in Prague, subsequent sessions by phone, and I'd return when face-to-face meetings were wanted.

Whenever I came to Prague, I called Karel. His greeting was always happy and welcoming, but he insisted I come to U Švejku. He wouldn't agree to come downtown again. When I urged him to come to one of the pubs or restaurants I preferred – nothing fancy or expensive, just regular pubs – he would refuse. "*Příliš nóbl!*" he'd sneer. Too posh. Nor was he interested in doing anything else. The pub had become a mainstay of his life, an essential part of his daily routine, and he refused to give it up.

I made that now-familiar trek across the park and down the street to the pub. He was there every afternoon, in the same seat at the head of the table with the same drinking buddies. I'd walk in, he'd look up and his face would light up as I crossed the room. There were good times, when we'd sit and talk, but there were times when the barman's slip had many strokes on it and he was already drunk, sometimes barely coherent. I'd leave, heartsick. He'd leave a phone message at the hotel the next day, apologizing, asking me to please come again. He was starting to look unwell, even frail. He had aged. The drinking was taking its toll. "Karel, please stop," I begged him. He'd shrug. I didn't know what I could do or say to change things.

———

On some of my trips to Prague, when he was free, Walter came with me. Realizing I would be coming often, he decided to look for opportunities to get involved in a project of his own. Through the Formáneks, he met Chip Caine, an American architect who'd married a Czech woman and lived in Prague developing real estate. A close business associate of Walter's in Canada was interested in investing in this emerging market, and Walter invested his associate's money in a high-end retirement home called Residence Classis that Chip was building in Průhonice, a wealthy suburb of Prague.

Walter loved the city. It was a thrilling, heady time to be involved in the country, and most of the action was in the capital, which was throbbing with life. New restaurants, cafés and shops were opening on every block in the centre. Office and apartment buildings were springing up or being restored everywhere.

What Walter didn't realize and we were to discover, to his and Chip's dismay, was the degree of corruption that was taking over the country. Czech oligarchs were establishing themselves and moving into positions of power and influence. One of the wealthiest men in the Czech Republic lived in Průhonice and admired the building, completed by then and partially occupied by senior residents. Using his powers of persuasion, he convinced the bank that held the majority of the project's financing – and also managed his own wealth – to call the project loan early, before the retirement home had attracted enough residents to begin turning a profit. The bank foreclosed, Walter and Chip lost their investors' money, and Residence Classis was lost. The existing residents had to be moved elsewhere and the building was taken over by the individual who'd had his eye on it. Walter was devastated. It was the first time in his entire career he had lost investors' money in one of his projects.

———

One day, when I called Karel shortly after I'd arrived, he said, "Come to a new place. In the centre, just off Old Town Square, called U Zlaté Trumpety. At the Golden Trumpet. That's my new meeting place." This sounded hopeful.

When I walked in, I was thrilled to recognize some of the old gang, Zlatá Praha and Spolek Pohodlí. Milan Udržal was there, a prosthesis on his leg. Milan Kohout. So both groups still existed. It was Karel who had avoided them, or been ostracized by them. Several gave a shout of welcome when I walked in and got up to hug me or shake my hand. It was almost like old times.

At some point in the evening, Karel told me he had news for me. "I've started painting again. It's nothing serious. Silly, really." He had a sheepish smile on his face. "Flowers. Flowers in vases. But – they may not be too bad – so far."

"Wonderful, happy news!" I cried. Maybe this could be the beginning of Karel getting back on his feet.

Later, he touched my arm and said, "I have something else to tell you." He hesitated. "I'm divorced."

The group was rowdy and loud. "What?" I said, caught mid-sip, unsure I could believe what I'd heard.

"Míša and I got a divorce."

"Are you serious?"

"It's been terrible between us. She's been an angel with what she's put up with – but I hated her sometimes, and she was tired of my boozing, tired of supporting the family or needing her mother's financial help. We've had it with each other and agreed to part."

"Even now that you're teaching? Painting again? Maybe not drinking so much?"

He shrugged. "In any case, it's over."

"So where are you living?" I said, trying to take it in.

"In my atelier. It's small – but it's all mine." My reaction was excitement and fear.

We walked together to the metro station and I caught the tram back to the Blue Key.

Walter had come with me this time and was awake, reading the *Prague Post*, the country's English language newspaper.

"Come and meet Karel next time, why don't you?" I said. It was important to me that Karel not be a secret. I wanted Walter to think of him as an old friend, interesting to me because of the magical time I'd spent in Prague so many years ago. I didn't know if he sensed the conflict I felt, the powerful pull I still felt towards this man. Perhaps if they met, the spell might be broken and I'd be freed.

Walter agreed. Karel did too when I made the same suggestion. We met at U Zlaté Trumpety on an evening Karel's group wasn't meeting. Walter and I got there first. I was apprehensive, but hopeful. Two worlds colliding. Looking at Walter out of the corner of my eye, I wondered what this was like for him, meeting an artist and a Czech, foreign, exotic. Walter was good at appearing calm and collected no matter what he faced. Was he anxious? Yet I knew his kindness and his integrity would see him through. And Karel? He too was a gentle soul, though he could explode into rages and rail at injustice. How would it be for him, meeting this successful, Western businessman? The man I shared my life with, and wouldn't leave for him? Both were sensitive, vulnerable souls. They would not hurt one another, or me, I was sure.

Karel arrived. I greeted him, and we kissed on both cheeks, the traditional Czech greeting.

"It's good to see you again after all this time," Walter said to Karel in English as they shook hands. "Since Kytlice."

Karel, of course, didn't understand, but he recognized the reference to Kytlice, where they'd met many years before, and it drew a smile of recognition.

"Yes!" he nodded, laughing. "Kytlice."

We pulled it off. Both men had enough social grace to be friendly and respectful and I, in turn, worked hard at bridging and translating. We found much to say to one another, about our boys, Walter asking about conditions in Prague, Karel curious about Walter's work and life in Canada. Over dinner and beer, we became friends. It was a brilliant evening, with much laughter. They liked one another, despite the vastly different worlds they inhabited. They were good men. I loved them both.

One day on a crisp late afternoon in late fall, Karel and I made an arrangement to meet at Malostranské Náměstí and walk through Malá Strana. As we walked down Nerudova, I was looking up at him, laughing, almost skipping, he reaching out and taking my arm, when I happened to look down the street, and there, coming up the street towards us, was Walter. He saw us just as I saw him, and his face blanched. He looked away and made a sudden move as if to turn, pretending he hadn't seen us, or intent on avoiding us. I ran to him.

"Walter! We were just saying goodbye, Karel is taking the tram home. Walk with us to the tram and then you and I will head back to the hotel, okay?"

The two men shook hands and we walked together to the square and waited for Karel's tram to arrive. I was full of regret. Not that we had done anything illicit. But Walter must have seen our happiness, seen the bond between us. A stab in the heart. More than anything, I didn't want to hurt him.

Walter and I were having dinner one evening at the home of Tom and Dáša Smit, friends we'd met through the Formáneks. Tom was a wealthy South African based in England. Travelling to the Czech Republic on business a few years ago, he'd met a beautiful Czech girl, Dáša, and moved to Prague. They were describing how they'd found the magnificent flat they lived in.

"I'd love to have a flat of our own," I said, turning to Walter. "The Blue Key is lovely but … it's not home."

"I think you need to be a citizen to buy a flat," Tom said. "Or own a registered company."

"Let's look into that," Walter said.

Dáša looked thoughtful, then told us about a friend named Franco, a wealthy Italian who travelled to Prague often and had bought and renovated a flat for his mistress, whom Dáša knew. Tired of waiting, she'd found another lover and moved out. "He's hoping she comes back – but she won't. I'll see what I can do."

Flats were available now. Real estate agencies had sprung up with flats for sale or rent, some renovated, some needing drastic remodelling. This sounded promising, and there'd be no agent's commission.

The other thing I had been thinking about was how wonderful it would be to actually be a Czech citizen; perhaps then I'd truly belong. I consulted a lawyer, Mr. Kubík, young, blond, earnest, and very knowledgeable. He spoke fluent English. He advised us that, yes, one had to be a citizen to own property. "Officially, having been born here, you are a Czech citizen already, you just don't have the papers to prove it," he said. "Did you ever renounce your citizenship?"

Both my parents had, but I hadn't, I told him.

"Good," he said. It was a complicated process, he explained, especially in my case, having been divorced and remarried. "We'll apply for a birth certificate and then a passport. You can't get a Czech identity card unless you have a permanent address here."

I told him we were looking into buying a flat and he agreed to act for us, should we find something. Over the next months, he navigated us through the intricacies of Czech bureaucracy. He accompanied me from one functionary's office to another while we were in Prague, then worked on my behalf in our absence.

Getting my papers was very complicated, including my having to have my divorce papers "superlegalized" and sent to the Supreme Court in Brno to ratify my divorce; only then could they recognize the legality of my marriage to Walter. "According to Czech law, I've been a bigamist since I married you," I said to Walter, laughing.

Next came the problem of my surname being different than Walter's, and even worse, that Adam's surname was a hyphenated combination of our two names, neither being common or approved-of practices in the Czech Republic. Adam's birth certificate had to be "superlegalized," witnesses found and sworn in, and Walter had to appear with me, produce witnesses, and swear that he was indeed Adam's father. We supplied Mr. Kubík with everything required, and waited.

———

In the meantime, in phone calls from Canada, I hounded Dáša. Couldn't she press Franco harder? She was working on him, she'd say. No luck so far.

Finally Walter and I arrived in Prague one day and called her.

"Good news – he's considering it," she said. "Let's go have a look – make sure you like it."

She picked us up and we drove to Vinohrady, actually zipping by the intersection where Růža had lived. Polská, I read as we turned down a one-way street. Dáša pulled into a parking spot across from a park. We stood in front of a building painted a pale butter yellow with white trim, directly across from the park.

Dáša led the way up to the third floor. Three doors on the landing, two an unpleasant mustard colour, one a gleaming, white enamel. She inserted the key into that door's lock, and we entered a beautiful, high-ceilinged apartment, fresh white walls, the light streaming in through two impossibly tall living room windows. A large bedroom with a bay window, a walk-in closet. A modern bathroom and kitchen. Across the street dogs frolicked on the grassy hillside, joggers ran and mothers pushed strollers along the paved pathways.

"Dáša, it's perfect!" I said. Walter loved it too. A few days later, Dáša called to say Franco had agreed. That evening she and Tom met us at their favourite restaurant to celebrate. "Here's to coming home," Walter said to me.

"To coming home," Dáša and Tom echoed, and we raised our glasses.

The coincidences were astonishing. I'd been born on Blanická Street and discovered it was three streets away, ending on the same park. My mother had probably wheeled me in my pram to the very same park. The Formáneks lived just two blocks away and Helena's flat was four blocks away, just off the square which was to become our locale for shopping, pubbing and café sitting. There was a metro stop on the square with

Wenceslas Square just two stops from our building, and the State Opera was twenty minutes of downhill strolling away.

Several weeks later I bought the flat. Franco had established the date of our meeting, and Walter couldn't get away. He was fine with my taking care of things, as the flat was to be registered in my name in any case.

Endless documents, signatures, stamps, a notary called in to witness everything, a flurry of talk – Czech, English, Italian, Dáša translating for Franco in fluent Italian. And at the end, I shook hands with Franco, and Mr. Šisl, the property manager, handed me the keys.

"And I have this for you," Mr. Kubík said once the others had left, handing me an envelope. I tore it open. My birth certificate. I held it in my hand and cried. My official birth number and the address where I was born, in their records all this time, as if I'd been here all along. I'd never had a birth certificate; all I'd had for identification was my Canadian citizenship document from 1951, when I was seven years old, and then later of course a Canadian passport.

Mr. Kubík handed me a second envelope. I tore it open – my Czech passport. I was not only a Czech citizen, but now a citizen of Europe. I threw it in the air, whooping with joy and hugged smiling Mr. Kubík.

I raced to the flat, opened the street door, ran up the stairs, across the tiled landing, unlocked my door and stepped inside. It was beautiful. Quiet, bright, fresh white walls, sunlight pouring in. The trees in the park shimmered with new life, the grass a vivid green.

Home at last.

———

Walter and I had a marvellous time furnishing it. We bought most of the major furniture at Ikea, including a blue and white sofa-bed, where Adam would sleep, we told each other. The most fun was finding Czech art in antique bazaars, oil paintings by lesser, earlier Czech artists; a mother and child, Czech landscapes, an ancient panorama of Prague in an elaborate gilt frame. My favourite was a framed graphic from 1940 by Josef Soukup that I hung in the vestibule, containing every aspect of Czech life and tradition in one unlikely scene. Underneath in calligraphy were the resonant words of the national anthem, *Kde domov můj?* Where is my home?

One afternoon I was at the flat alone, waiting for a delivery, sitting in the living room, looking with delight at the home we were creating, when I was overcome with a profound sadness. So many people I loved were gone. My mother and father would never see this, never share in our good fortune; grandfather and Uncle Paul, Růža, Malý Pavel, his wife Helena – all gone. I busy myself, I thought, with my new life here, with my projects and work, new friends and contacts. All that is a thin surface laid over a deep emotional sea, full of changing tides and currents, all the way back to my life here as a child, the harrowing escape, the songs and stories, the yearning that seeped into my very bones.

I made myself a cup of tea and took it into the bedroom. With our wonderful Czech bed we'd bought two great pillows. I'd bought them thinking of my mother's pillowcases, a set of oversize, almost square monogrammed pillowcases that had been part of her trousseau. I'd imagined her sitting in the apartment on Jugoslávská with my grandmother, sewing her elegant initials, *MK*, Martha Kratochvílová, on her fine cotton pillowcases, duvet covers and sheets – which I'd asked for many years ago and she had given me. They had languished in the back of a closet in Canada, unusable, the sizes so different. I can use them now, I thought.

My mother wasn't able to find contentment and luxuriate in her life, because home and happiness always lay elsewhere. Well, look what I've done, I smiled, standing up, stretching. I have created a place for her monogrammed pillowcases. I will bring them from Canada, put them around these plump luscious pillows, and honour her. Could I be happy and luxuriate in my life at last, as I'd wished so much for her?

Chapter 25

"HOW'S THE PAINTING COMING ALONG?" I ASKED KAREL THE
next time we met. We were at U Švejku again, a month or so
later, and I was in Prague alone.

He shook his head. "Painting flowers is meaningless – as
bad as happy peasants hauling sheaves of wheat."

"Then paint something else!"

"A while back when I needed the money, I was doing some
portraits – they actually weren't half bad. But I just don't have
it anymore."

He was silent for a moment, took a long pull on his beer,
then added, "Your niece Helena called and wants me to do a
portrait of her and Markéta." It turned out Helena had bought
one of his flower paintings. Karel had called her, needing the
money. "I told her I wasn't painting anymore."

"Karel, what a great opportunity. Do it!"

"It's been too long."

"Really, give it a try! It could get you started again."

He stared at me. "You think I should?" I could see the fear
and the desire fighting it out.

He lit a cigarette with shaky hands. "I don't know if I have
the courage."

"It's Helena – she's practically family. If it doesn't work out, you've lost nothing."

"She's offered to pay for the supplies. I wouldn't charge her if she didn't like it. But I couldn't afford to return her money."

"She wouldn't want you to. But I think she'll like it – she knows your work."

"I'll think about it."

"Do, please." I felt immensely grateful to Helena for the idea. It could get Karel back on his feet. Clearly painting was essential to his survival.

"I've wanted to do another portrait of you for a long time," Karel said tentatively. "Would you be willing?"

I imagined sitting for him again, watching him work, Karel focused, happy and productive. I nodded, unable to speak, then managed, "I would."

He took a drink. "All right then. I'll do it. First theirs, then yours." Triumphantly, we raised our steins and sealed the deal.

"Where shall we sit for you?"

"I was doing them differently. A friend of mine is a great photographer – or would be if he'd quit drinking long enough. I get him to take photos of the subject and I paint from that." A flare of regret – no sitting for him after all.

"How about we meet Saturday morning – if the weather's good – for the photo session? I'll line up the photographer, you ask Helena and Markéta."

Saturday morning, Helena, Markéta and I met at U Švejku and had a couple of beers with Karel and his friend the photographer – whose name was also Karel, it being one of the most popular men's names in Czech, after King Charles, the greatest of Bohemian kings – and the rest of the guys, already sitting at their usual table. Karel the photographer was a serious alcoholic.

"I warned him he'd damn well better be in shape to do the photography," Karel said.

The photographer was drinking soda water, his hands shaking, his face pale, his fat body white and trembling. He was sweet, eager, accommodating, clearly anxious to do a good job.

In the park across the road, Karel became our director, instructing the photographer what settings and backgrounds he wanted, angles, close-ups, telling us how and where to sit, what to do with our hands, lift your head a little, look at me, now off into the distance.

Helena gave Karel instructions right back. "I want my ancestors to think, 'She was a fine-looking woman!' when they see their great-grandmother's portrait on the wall. Don't paint me too *pneumatická!*"

The sun was shining, a warm mid-morning in late May. We moved from pose to pose, hamming it up, swinging on the swing set, laughing, silly, serious at times, a wonderful, happy day. We were creating memories that would be fixed forever by Karel's creation.

Hours later we repaired to the pub while Karel the photographer took the film to a Fuji shop down the road. He brought back negatives, contact sheets and a few prints which we passed around. Karel would choose the ones he liked, and we'd meet again to see if we agreed.

Karel the photographer, his job done, ordered his first beer and was transformed. He relaxed, his shaking stopped, his anxiety vanished, and he sat back in his seat, affable, easygoing, restored. Jesus, what this goddamn booze does to people, I reflected. And I get sucked right into it myself, drinking along with the rest, accepting it, in fact loving it, as part of this Bohemian lifestyle. Yet so many lives destroyed.

Congratulating one another on a great day, and full of exhilaration, Karel and I parted from the others.

"Let's go to Šárka – it's beautiful this time of year," Karel said to me. We took the tram and strolled down the steep path to the large, wilderness ravine, its craggy cliffs rising above us.

Pointing to a grove of trees on a distant hillside, Karel said, "We made love there once." Long ago, and lost to me now.

We spent the afternoon walking through the park, stopping at pubs or cafés along the way. We talked and talked, about life in Prague now, life in general – happiness, art, loss, change; it was amazing how much we always had to say to one another. We laughed, several times we were close to tears. At times I took his arm, or he'd reach out and take my hand. When night fell we were back in Dejvice and back in the pub, not wanting to part. Midnight came. The trams and metro stopped.

"Let me come back to your studio," I begged. "I don't want to go back alone." Karel assented. It was a tiny bachelor flat with a studio bed, an armchair, a table and kitchen alcove. In one corner was a shelf piled with art supplies. A collapsed easel was propped against the wall. Karel offered me a drink. I took it. We stared at one another. He downed his.

"You sleep in the bed. I'm fine sleeping in the chair, I've done it often," he said, and went out to the washroom.

I took off my clothes, all but my panties and silk camisole, and slipped under the covers of the studio bed. Karel came back. I held out my arm.

"Helenko, I can't," he said. "I want to, desperately. But the years and the drinking have done me in. I simply can't."

"I don't care about that," I said. "I just want you near me."

He lay down beside me, still in his shirt and jeans. How exquisite to have him so near. Tentatively I put a hand on his arm. Like chaste children we lay awake, talking quietly, taking comfort in one another's presence, until we fell asleep. In the morning, he brought me a cup of coffee, his expression tentative, a composite of happiness, sorrow, regret. I felt sorrow at not being together, at the events that had parted us, and gratitude that we still had one another even in this way. I dressed, and after a quick embrace, left.

———

Karel had terrible news for me the next time I was in town. He'd been put on probation at the school. "Those bastards, those self-righteous assholes," he raged. "Somebody ratted on me – so I'd had a few beers. Big deal." Turned out he'd been showing up to class drunk or not showing up at all. "Hauled me out of class and made me blow into some goddamn instrument that proved I was drunk. Me, an academic painter, one of their best instructors. They're lucky to have me in their fucking school!" He'd been given a warning – if he was caught drunk again, he'd be fired.

"Karel, that does it," I said. "You absolutely have to stop drinking." I used every argument, every entreaty I could come up with. "And quit feeling sorry for yourself. You have to take this seriously."

He calmed down. "You're right, I do. I promise."

———

Several months went by before I saw Karel again. "Come to U Zlaté Trumpety," he said when I called. There he was when I walked in, sitting among his friends, the usual raucous scene. He looked good – animated, happy. He greeted me with a hug, ordered me a beer and pointed at the glass in front of him.

"Soda water," he beamed. "I haven't had a drink since that evening with you." He had kept his promise. "Things are good at the school, too. I apologized to them. I can be an idiot."

"You can."

"Guess what else!" he went on. "I've been painting since then. Helena and Markéta's portrait is finished – and it's not bad at all. In fact Helena loves it." I could have jumped for joy. He was lucid and full of plans. "Next I'll start on yours. I'm going to call it *The Return*."

"I'm honoured. That's what this is, all right." We talked and laughed, and were happy.

The photo for Karel's new portrait of me to be titled The Return.

Helena invited Walter and me for dinner, along with the new man in her life, Pawel – the Polish form of Pavel, or Paul – a charming, warm, fun-loving man in his fifties, who kissed my hand when introduced to me. He was a reporter for Polish radio and television on current events in the Czech Republic. Markéta and her fiancé Zbyněk were there. Karel's portrait of Helena and Markéta hung in her dining room, beside his flower painting. It was beautifully rendered, capturing their essences, Helena, her head tilted a little to one side, her expression wistful yet contented, Markéta staring directly out at the viewer, serious, intense.

"Your commissioning this saved Karel," I said to Helena.

"He's worth saving," Helena said, "and we're thrilled with the portrait."

"Now I'll start on yours," Karel said when I next saw him. He continued to order soda water and tea, despite what the others were drinking. I gave him five thousand crowns for materials to begin working on my portrait.

One night the following year the phone rang late at night. A chill ran through me. A premonition? It was Karel. "Why aren't you here?" he demanded, his voice thick. He was terribly drunk.

"You're drinking again!" I yelled. "What happened?"

"I proved I could quit if I wanted to," he said. "Well, I don't want to anymore." He went on, railing, lamenting, becoming incoherent, then crying again. "Why aren't you here? When will you come again?"

"Next month."

"Come sooner!"

"I can't. I'll see you next month," I said, and hung up.

Karel, I cried silently, don't do this.

———

The next time I was in Prague, I called. He asked me to meet him a U Zlaté Trumpety. There was something about his voice that worried me, frightened me. When I walked in, the first thing I noticed was the beer in front of him. He threw me a glance that frightened me more.

"It's bad, Helen," he said when I'd sat down. "I've been thrown out of the school." I stared at him, speechless. "I wasn't even drunk!"

"What then?" I whispered.

"I've been charged with insubordination. All because I refused to blow into that damn tube again. Nobody but the police has the right to make you do that. A buddy of mine told me that. So when they asked me to, I refused. On principle! I hadn't had a drink in months – you know that! I told them so, and that they didn't have the right to make me do it. But they charged me with insubordination anyway and threw me out!"

I was close to tears. On stupid, stubborn principle. They figured they had the right despite what some idiot pub buddy of Karel's claimed.

"So I started drinking again – at the injustice!"

"Might they take you back, if you apologize, explain?"

"No. I've burned that bridge."

"Other schools? Teaching privately?"

He shook his head, drank.

"What are you going to do?"

"I don't know." We sat in silence, contemplating one another. I wanted to enfold him in my arms and I wanted to rage at him.

"You owe me a portrait."

"I know." He shrugged.

"Start working on it. Other things will come up in the meantime, other ideas. Start, please!"

"I'll try."

We walked through Old Town Square, full of tourists and Praguers, the outdoor cafés bursting with life, with music, the magnificent buildings glittering with light. Crossing the river, we stopped to lean over the parapet, breathing in the soft night air, the river flowing swiftly beneath us, the castle luminous above. There was the Summer Castle, and I saw myself again walking through the park at dawn after the ball, back to my room on Nosticova, full of love and yearning for this tragic man, now nearly sixty years old, still beloved.

I took his arm and he walked me back to my metro stop. So much life had been lived between us. So many years of loss and love.

"I'll be back in June," I said. "Please take good care of yourself," I said. "Please."

He held me tight for a moment and watched as I disappeared down the escalator into the station.

Walter and I were back in June, less than two months later. I called Karel. "You're here!" he cried. "Come to U Švejku. Right now."

"No," I said, "I won't come there. Somewhere else or not at all."

He was silent a moment. "Tomorrow afternoon then. There's a sixtieth birthday party for Tomáš. You know our old Zlatá Praha ritual – you make it to sixty, you host a celebration and you're declared a president. That'll be me next year." He laughed – a rough, bitter laugh. "Come with me. Meet me, four o'clock, Hradčany metro. Will you?" I agreed.

He was late. I waited for him there and finally I caught sight of that familiar khaki jacket and jeans. But the stride I'd known so well was gone. He was unsteady on his feet and walked with a shuffle, his steps small and slow, like an old man's. He saw me and waved. When he came closer, he smiled. I reeled back. One of his front teeth was missing. He reached out and hugged me. He smelled. He was thin, lost in his clothes. He must have forgotten his belt, his pants hanging low like a skateboarder's. His face was grey, sallow. He looked emaciated. When he spoke, his eyes wouldn't focus.

"This way," he said, turning up a side street. I caught up with him.

He waved a paper tube. "A present for Tomáš," he said.

"You're painting?"

He laughed harshly. "No. It's an old one I found. One of the few I have left. He can have it." After a moment's silence, "I don't paint any more. I'm finished with all that."

Out of the corner of my eye, I saw him reach into his jacket pocket and surreptitiously pull out a mickey. He took a quick gulp and dropped it back into his pocket. I stood staring after him, shocked.

"Oh my God, Karel, what's happened?" He didn't answer. He lurched forward as we entered a small park.

"Let's sit for a minute," he said, sinking down on a bench.

"What happened to your tooth?" I asked.

"How the hell do I know?" he barked. "I've got wounds and bruises all over me. I've no idea how they got there."

"Jesus Christ," I whispered.

He reached into his pocket and took a drink, then put the bottle back in his pocket. He saw the look on my face. "I'm sorry, Helen," he said, his shoulders slumped, his eyes down.

I was crying now. "You have to stop, Karel."

"I can't."

"You can. You have to. You've done it before."

"I can't any more. I have to drink."

"What do you mean?" I said. "Are you sick? Is something the matter?"

"No!" he said angrily.

"Then why do you have to?"

"I'm in terrible shape, physically and mentally – I know that, and it's my own fault. I deserve everything that's happened to me. I have to drink just to cope."

"You can't do this!" I cried. "I need you here! Prague isn't Prague without you. What will I do without you here?"

I looked at him, the sun in my eyes. "You are so beautiful," he said. "You have the most beautiful eyes I have ever seen. Cerulean blue."

At that moment a little dog ran over and jumped up, his paws resting on my knees. I rubbed its ears and stroked it, and spoke to it in English, softly and sweetly – blessed relief – and then it moved over and jumped against Karel's knees and he played with it too, a brief moment of innocence and simple joy. Then the dog ran off after its master.

Karel turned to me. "May my boys forgive me – what I regret more than anything else in my life is losing you," he said. He reached forward and grazed my cheek with the back of his hand. "*Lásko má.*"

Tears streamed down my face. I had to turn away. How much of this was my fault? Was this happening to him because of me? I'd often raged at the country that had destroyed their very best, the sensitive, the aspiring, the creative. But what part of this lay at my door? Would he have been happier, his life better, if I'd never come to Prague, never descended those stairs at Rubín late that night?

Karel roused himself, stood up and walked away towards a stand of trees. I was shocked to realize he was urinating. Instead of coming back, he zipped up and walked toward the far side of the park. I had to run after him, carrying his gift. When I caught up with him, he muttered something about not being able to find me, seeing only blackness. That's how he was – he'd be present and coherent one moment, take a swig of vodka and be gone, incoherent, lost.

We walked, him in the lead, until we came to a garden restaurant with tables and chairs and gaily coloured umbrellas. Well-dressed people stood around, laughing and chatting, drinks in their hands. The celebrants, a handsome couple, surrounded by friends. People looked at us, looked away. I recognized some of Karel's old friends, including Milan Udržal, sitting at a nearly table. I nodded to them. Karel didn't acknowledge them. We made our way inside and to the bar. No one spoke to us.

"What will you have?" Karel asked me. What should I do? "A glass of red wine."

"Two," he told the bartender. We took them to a table and sat down.

Karel waved the tube. "I'll take this inside to Tomáš. I'll be right back."

After what seemed like a very long time, I saw Karel coming back. He was staggering. He sat down without looking at me. "The bastards. I don't give a shit about them. Let him shove it up his ass." I gathered that his gift had not been well received. He reached for his glass of wine. "I can't drink this," he said. "Let's get out of here."

I felt everyone's eyes on us as we made our way past them and out the door. I took Karel's arm until we were outside, in the sun again. I was terribly ashamed.

"I need to go home," Karel said.

We walked along the sidewalk back toward the Hradčany tram stop. He lurched and slipped off the sidewalk, catching and righting himself just before falling. I grabbed his arm, but he shook me off, barking, "I can walk!" Finally he turned to me and said, his voice contrite, "Helenko, please help me. I can't make it on my own."

I took his arm. We walked together with me steadying him, at times holding him up, all the way to his tram stop. He was going one way, I the other. I waited with him until his tram arrived. People waited, staring with disapproval as he hauled himself up the steps. I watched him collapse into a seat. He didn't look at me. I was sick with shame, anger and sadness.

He phoned me the next morning and apologized. "I was drunk," he said. "Did I do anything terrible?" Your being so drunk *is* doing something terrible, you idiot, I thought.

"No," I said, "you didn't do anything terrible. Please take care of yourself."

I left Prague a few days later without seeing him again.

Chapter 26

A MONTH LATER, EARLY ONE EVENING IN JULY, I WAS working in my office at our home in Toronto when the phone rang. I picked up the receiver to hear a woman's voice, tentative and halting, speaking in Czech.

"*Dobrý den. Je to paní Helena?*"

"*Ano,*" I answered.

"This is Míša Zavadilová." She paused. My mind laboured to switch gears to this other language, this other world. Míša Zavadil. Karel's ex-wife. Calling *me*? "We don't know one another," she continued, in Czech, "—well actually we met once long ago in Kytlice, at the cottage."

A chill went through me. Of course I remembered. But why was she calling me? "*Ano, ano,*" I said. Yes.

"I hope I'm not disturbing you or intruding on you and your family," she went on. No, not at all, I assured her.

"I'm afraid I have bad news." She hesitated. "I thought you would want to know."

"What is it?"

"It's Karel. He fell in the street a week ago and hit the back of his head on the sidewalk."

"Oh my God. Will he be all right?"

"He'd been drinking. He was drunk."

"Yes, I know, I know," I said impatiently. "The last time I saw him, I had to help him walk. How is he? Tell me!"

"The fall shattered his skull. He never regained consciousness. He died yesterday morning. I found your phone number in his wallet. The only number he had."

A flood of the most immense grief washed over me. I had to get off the phone. I couldn't think of the proper terms to express my sympathy for her loss, or her sons'.

"I'm so sorry," I managed to say. "Thank you for calling me. I'm sorry, I have to hang up."

"I think I know how much you two meant to one another," she said.

"Perhaps we could talk again later," I said.

"The funeral is the day after tomorrow. Very short notice, I know. I don't suppose you can come?"

The day after tomorrow. His funeral. No. I couldn't.

"I'll mail you the death notice," she said. "Would you like me to?"

"Yes, I would like to have it," I said. His death notice.

———

I sat at my desk and despite the warm evening, I started shaking. I sat for a long time, staring ahead, frozen. Outside night fell and I sat in darkness. Prague without Karel. I couldn't imagine it. To not be able to call him and have him exclaim, "*Helenko! You're here! Come and meet me!*" To not be able to walk into U Švejku, to see his face transformed by a smile. To never hear the words, *Lásko má* again.

As though from a distance, I was amazed and curious about my own shock, like an accident victim staring at his shattered limbs. Didn't I see it coming, given the state he was in the last time I saw him? That desperate need to drink, how gaunt he looked, the gaping hole between his front teeth. Somehow I'd hoped he would recover. Hadn't he done it before?

I buried my head in my arms and wept.

———

As I went through my days over the next weeks, I was astonished at how profoundly Karel's death affected me. Flashbacks. The songs. *Řeka Lásky*, River of Love. *Nedělní Ráno*, the Czech version of Sunday Morning Coming Down:

> *A proč divný smutek mívám*
> *to snad se nikdy nedovím.*
> "And why do I have such a strange sadness?
> Perhaps I'll never know ..."

Karel saying to me, it's true, you know, there's truth to those words.

———

Vivid memories, wild thoughts. His death was Míša's fault, she should never have married him, knowing he loved someone else. She trapped him into an unhappy marriage and he became an alcoholic as a result. All on her.

Why is this so huge for me? I asked myself. The thought: I wonder if I've truly lived since then, since being thrown out of Czechoslovakia. Or maybe even since our escape, when I was four years old and lost so much. Helena said once that

Karel lived in the past, coming to life telling stories of our time together, sharp and clear in his mind as though they'd happened just yesterday. It's true for me too, I realized. Karel had been a backdrop to my life all this time.

I felt disloyal to Walter thinking these thoughts. I hated the thought that having loved Karel for so long was at the expense of my relationship with Walter. I couldn't have created a better life than the one Walter and I shared. Did I wish I'd stayed and been with Karel all these years? No! Especially if he'd continued to drink. Could I have prevented it, saved him? There was no way of knowing. I'd simply loved him – and it had nothing to do with Walter. I was discovering through my grieving, through the incredible, ongoing pain, how important he'd been to me. I kept seeing us sitting recently at U Zlaté Trumpety, with Walter and Helena and Markéta, Karel telling stories, talking to me, so full of life and kindness and sweetness. So full of life.

Lásko má, he'd say to me after walking me back to my hotel. He had loved me all that time, and I him. Just to be able to do that was enough. Meet, go for a walk, talk. So much history – yet we'd been together barely more than a year.

I couldn't imagine going to U Švejku, to U Zlaté Trumpety, and he not there, never there again – his smile, his khaki jacket, his slightly slouchy walk, his moustache, his fine brown hair.

———

I didn't get back to Prague until October, when I'd committed to delivering a workshop I called "Creating Your Future: How to Create the Life You Want" at the American embassy. The workshop successfully over, I began the main thing I had come to do – to discover Prague without Karel. I left my flat – so welcoming and comforting – and walked down Polská to Wenceslas Square, choosing the broad pedestrian boulevard that ran down its centre, then through the narrow streets that opened up into Old Town Square, to U Zlaté Trumpety. It was just noon. I stood in the doorway – nobody there but a few tourists having lunch.

I checked all our favourite places. Standing on Charles Bridge, I watched a young man rowing a boat, his partner sitting in the stern, her face uplifted toward the autumn sun. As always, I went to Kampa, looked across the Čertovka River at my two windows. Then to U Fazole and stood in the court-yard, the aroma of baking pastries wafting from the bakery that had taken over the coach house.

Karel's absence was everywhere, and I was lost. Prague was transformed, lonely, meaningless. It was nothing but buildings, cobblestones, trams – impersonal and cold.

Exhausted, I sat in my flat, wondering what to do. I needed to stop looking for him. How could I teach my heart what had happened? Finally it came to me; I called Míša. She was friendly and agreed to meet me the next day at the Slavia Café on the river.

"I don't know if I'd recognize you," I said. "It's been twenty years."

"I'll have no trouble recognizing you," she cut in. "I'll know you from your portrait."

A brown-haired woman stood in front of the café. Tall and lanky, a little stooped, she wore a long brown skirt and a quilted jacket. We locked eyes.

"*Helenko?*" she said, reaching out her hand.

The name Karel had called me. She led the way into the café. She was a mild, kindly woman with nervous hands. We ordered our coffee. I thanked her for meeting me, told her I still couldn't believe it was true.

"I'm sorry I wasn't at the funeral," I said. "That would have helped."

"It was very quiet, very short."

"Who was there?" I asked. "Who spoke?"

"There were very few people. No one spoke."

"No one? His friends? Spolek Pohodlí? Zlatá Praha?"

"Nobody from either one. We played a couple of songs he liked by Johnny Cash, his favourite singer. Desolation Road was one of them. Neither my sons nor I could bring ourselves to speak. What could we say? His life was a tragedy."

I asked after her sons. I hadn't thought much about how it was for them.

"They're having a hard time. He was difficult, but they loved him despite everything. If you want to see where he's buried, my sons could take you. They visit every now and then."

No, I thought. Not yet.

Míša was treating me as a friend, showing no sign of anger or jealousy.

"It was very kind of you to call me," I said.

"You meant a lot to him."

I asked her to tell me again, to describe what had happened. I needed to hear it again, to make it real, believable. She told me of his fall, of a neighbour coming home and finding him lying in the gutter, calling an ambulance; of his lying unconscious for a week in the hospital. He'd been coming home from the pub. "Or wherever," Míša sighed. "They said if he'd recovered consciousness, he wouldn't have been right. His brain was severely damaged."

"Míša, why did he start drinking so deliberately, so desperately, at the end?" His broken teeth, the bruises.

"I don't know," she said. "He never got over losing his job at the Academy. He became unbearable after the revolution. He became abusive towards me, something he'd never been. Ashamed, he'd disappear for days at a time, hiding out in his atelier. We were afraid he'd killed himself. He'd come back until the rage came over him again. We both agreed it was best to split up. I was so happy when he got the job at the graphic school and even stopped drinking for a while. But they let him go, and it was downhill from then.

"I still took care of him," she continued, "doing his laundry, shopping for him, bringing him meals. I couldn't let my children's father go around like a homeless man."

He'd called her an angel. I understood.

"If I hadn't been a social worker, I couldn't have stood it as long as I did," she said. "I treated him like one of my clients."

I asked her question after question. There were so many things I hadn't known about him. Karel and I had been together for a year; she'd been with him for thirty years. He'd never spoken about his family or his childhood. We had lived purely in the present, from one shining day to the next.

"His parents were poor, though his father was a functionary in the Communist party. He'd been in a concentration camp, Dachau, during the war. Both parents were rabid communists. They worshipped Stalin and our own traitorous leader, Gottwald. When the Russians invaded in 1968, they wished they'd stay forever. They believed all that bullshit propaganda. What he lived through with his parents was total insanity

– and he an artist and dissident. And yet he loved them, loved them desperately. Imagine how that screwed up his head."

I listened intently, hungry for everything she could tell me.

"His mother was an alcoholic, had bottles hidden all over the apartment. He was boisterous as a child, and his mother couldn't manage him. She'd scream at him and beat him. His sister, thirteen years older, married with children of her own at the time, told me she'd pitied him, wished he could live with her.

"Most of all, he couldn't figure out his stance toward things. He was lost. It killed him to have joined the party. He'd have been better off if he'd never agreed. If he lost his job, so be it. But he signed on, and paid for it anyway sixteen years later. Do you see? How could he not have joined, given his love for his parents, and what they'd done to get him educated and into his beloved Academy? Yet how *could* he have joined, given his dissident circle and his artist's sensibilities? He was a sensitive soul. I think he drank to try to make himself tougher, stronger."

I thought of how I'd railed at him.

"After the revolution, he became a pariah. When I married him, even my friends were shocked at my marrying a communist. People are stupid.

"He was like a wounded bear," Míša continued. "I don't believe it would have been any different with you. I bore the brunt. In the end, you can consider yourself lucky, Helenko."

A novel perspective. I was amazed at her. She felt no blame towards me. I didn't let myself off so easily, certain that I bore some responsibility for what had happened to him.

"I often said to Karel, these last years, how I wished I could come along to his meetings with you," Míša said. "I'd have liked to get to know you. But he refused." So she didn't know. I wouldn't have welcomed her joining us on our walks through Prague.

I asked her if Spolek Pohodlí and Zlatá Praha were still meeting. Yes, she told me, but in a different place, in a café on a side street near Nerudova, a café tourists hadn't found yet called U Zavěšenýho Kafe. At the Hanging Coffee. "Once a month on a Wednesday, I'm not sure which one. Karel never invited me. But you could go," she said.

"Maybe I will," I said.

Míša put her hand on my arm. "Helenko. I want to tell you something. He may have married me ... but you were always the one. The only one."

The stone in my chest lightened a little. How generous of her to say this to me. I wondered how difficult it had been for her to live with that.

As we parted at the door, she kissed me on both cheeks. "Call me if you want to meet again," she said. "Perhaps we could be friends."

I climbed steep Nerudova Street and found the café, a tiny storefront covered with ivy. Peering through the dark window, my hand on the doorknob, I hesitated, and turned away. Perhaps another day.

Helena had told me a good friend of hers knew Milan Kohout, Karel's old friend and a member of Spolek Pohodlí. She called her friend, got his number for me and I called him. He lived in the country but agreed to come to town to meet with me at U Glaubiců.

He had white hair and a white moustache, but his smile was just as infectious. We greeted one another like old friends. It helped to know Karel's Bohemia still existed, and I still had some access to it.

"Milan, you look just the same," I said. "I'd recognize you anywhere!"

"You too," he said. "Just as beautiful."

"Hardly," I said. "Fill me in, Milan. Help me understand what happened to Karel."

"He dropped out," he said. "The art world shunned him – because he was a communist! Can you believe it? Even his so-called friends. He was in a rage most of the time, impossible to be around."

"Tell me about back then, when I got thrown out."

"Honza was an informer, paid two thousand crowns every time he gave the police some information, the bastard. We threw him out. I've no idea what's happened to him."

We drank our beers and reminisced. The steamboat ride, the apartment awash with soup. All the good times.

"Come to one of our meetings, first Wednesday every month, to U Zavěšenýho Kafe," Milan said. And as we were parting, he added, "One day you and your husband could come visit me in the country. You remember, you and Karel were there once, sleeping in the hayloft."

"Oh yes," I said, "I remember."

Chapter 27

THE FOLLOWING YEAR, ADAM, NOW TWENTY-FIVE, APPLIED for Czech citizenship, being entitled to it as the child of a Czech mother. It was fairly straightforward, now that I had all my documents in order. Wonderful Mr. Kubík took care of the details and the final papers were ready for Adam's signature. In the spring, Walter, Adam and I came to Prague to celebrate his becoming a Czech. We took Mr. Kubík out to dinner and raised our glasses to Adam.

"You are now a citizen of the European Union," Mr. Kubík said, "meaning you could work anywhere in Europe, should you follow your mother's footsteps and be drawn to Europe."

"Maybe I will," said Adam. "I love Prague. I'd love to work here one day – once I've established myself a bit in Canada." Adam was working as a writer in an advertising agency.

———

One morning I said to Walter at breakfast, "There's something I'd really like to do. Let's invite everyone out to dinner together – Míša, her boys, Helena and Markéta. Míša and her sons must have had it pretty rough, and I'd like us to connect with them." Walter and Adam were all for it.

Our reservation was at Wings, a restaurant just off our square. We met in front of the church and introductions were made all around. I met Karel's sons, whom I had last seen at their cottage in Kytlice when they were eight and ten years old. Karel Jr. was thirty now. He was tall and thin, wore glasses and had a short beard. An artist and an intellectual. As we shook hands, I was struck by how alike he and Adam looked. Míša commented on it as well, and we laughed at the extraordinariness of it. "I swear I was in Canada when he was conceived!" I joked, absurdly. Martin, now twenty-eight, was dark-haired and fine featured, more withdrawn than his brother.

"I still remember you showing us that big red Citroën," Karel Jr. said to Adam as they shook hands. "I'd never seen such a beauty!"

"I'm very sorry about your father," I said to the boys. They nodded, muttered their thanks.

The eight of us walked the two blocks to the restaurant and were ushered into the private room at the back, where we took our places at a large oval table.

We ordered drinks, the food came, and though it started slowly, the conversation swelled and soon we were talking as though we'd known each other for years. As though we were family. We spoke in English and Czech, translating as needed.

"I have a small exhibition coming up in a couple of months," Karel Jr. said. "I don't know if you'll all be here, but please come if you are." He gave us the details.

"One day I'd like to come to Canada to improve my English," Martin said. "Do you think I could find a summer job in Toronto? Any sort of work – busboy, whatever, that will pay my way and get me among people speaking English."

"I could ask around," Walter said. "Why don't you send me your resume?"

Adam said he'd been thinking of spending some time in Prague and seeing if he could work there. "I don't speak Czech, though, and I hear it's a tough language to learn."

"That's true," Karel Jr. said, "but I'm sure you've noticed all the awful English translations everywhere – on ads and posters, even opera surtitles. You could do editing, correcting and proof-reading." Adam liked the idea.

"We'd be happy to show you around," Martin added, "introduce you to our friends."

Helena and Míša chatted amiably. When Míša learned Helena was a dentist, she asked tentatively if she was taking new patients. Helena said, "In your case, of course I would." Míša signed up both her sons.

Walter and I smiled across the table at the magic circle of friends and family we were creating.

———

On the sidewalk as we were saying our thanks and goodbyes, I took Míša aside and told her I wanted to visit Karel's grave now, on my own. In my notebook I wrote Praha 6, Kostel U Svatého Matěje. St. Mathew Church. Bus 131 from the Hradčany metro station. Prague 6 was Dejvice, Karel's stomping grounds. So he wasn't far from home or from his studio – or from his local.

"The cemetery surrounds the church. Zavadil and Beránek are the family names on the headstone. His father bought it years ago, the second name Karel's sister's married name. It's not a large cemetery. You'll find it."

That afternoon I left Walter and Adam to themselves, took the tram to Malostranské Náměstí, and after stopping to buy some paper and an envelope, climbed up Nerudova Street and pushed open the door to the café, U Zavěšenýho Kafe. It was a cozy café, intimate and eclectic, with extraordinary objects covering every surface, humorous, clever, both kitsch and the real thing. Sculptures and paintings everywhere. And on the walls, framed black and white photos of large groups of people, old and young, sitting and standing, posing in front of the café. Lots of dogs.

"Who are these people?" I asked the man behind the bar.

"Regulars. Every year we take a photo of them."

"Is the Spolek Poholdí or Zlatá Praha among them?"

"*Ale jo!*" he exclaimed, and came around from behind the bar. "There, and there, these three people, this man, these two women. They're all members of one or the other."

I stared at the photos.

"A long time ago I sat with them," I told him.

He smiled. "Great bunch. Lucky you!"

Yes. Lucky me.

Taking a table in the back room, surrounded by wild artwork and an ancient upright piano, I ordered a coffee and looked around. Karel would have celebrated his sixtieth birthday and been feted as one of the presidents of Zlatá Praha. His photo should have hung there.

I took the paper and pen from my bag, and wondered what I wanted to say to Karel. I have been terribly selfish, I suddenly realized, appearing out of the blue, a woman from another world, a world utterly inaccessible to him. I abandon him, showing up twelve years later, and keep coming back over the years, needing him to be there for me. I leave again and again, unwilling, he knew, to ever leave Walter. How could I not have realized how hard it must have been for him? Tears filled my eyes. Forgive me, Karel, I whispered, for the pain I caused you.

And then a wave of intense gratitude washed over me. For making me part of his world, and helping me find mine.

I picked up my pen and began to write. When I was finished, I signed it, put it in the envelope and wrote *Karlíčku* on the front. As I was paying for my coffee, I said to the barman, "Would you allow me to hang a photo of a friend of mine? He was one of the founders of Spolek Pohodlí and a member of Zlatá Praha, but he died. He would have been a regular here. His photo should hang here with the others."

"You'll have to ask the owner. She's here at the bar every day around five or six o'clock."

"I'll be back."

Back at the flat I had a photo of Karel sitting with my portrait hanging on the wall behind him, a photo he'd sent me just after I'd been thrown out of the country.

The next afternoon I took the bus out to the cemetery. It was beautiful, gnarled ancient trees sheltering the gravestones. The church and the cemetery were perched high on a hill, overlooking the great ravine, Šárka, where Karel and I had walked together. I searched, walking up and down the rows of graves and finally found it. A modest grave, covered with myrtle groundcover, with a few flowers and red candles on the gravestone. To my disappointment, there were no names or dates – just the two family names. I had hoped to see Karel's. But it didn't matter. I stood there and spoke to him, telling him everything that was in my heart. I asked for his forgiveness, then thanked him for everything we'd had together. I repeated the words that had been printed on his death notice: "*Kdo v srdcích žije – neumírá.*" Those who live in people's hearts – never die.

I found a flat rock nearby and scraped the earth away from a corner of the grave, placed the letter in the hollow and covered it with earth. "*Pa,*" I said, getting up. Bye. And I walked through the rows of gravestones, red candles flickering in the twilight, back to the bus stop.

———

The next day, I had a copy of the photo of Karel made, with a white border below. There I wrote, in Czech,

> Karel,
> Thank you for everything you gave me –
> your love, your art, your world.
> Thank you for bringing me home to
> my world.
> Know that you were deeply loved.
>
> Helena

I slid it into a silver frame.

———

Back at U Zavěšenýho Kafe that evening, I was introduced to the owner, who sat at the bar, a woman around my age, drinking, smoking, laughing, chatting with friends. I introduced myself and made my request. "Who was your friend?" she asked. I told her. "Of course!" she said. "We knew him," her friends said. One of them, a man with long hair and a beard, turned out to be the artist whose murals covered the café walls. I produced the photo. "Of course we'll hang it," the owner said.

Outside, walking down Nerudova, I stopped and took a deep breath, looked up at the deep, star-filled sky, heard the symphony of laughter and conversations of passersby and noticed the glorious evening all around me. I wanted to laugh, to run, to skip, suddenly light, weightless – free.

I was seized with a desperate urgency to get back to the flat. Walter came to meet me at the door.

"Let's go out." I said. "Let's go to the Grand Café Orient." One of our favourite places off Old Town Square.

We walked across the street and through the park, stopping at the crest of the hill, as we often did, to see Prague glittering below us. Down Wenceslas Square, alive with shoppers and strollers, past the Ambassador Hotel, where we'd stayed the very first time I'd brought Walter here. He reached for my hand and held it. Across Na Příkopě, past the bank where my father had been director, past the café where my parents had met. Walter knew my landmarks now as well as I did.

We climbed the circular steps to the café on the second floor and slid into the elegant banquette upholstered in striped green brocade. The waiter greeted us like old friends. "The usual?" he said.

"No," I smiled. "We'll have a small bottle of champagne."

"Great idea," Walter said. He was watching me. "You look different. What's going on?"

"I *am* different," I said. "Something that's had hold of me for a long time has finally lifted." He raised his eyebrows.

We were silent while the waiter opened and poured our champagne. Walter raised his glass.

"To Prague. To us."

We clinked glasses and drank. I stared at him. Had he always been so handsome? His hair was black streaked with silver now, longish, combed back from his forehead. Over the years people had told him he looked like Paul Newman, like Jack Nicholson, and more recently like Clint Eastwood. I felt as though I was seeing him for the first time. I could see every one of his eyelashes, his strong eyebrows.

"What is it?" he asked.

"Here's to you, darling," I said. What could I say to him, this man who had brought kindness, generosity and absolute trust into my life? This man who'd been determined to fulfill my every dream. Karel's life had been a tragedy. Mine might have been too, if Walter hadn't been the man he was. I told him what his patient love and acceptance had meant to me.

"You've said many times over the years that I saved your life," I said. "Well, you also saved mine."

He took my hand, and we sat in silence, contemplating one another.

"Were you ever worried about my relationship with Karel?" I asked him.

"I was terrified – but prayed you loved me enough to stay."

Another regret I'd have to live with. "I'm sorry for what I've put you through."

Walter interrupted me. "You have nothing to apologize for," he said. "Nothing."

We raised our glasses. I leaned my head against his shoulder. Tears rolled down my cheeks. Despite my new lightness, I felt an old, deep grief, which I supposed would always be there.

But I could live with that now.

———

The End

Walter having fun during our travels through Europe, outside the Louvre

Printed in Canada